Other
Peoples'
M·y·t·h·s

Other Works by the Author

Tales of Sex and Violence
Dreams, Illusion, and Other Realities
Women, Androgynes, and Other Mythical Beasts
The Origins of Evil in Hindu Mythology
Siva: The Erotic Ascetic

Works edited and co-translated by the Author

Textual Sources for the Study of Hinduism
English-language edition of Yves Bonnefoy's *Mythologies*
(under the name of Wendy Doniger)

Other Peoples' Myths

The Cave of Echoes

Wendy Doniger O'Flaherty

The University of Chicago Press
Chicago and London

Acknowledgment is gratefully made for permission to reprint the following copyrighted material:

Four lines from W. H. Auden's "In Memory of W. B. Yeats" are reprinted from *Another Time,* New York, 1940, by permission of Random House, Inc.

Robert Frost's "Fire and Ice," copyright 1923 and renewed 1951 by Robert Frost. Reprinted from *The Poetry of Robert Frost,* edited by Edward Connery Lathem, by permission of Henry Holt and Company, Inc., New York, and, with acknowledgments to the Estate of Robert Frost, by Jonathan Cape Ltd., London.

Two lines from "Ol' Man River," music by Jerome Kern and lyrics by Oscar Hammerstein II. Copyright © 1927 T. B. Harms Company. Copyright Renewed (c/o The Welk Music Group, Santa Monica, CA 90401). International Copyright Secured. All Rights Reserved. Used by Permission.

Nine lines from A. K. Ramanujan's "Prayers to Lord Murughan" are reprinted from *Relations,* Oxford, 1971, by permission of Oxford University Press.

The University of Chicago Press, Chicago 60637
The University of Chicago Press, Ltd., London

Copyright © 1988 by Wendy Doniger O'Flaherty
Preface © 1995 by Wendy Doniger
All rights reserved. Originally published 1988 by Macmillian Publishing Company, A Division of Macmillan, Inc.
University of Chicago Press Edition 1995
Printed in the United States of America
13 12 11 10 09 08 07 06 05 04   7 6 5 4 3

ISBN 0-226-61857-9 (pbk.)

Library of Congress Cataloging-in-Publication Data

Doniger, Wendy.
    Other peoples' myths : the cave of echoes / Wendy Doniger O'Flaherty.
        p.   cm.
    Originally published: New York : Macmillan ; London : Collier Macmillan, c1988. With new pref.
    Includes bibliographical references and index.
    1. Myth.   2. Storytelling—Religious aspects.   3. Religion.   4. Myth—Study and teaching.   5. Storytelling—Religious aspects—Study and teaching.
    6. Religion—Study and teaching.   I. Title.
    BL304.D55   1995
    291.1'3—dc20   95-18927
                                                                                          CIP

⊗ The paper used in this publication meets the minimum requirements of the American National Standard for Information Sciences—Permanence of Paper ᷆ Printed Library Materials, ANSI Z39.48-1992.

for Mircea and Christinel Eliade

and for Brian,
who taught me the meaning of Nietzsche's dictum:
"Aus der Kriegsschule des Lebens:
was mich nicht umbringt, macht mich stärker."
—*Götzen-Dämmerung* 1.8

Contents

Acknowledgments

This book is a not a collection of essays, though several pieces of it have been published separately. It is, rather, a tapestry of threads (*sutras*, as the Hindus and Buddhists call the "threads" of their sacred books), a kind of *bricolage*, that grew into a book as I expanded a corpus of ideas in published articles and nourished them on feedback from public lectures. I am therefore grateful to the editors of several journals and to my hosts at several public lectures not merely for permission to republish materials here but for supplying the very substance of these revised chapters, for pointing out places where I had not thought things through properly, and for offering me more stories on my themes.

It all began with a 1980 *Daedalus* article ("Inside and Outside the Mouth of God: The Boundary between Myth and Reality"[1]), which formed the armature for what was to become chapter 7; I am grateful to Jonathan Z. Smith and Stephen Graubard for this initial inspiration. A much later version of this chapter formed the basis of my address in honor of Mircea Eliade at the Sorbonne in June 1987.[2] Parts of chapter 6 emerged from a May 1987 inaugural lecture for the Mircea Eliade Professorship in the History of Religions,[3] and chapter 5 from an article "Dionysos and Śiva: Parallel Patterns in Two Pairs of Myths."[4]

The heart of chapter 4 came from a 1985 *Criterion* article ("The Good Shepherd/Tiger, or, Can One Have an Eclectic Religion?"[5]) and was further developed in my keynote address to the Midwest branch of the American Academy of Religion in March 1986; my Arnold Lowe lecture at Macalester College, in Saint Paul, in April 1986; my presentation at Brian K. Smith's panel on sacrifice at the November 1986 meeting of the American Academy of Religion; and an article in the *Festschrift* for Zwi Werblowsky.[6]

My 1984 Humanities Open House Lecture ("When Is a Classic Not a Classic, or, Who Says the East Is Mysterious?") and my 1985 "Aims of Education" lecture, both at the University of Chicago,[7] started me on the materials for chapter 3, which in turn led to several addresses and articles: two for the Smithsonian Institution in Washington, D.C.;[8] a presentation at the Association of Asian Studies meeting in March 1986;[9] an NEH seminar at the University of Chicago in June 1986;[10] the keynote address to the National Federation of State Humanities Councils, in Washington, D.C., in September 1986;[11] the keynote speech for the Eaton Conference of Science Fiction Writers, April 11, 1987;[12] and a presentation, "Can a Humanist Compare Religions?", at the Ohio State University, 8 May 1987.

Chapter 1 is based upon my November 1985 Presidential Address for the American Academy of Religions,[13] and my "Last Lecture: Memory, Death, and Experience."[14] Chapter 2 was written last, in an attempt to tie up a lot of loose threads, as it were; but it benefited greatly from the class on the *Timaeus* that I taught with David Grene and David Tracy.

In the summer of 1986, I tried out an early version of the whole book in a series of lectures at the University of Canterbury, Christchurch, New Zealand.[15] All along the way, I exposed draft after draft to my great friends and critics, the Davids (Grene, Brent, Tracy, Shulman, and White), and to A. K. Ramanujan and Ed Dimock. David Carrasco gave me a most painstaking, sympathetic, and detailed critical reading of the penultimate draft, which greatly improved the book. I am, as always, deeply indebted to my students, with whom I argued each case (like Father William with his wife), particularly to Laurie Patton (who also typed a penultimate version), to the students in my class on sacrifice (particularly Kay Read, Mary MacDonald, Jon Walters, Beatrice Briggs, Philip Arnold, and Michael Allocca) and to all those students who (together with my son Michael) have allowed me to quote their work.

Best of all, Brian K. Smith read draft after draft after draft, each one alleged by me to be the very last one but inevitably followed apace by a complete revision, which he dutifully read again, flagging neither in fiery enthusiasm nor in icy criticism.

This book is a collection of stories, many of which were told to me by friends, colleagues, and students (three often intersecting categories). In addition to my main suppliers, acknowledged above, each of the following has given me at least one good story: Wayne Booth, Norman Bradburn, David Carrasco, Arthur Cohen, Ed Dimock, Joseph Edelheit, Nancy Falk, James Fredericks, Steve Gabel, Chris Gamwell, David Graeber, Andrew Greeley, Zanvel Klein, Tom Lawson, Bernard Lewis, David Loehr, Mary MacDonald, Bill Parker, Laurie Patton, Roy Rappaport, James Adam Redfield, Arshia Sattar, Larry Sullivan, Frederick Turner, Dick Underwood, Irena Vasquez, Jon Walters, and Paul Wheatley.

Finally, just as the book was taking final shape, I was invited to give the first Mircea Eliade Lectures in the History of Religions at Western Michigan University in Kalamazoo. This seemed an uncannily appropriate invitation to receive at that moment; this book, more than any I have ever written, was inspired by the work and the life of Mircea Eliade. I am therefore deeply grateful to Western Michigan University for honoring me in this way, particularly indebted to the anonymous donor of the lectureship, and happy to publish this book as the 1988 Mircea Eliade Lectures in the History of Religions.

Mircea Eliade died while I was writing this book. I dedicate it to his memory and to the living presence of Christinel Eliade.

Wendy Doniger O'Flaherty
Chicago/Inwood/Truro, 1988

Preface to the 1995 Edition:

I am so grateful to the press for snatching this book from the jaws of the Murdochian dragon and giving it a second life. I have continued to think and write about myths since 1988, and I have learned a lot from reviews of the book and from student response to it in my own teaching. There is one point in particular which has proved controversial and on which I have come to modify my opinion: the assertion (in chapter 6) that it is harder to change rituals than to change myths. I still believe that this is basically true, and I still stand behind the arguments in that chapter, contrasting the problems inherent in changing rituals with the advantages offered by changing myths. But I now think that I both underestimated some of the difficulties that arise when one changes myths and overestimated the difficulties that arise when one changes rituals; and I would want to say more about the degree to which myths and rituals are interrelated, so that it is almost impossible to change one without changing the other in some way. This shift does not seem to me to justify rewriting the book, merely to merit this caveat to new readers. You might say that I have found it easier to change my own myth about the ease of changing myths than to change my own ritual of publishing.

Other
Peoples'
M·y·t·h·s

Introduction

This book is about the stories that people have told about others. More precisely, it is concerned not so much with stories *per se* as with stories about stories—metastories, or, more specifically, metamyths. What do we learn from the stories that we have told, and that other peoples have told, about the *stories* that people tell? We learn something special when we focus on the stories themselves, the myths: for myths, narratives, are not merely the medium through which knowledge about others is transmitted. Myths themselves are objects to be known; the medium of myths is in one sense the message. Myths are about the human experiences and events that we all share—birth, love, hate, death—, and one of those experiences or events is *storytelling*.[1] Storytelling is one of the few truly universal human bonds; people in all times and places have sat down at night and told stories. Putting together words to reproduce events that engage the emotions of the listener is surely a form of art that ranks among the great human experiences.

Martin Buber tells a good story about telling a good story:

> A rabbi, whose grandfather had been a disciple of the Baal Shem, was asked to tell a story. "A story," he said, "must be told in such a way that it constitutes help in itself." And he told: "My grandfather was lame. Once they asked him to tell a story about his teacher. And he related how the holy Baal Shem used to hop and dance while he prayed. My grandfather rose as he spoke, and he was so swept away by his story that he himself began to hop and dance to show how the master had done. From that hour on he was cured of his lameness. That's the way to tell a story!"[2]

Metamyth as Method

The myths do not merely tell us of encounters with strangers; they are, themselves, on a plane once removed, such encounters for us. Through this methodological struggle with myths, we can raise certain basic questions of human meaning. What do we learn from the stories that human beings have told about strangers, animals, gods, and children? We may learn a lot about others, and about myths, from our own myths about others. And we may learn even more about others by studying their stories about themselves and their

1

stories about others. But we also learn things about ourselves by studying these stories. For as we progress, we may find that we are among the others in other peoples' myths.

What do we learn by reading the stories told by others about others? We do have stories composed by people whom we consider other, and these are the best sorts of stories that we can use to enter into the world of others in general. For, setting aside the claims of authorship made by most sacred scriptures, we have no stories composed *by* gods. (Nor do we have any stories composed by animals, or many composed by children—though we do have some, and we have many stories composed *for* children). But stories—myths—are one of our only sources of knowledge about the gods. And stories told by other peoples are one of our best sources of knowledge about them.

So the stories are the method in this book; there is no other. Stories reveal things that are not easily gleaned from the harder disciplines. Other people have, of course, demonstrated alternate ways of getting inside other cultures, including art in general, though not without raising certain problems that I shall discuss in chapter 2, and ritual, whose dangers we shall encounter in chapter 5. Art and ritual are powerful supplements to myth in the cross-cultural enterprise. But these ways are not my ways, and indeed I think (though I certainly cannot prove) that myths are the easiest way.

But the stories are not designed as arguments, nor should they be taken as arguments.[3] Rather, the stories provide us with metaphors that make the arguments real to us; the metaphors of the hunter and the sage and the cave of echoes help us to approach certain problems of otherness. For me, they are a way of thinking that works better than the development of a step-by-step argument. The reader may wonder, from time to time, whether I have gone off on a tangent, telling stories and losing the thread of the point that I want to make. But the stories *are* the point that I want to make; I am telling methodological stories about the stories I am telling. Methodologies, after all, are stories too, and every storyteller is a methodologist.[4]

Strangers, Animals, Gods, and Children as Others

The "others" in this book are the people who cluster on the borders of what we define as ourselves—our Western, human, mortal, adult nature: they are strangers (primarily in the sense of non-Westerners), animals, gods, and children.

There are several disciplines devoted to the attempt to understand how others think. Anthropologists try to find out how other peoples think; zoologists attempt to imagine how animals might think; theologians try to imagine how gods must think; and child psychologists attempt to find out how children probably think. In the early years of the social sciences, foreigners, animals, and children were regarded as forming a coherent group, to which another group, the insane, was usually added and in which certain of the non-Westerners were usually called "savage" or "primitive." Some of the qualities regarded as inherent in this group were admired (their supposed innocence, purity of vision, natural religiosity, etc.); some were despised (their backwardness, or brutality, or low cunning). In general, when they were admired it was by those who felt that there was in fact a grey area of overlap between us and them, an area in which the qualities that we shared with them, good qualities, lay dormant in us and might perhaps be reawakened through contact with them. When they were despised, it was generally by those who felt that they were categorically different from us, utterly nonhuman, though they were also despised by those who feared that we might, in fact, share with them our darker qualities, qualities that science and progress hoped entirely to expunge.

Of course, non-Westerners, animals, gods, and children do not form a natural group. Animals are not the same as gods (we have all seen animals . . .), nor are children like "primitives." But the fact that we tend to *regard* them as a coherent group has important implications for our self-understanding. In the narrative which is this book, my principal actors will be gods and animals, with foreigners playing only supporting roles[5] (except, of course, as the authors of many of my scripts) and children still further in the background, almost offstage. But all four groups are essential to the plot.

Why are these others important to us? We see in them not what they are, or at least not just what they are, but what we think *we* are as distinct from them. Still foundering in the wakes of colonialism and positivism, we tend, arrogantly, to define ourselves as not them: "We are not strangers, because we share a culture that they do not share; we are not Hindus (for instance), because we are not immoral or stupid or unscientific. We are not animals, because we are not vicious or irrational; we are not gods, because we are not immortal; we are not children, because we are mature." Because they are by definition not us, these others populate a territory at once strange and familiar, within which we search for our answers to certain basic questions of human meaning.

The gods are the final others, the defining others in all myths; and the myths tell us that the gods come among us most often in the form of those other others—animals, strangers (both in the sense of foreigners and in the sense of outsiders within our own culture), madmen (if we are to include them as fringe members of this group outside the group), and children. One of Zeus's most important epithets was Xenios—the god of those who come to us as strangers, and whom we must receive as our guests lest we provoke the wrath of Zeus; for Zeus himself might take the form of a stranger. Of course, all gods are other,[6] since they are other than mortal, but some are more other than others, and it is these gods—those who are defined as outsiders within the very cultures that worship them—to whom I shall pay particular attention in chapters 4 and 5, the Hindu god Rudra/Shiva and the Greek Dionysus. More generally, a divine Other who plays a major part in this book is Death, who comes in the guise of a stranger, the ultimate other, in many myths. Interwoven throughout the chapters of this book are two great myths about death: the myth of Christ's passion, together with the ritual of the Eucharist,

which celebrates that myth; and the Hindu mythology of rebirth, together with
the ritual of animal sacrifice that accompanies that mythology.

The Argument

My argument, such as it is, stripped down to bones for theory seekers to suck
dry, is but the mere skeleton on which the stories themselves will provide all
the flesh, and all the meaning. Though I have taken just a few paradigmatic
myths and set them in a rather extended exegesis, my questions are posed
through seven central myths, each designated in the subtitle of a chapter,
which act out the implications of the problems and of certain possible answers
to them. The warp of the book, as it were, is formed by the questions that each
chapter sets out to explore; the weft is formed by the thread of images and
anecdoctes (or mini-myths) that are woven in and out of the arguments. What
unites these stories is not so much the thread of the philosophical discourse in
which they are situated, the warp, but the themes that recur in the narratives,
the weft, particularly the themes of strangers, children, animals (especially
fish), and gods. The resulting fabric is not an answer to the questions but
rather a tapestry of myths within which the questions are set in a traditional
narrative context. This context is offered as a place from which readers may
set out to find their own answers; and it may even provide some readers with
a kind of treasure map with which to set out on the path to the discovery of
their own myths.

　　To begin with, I should define who "we" are, though this "we" will
undergo modifications in focus from chapter to chapter. The term "we" is
problematic, though I cannot see how to do without it. Whenever I use it, I am
reminded of what Tonto said to the Lone Ranger when they found themselves
surrounded by hostile Indians and the Lone Ranger said to Tonto, "What are
we going to do?" Tonto replied, "What do you mean, 'We?', white man?"[7]
There is as much of a multiplicity of "we's" in the West as there is of "they's"
in the more notoriously multiplicitous world of Hinduism. In undertaking the
comparison of religions, we (I!) tend to regard ourselves as spokespersons
for our own tradition; but of course this is not so. To presume to speak for an
"us," rather than just for a "me," is merely to indulge in a transformation of the
claim to speak for an "it," that is, to have complete objectivity. I have certainly
not studied the Western tradition with even a fraction of the attention that I
have devoted to Hinduism. I can only stand, personally, as a spokesperson for
the several particular parts of the Western world that I grew up in: I speak
as a woman, a mother, a Jew, a horsewoman, a mythologist—"I's," like "we's,"
are innumerable. This book is in a way my intellectual autobiography; when
I speak of the challenges and dangers of confronting other peoples' myths,
of the relationship between Judaism and the history of religions, of loving
or hating the culture that one studies, I speak out of my own experience of
these challenges and dangers. For the great myths, though not the rituals, of
Hinduism and Catholicism have become a deep and ever-growing source of
personal religious understanding for me.

But I do want, nevertheless, to speak for several other "we's" in this book. In Chapter 1, I wish to speak for historians of religions. In chapters 2 and 3, I wish to present the viewpoint of the people whom I am attempting to define in those chapters, by implication in my definition of the classics: the people who define themselves as "the culture," the people who control the body of literature that *they* refer to as "the classics." This is not really a circular definition: I am speaking of those people in the West, generally but not only white male Christians, who have designed and benefited from the European and American systems of formal education over the past few centuries. This means that I have necessarily excluded from this discussion the many groups who have never been a part of this culture and who therefore have not lost *those* classics, never having had them. Instead, these people often have classics of their own that they have never lost at all, or they are inspired to create other, alternate traditions that eventually come to play the role of traditional classics for them. Such groups would include blacks, who celebrate the gospel in their own way, within their own oral tradition; Orthodox Jews, whose primary source of meaning has always been and continues to be the Hebrew tradition of the Torah and the Talmud; the Amish; the Quakers; the Shakers; in short, the many, many Others, ethnic and religious groups who have maintained their own nonmainstream traditions, often both despite and because of pressures to assimilate to "the" culture. Their story would be another book. Finally, in chapters 5, 6, and 7, I shall try to speak to, if not for, several groups of Americans who find themselves in several different stages of demythologization: the un-demythologized, the demythologized, and the remythologized. The book in general is *not* addressed to the thoroughly unmythologized—people who have never had, and never will have, any inclination to take myths seriously; it assumes that the reader has some personal interest in myths.

So much for "we"; let us turn now to the argument of the book.

The seven chapters set forth seven stages (in the dramaturgical rather than logical sense of that word), on which the myths act out seven sets of problems posed by our approach to other peoples' myths. Chapter 1 uses the Indian metaphor of the hunter and the sage to examine the problems that arise when scholars who study other peoples' myths integrate that study with their own personal search for meaning. To meet some of the challenges posed by this enterprise, we must first consider our own assumptions about our own myths. Chapter 2 uses the metaphor of the cave of echoes to argue that we think of myths as lies, and that we have lost our own myths. It traces back to Plato the definition of a myth as a lie, proposes an alternate definition, and points out the advantages and disadvantages of the theory of archetypes that ultimately derives from Plato. Chapter 3 argues that we have lost not only our own myths but our own classics in general, a broader category that overlaps with that of myths. This loss becomes the more apparent when we see how other cultures preserve their myths in ways inaccessible to us, given our cultural definitions of fluidity and fixity.

Chapter 4 uses the metaphor of "If I were a fish" as an entry into the extreme case, mythologies about animals, animals who may represent human strangers (barbarians and foreigners), or gods, or the darker sides of our own natures. What problems arise when we attempt to understand the thoughts (myths) of animals (other people)? What problems arise when we attempt to understand the thoughts of animals who are regarded as gods?

Chapter 5 asks, What stories are told about people who enter into other peoples' myths, especially when those myths involve them in rituals? What happens when they resist? How does the myth-and-ritual force itself upon them? What are the dangers of converting, and the dangers of not converting, to a strange myth-and-ritual? Chapter 6 asks, How is the audience absorbed, willingly or unwillingly, into the story when it is enacted in the ritual of theater? How can a myth survive without a ritual, or a ritual without a myth?

Chapter 7 picks up the thread of chapter 1 by returning to examine the experience not of the people depicted within the myths but of the people who study myths. We may regard other peoples' myths as bizarre stories that have nothing to do with us, as stories about other people, as stories about how others ought to be, as stories about us, or as stories about how we ought to be. How can we find our own stories in other peoples' myths? We may find our myths now not so often in our own communal religious settings (or rituals) as in unexpected places in our actual lives. And if we are in danger of missing them or resisting them when we find them in our lives, we may recognize them and accept them better if we have already met them in other peoples' myths.

But before we begin to contemplate the possible benefits of absorbing other peoples' myths (as we shall do in chapter 7), we must face up to the three levels of obstacles that have to be surmounted on our mythical quest: the intellectual problem of sympathetic objectivity (chapter 1), the emotional problem of empathetic understanding (chapter 4), and the religious problem of conversion and resistance (chapters 5 and 6).

And we must, moreover, make certain distinctions, in order to decide what sort of use we may attempt to make of other peoples' myths. On the first, easiest, and perhaps most superficial level, we can use other peoples' myths merely as stories, as data, as a means of finding out the mysterious and fascinating ways in which other people on the planet earth think about things. This level, the travelogue level, which we shall encounter in chapter 1, is hard enough to master well. Second, we can treat them as a source of information about the human condition that we all share, as a source of data about our own lives, or, going a little bit further, we may regard them as explanations of *why* things are as they are. These approaches, which we shall examine in chapters 4, 5, and 6, still remain on the descriptive level. Third, as we will see in the concluding chapter, we may go on to a programmatic or exhortational level; we may take other peoples' myths as a source of advice about what to do about our lives.

Other Scholars' Myths

The Hunter and the Sage

A myth may be, among many other things, the incarnation of a metaphor.[1] One metaphor that we often use to describe complete sympathy with or understanding of someone else is "getting inside someone else's head." This does not, to my knowledge, occur as a figure of speech in Sanskrit, but the image that it conjures up is often literally depicted in Indian mythology, where a person may "get inside" another person's head (that is, his mind, his mental software) by actually going inside the physical space of his skull (that is, his brain, his mental hardware) and indeed pervading his entire body.[2] The theme of entering someone else's body is a popular one in Indian literature; any respectable yogi can do this trick, which may lead to embarrassing or amusing situations (as when the mind of a yogi enters the body of a whore, and her mind enters his body in return).[3] I propose to use an Indian myth to dramatize our own English metaphor, in order both to demonstrate one of the cross-cultural uses of mythology (that is, to show how we may legitimately see in a myth a meaning different from what its own culture sees in it) and to create an image with which to think about such cross-cultural uses (an image about scholarship).

The Hunter and the Sage

The most striking dramatization I know of the metaphor of "getting inside someone else's head" is a myth that occurs in the *Yogavasishtha*, a Sanskrit philosophical treatise composed in Kashmir sometime between the tenth and twelfth centuries A.D. The myth is the story of a hunter who meets a sage who has entered another man's body and lodged in his head:

One day a hunter wandered in the woods until he came to the home of a sage, who became his teacher. The sage told him this story:

In the old days, I became an ascetic sage and lived alone in a hermitage. I studied magic. I entered someone else's body and saw all his organs; I entered his head and then I saw a universe, with a sun and an ocean and mountains, and gods and demons and human beings. This universe was his dream, and I saw his dream. Inside his head, I saw his city and his wife and his servants and his son.

When darkness fell, he went to bed and slept, and I slept too. Then his world was overwhelmed by a flood at doomsday; I, too, was swept away in the flood, and though I managed to obtain a foothold on a rock, a great wave knocked me into the water again. When I saw that world destroyed at doomsday, I wept. I still saw, in my own dream, a whole universe, for I had picked up his karmic memories along with his dream. I had become involved in that world and I forgot my former life; I thought, "This is my father, my mother, my village, my house, my family."

Once again I saw doomsday. This time, however, even while I was being burnt up by the flames, I did not suffer, for I realized, "This is a just a dream." Then I forgot my own experiences. Time passed. A sage came to my house, and slept and ate, and as we were talking after dinner he said, "Don't you know that all of this is a dream? I am a man in your dream, and you are a man in someone else's dream."

Then I awakened, and remembered my own nature; I remembered that I was an ascetic. And I said to him, "I will go to that body of mine (that was an ascetic)," for I wanted to see my own body as well as the body which I had set out to explore. But he smiled and said, "Where do you think those two bodies of yours are?" I could find no body, nor could I get out of the head of the person I had entered, and so I asked him, "Well, where *are* the two bodies?"

The sage replied, "While you were in the other person's body, a great fire arose, that destroyed your body as well as the body of the other person. Now you are a householder, not an ascetic." When the sage said this, I was amazed. He lay back on his bed in silence in the night, and I did not let him go away; he stayed with me until he died.

The hunter said, "If this is so, then you and I and all of us are people in one another's dreams." The sage continued to teach the hunter and told him what would happen to him in the future. But

the hunter left him and went on to new rebirths. Finally, the hunter
became an ascetic and found release.[4]

This remarkable story has many meanings that we may use for our own
purposes, but first let us try to understand it in its own terms. In its own
context, this is a myth about doomsday and ontology. An ascetic sage tells the
tale of entering the body of a dreamer who is a married man—entering his
breath, his head, and his consciousness. The sage inside the dreamer dreams of
the same village that the dreamer was dreaming of, and becomes a householder
like him. His "outer," or original, body does not simply decay in the absence
of the conscious soul (as it does in many tales of this type);[5] it is destroyed
by a fire that burns the hermitage in which the outer body was lodged. This
is a strange fire: it came from the doomsday flames that the sage dreamed
about when he was lying asleep in that hermitage (and inside the body of the
sleeping man that he had entered). Moreover, whereas the first doomsday fire
seemed real to him, so that he wept to see it destroy the inner world, this
second doomsday fire seemed to him to be nothing but a dream, and a *déjà
vu* dream at that, so that he did not feel any pain when it burnt him. Yet the
first fire did *not* burn his outer body, because he merely saw it in another
man's dream, while the second fire did burn his outer body, because he saw
it in what had become his own dream, too. Since he had dreamed his outer
body into nonexistence, he was physically trapped inside his dream world.

Indeed, the dreams within dreams in this text are even more complex
than may appear from the narrative as I have just presented it.[6] For the story of
the hunter and the sage is embedded in the *Yogavasishtha* in a complex web
of interlocking narratives. As we read the story of the hunter and the sage,
we become confused and are tempted to draw charts to figure it all out. It is
not clear, for instance, whether the sage has entered the waking world or the
sleeping world of the man whose consciousness he penetrates, and whether
that person is sleeping, waking, or, indeed, dead at the moment when we meet
the sage. But as the tale progresses, we realize that our confusion is neither
our own mistake nor the mistake of the author of the text; it is a device of
the narrative, constructed to make us realize how impossible and, finally, how
irrelevant it is to attempt to determine the precise level of consciousness at
which we are existing.[7] We cannot do it, and it does not matter. We can never
know whether or not we have become trapped inside the minds of people
whose consciousness we have come to share.

Inside the dream village, the new householder (*né* sage) meets another
sage, who enlightens him and wakes him up. Yet, although he is explicitly said
to awaken, he stays where he is inside the dream; the only difference is that
now he *knows* he is inside the dream. Now he becomes a sage again, but a
different sort of sage, a householder sage, inside the dreamer's dream. While
he is in this state, he meets the hunter and attempts to instruct him. But the
hunter misses the point of the sage's saga: "If this is so . . .," he mutters, and
he goes off to get a whole series of bodies before he finally figures it out. The

hunter has to experience everything for himself, dying and being reborn;[8] he cannot learn merely by dreaming, as the sage does.

But let us now set aside the metaphysical complexities of this story, its primary locus of meaning for the Hindu reader or hearer, and extract instead a point that we can apply to a very different concern, the nature of the experience of the scholar who studies other peoples' religions.

Scholars and People

Let us attempt now to get outside the head of the author of that myth and to translate into our own terms the metaphor of the hunter and the sage as ideal types, extreme types never actually encountered in their pure form. If we return to the metaphor that is enacted in this parable, the hunter is the person who cannot get inside other peoples' heads and so is driven by his emotions to go on being reborn himself over and over again, in order to have the series of experiences that are the necessary prerequisites for enlightenment. But the sage, who *can* go inside other people mentally, mentally experiences countless lives without ever having to be reborn.[9] There are two different ways in which one can get inside another person's life: one can be reborn inside various bodies, and live many lives, as the hunter does; or one can use mental powers to get inside other peoples' heads and learn about their lives, as the sage does. Hunters and sages can be taken as two types of people, the sort who have to experience everything physically in order to understand it, and the sort who think that they can understand things merely by learning about them. Hunters are ordinary householders; sages are artists and intellectuals.[10] In Indian terms, sages are Brahmins, hunters are Kshatriyas.

To be a hunter one need not necessarily believe literally in the doctrine of transmigration; one might be able to live several lives within a single rebirth, living a life in one career and then in another, in one country and then in another, with one person and then with another. So too, to be a sage in a myth one might literally enter another person's head, as a yogi does, but to be a sage in real life one might simply enter other peoples' consciousness through some other, milder means, perhaps by entering their myths. I will use the image of the sage to denote the person who mentally enters the nonphysical essence of other people, in contrast with the hunter who physically, through his body, experiences many lives.

We are all hunters, whether we know it or not, but the ones who know what it means to be a hunter are sages. Since sages *believe* that they are experiencing many lives, they can do it on purpose; hunters live their multiple lives unknowingly, helplessly. The sage is always part hunter because he is a human being and therefore an emotional, experiential creature; but because he is a sage, he is always trying to be what he cannot be: entirely free from the hunter within him. That is, the sage has a hunter in him in addition to a sage, just as Dr. Jekyll had in him both the evil Mr. Hyde and the good Dr. Jekyll; but the hunter may not have a sage in him, just as Mr. Hyde did not have Dr. Jekyll in him.[11]

The sage in our story enters what in Sanskrit is called *manas* (translated as both "heart" and "mind," in contrast with *hridaya,* usually translated simply as "heart," with which it is cognate). *Manas* is the organ that is responsible for both reason and emotion, the place where one does algebra but also the place where one falls in love. This term provides a good example of the way in which Indian thought fails to distinguish between some of the categories that we tend to think of as inherently polarized,[12] for, as we shall see, we tend to demarcate rather sharply people who are ruled by the heart and people who are ruled by the head. Indians do not do this; the Indian sage experiences life through both the head and the heart, although he tries not to experience it with his body.

E. M. Forster describes a shrine in India that was created when, according to legend, a beheaded warrior contrived somehow to continue to run, in the form of a headless torso, from the top of a hill, where he left his head, to the bottom of the hill, where his body finally collapsed; at the top of the hill is now the Shrine of the Head, and at the bottom, the Shrine of the Body.[13] This seems to me to be a useful parable for much of Western civilization, certainly for that fraction of it that studies religion. A similar metaphor is provided by the mythical beast once described by Woody Allen: the Great Roe, who had the head of a lion and the body of a lion, but *not the same lion.*[14]

If we apply our root metaphor to scholars of religion (who would be superficially classified, as a group, as sages, in contrast with people who just *are* religious, the hunters), we might further distinguish within the group of sages a subgroup of hunters, who assume that their own personal experience of religion, their own religiosity, is a sufficient basis on which to understand other peoples' religions, and another subgroup of sages, who assume that they must *go inside* other cultures (through their texts, perhaps, or through personal observation of their rituals) in order to understand them.[15] We might then further divide this latter subgroup of sages into a sub-subgroup of hunters who prefer to do their learning by going there, experiencing, doing fieldwork (the more anthropological branch of the family) and another sub-subgroup of classical sages who prefer to do their learning in their armchairs, reading texts (the more classical branch of the family). And, finally, we might go on to divide either of the sub-subgroups of anthropological or classical sages into one sub-sub-subgroup of hunters, who allow themselves to react emotionally to their learning experiences, and another of sages, who attempt to remain as objective as possible toward the people that they are studying.

Scholars of religion tend to regard themselves as Great Roes, not realizing that they have the head and the heart (the *manas,* in Sanskrit) of the same lion.[16] But this is an unfortunate schizophrenia. Good hunters *do* have sages in them, sages that bring some degree of self-awareness to the hunting; bad hunters do not. But good sages, on the other hand, always have good hunters in them. To deny the experiential component is not merely elitist; it is to deny the essential humanitarian component in the study of religion.

Indian aesthetic theory calls the sympathetic reader or member of the audience the one "whose heart is with [the poet or actor]," the *sa-hridaya* (or sym-pathetic), whose heart melts in response to poetry or art.[17] But the narrow-minded scholar's heart is hardened and encrusted by his reading of dry metaphysical texts. The accomplished sage becomes *sa-hridaya* when he shares the heart of the person with whom he sympathizes. The narrow-minded scholar is the sage who wants to live entirely in the head and never in the heart; he is the sage who attempts utterly to deny his inevitable hunter component. The sympathetic scholar is the sage who acknowledges his need to live both in the head and in the heart; who accepts his hunter component, though he attempts to deal with that aspect of his nature with greater self-awareness than that of the hunter who lives only in the heart and never in the head. Just as there are sage hunters, there are hunting sages. The hunting sage is my idea of the right sort of historian of religions.

The Sage's Myth

Let us turn for a moment to the problem faced by sages, people who enter other peoples' heads. In India, sages are enlightened wise men, gurus or priests. In the West, sages belong to another category of professionals or specialists: scholars, humanists such as classicists and anthropologists. Classicists (by which I mean not just people who read Greek and Latin but, more broadly, all those historians, philologists, and other humanists and social scientists who deal with the past) attempt to enter a world that is perhaps as foreign and unattainable as any world can be—the lost world of people who are now dead, but who may once have lived where we live now, or have spoken ancient forms of languages related to our own. Anthropologists, who do not usually travel in time, make all the greater effort to travel far in space, to the farthest reaches of Otherness. And anthropologists are storytellers: the word for "anthropologist" in Tok Pisin in New Guinea used to be (and unfortunately no longer is) "story-master." But although anthropologists pride themselves on entering other peoples' heads (that is, their thoughts), they also pride themselves on *not* entering other peoples' hearts (that is, their emotions and their lives).[18] Malinowski once remarked, "I see the life of natives as . . . as remote from me as the life of a dog."[19] Nevertheless, sometimes anthropologists *do* enter the hearts of the people that they study, just as nonprofessionals (hunters) do.

People who study myths constitute a subcaste of historians of religion, more precisely a half-caste formed through an illicit liaison between anthropologists and classicists. Mythologists, too, are Western sages, and like other sages they are also hunters. To the extent that they are sages, mythologists may enter into other peoples' heads (that is, understand other peoples' myths). But to the extent that they are hunters, mythologists, like other sages, may also enter into other peoples' hearts and bodies (that is, *live* other peoples' myths). Like other sages, they do absorb, if only, sometimes, unconsciously, myths that become *their* myths, that become personally meaningful to them.

It may be recalled that after a while Mr. Hyde took over Dr. Jekyll's life: Dr. Jekyll could not help being Mr. Hyde, and could not get back into his existence as Dr. Jekyll. In our Indian text, the life of the man whose mind the sage entered became the sage's life. In that story, the sage who began his scientific experiment in cold blood became drawn helplessly into the life of the man whose head he had entered (a householder, whom we may call a hunter in the broad sense in which we are using that metaphor). Once he made the dreamer's dream his own dream, he forgot that he was a sage; he became a hunter. Yet, eventually, still within that dream, he awakened to become another sort of sage, a sage inside a hunter.

What meaning does this story have for us? On some deep level, I think, all truly creative scholarship in the humanities is autobiographical, but it is particularly evident that people who traffic in myths are caught up in them, *volens nolens*. This has certainly been true for me. In 1971, when I was struggling to come to terms with the death of my father (my first major experience of inexplicable and unjust evil), I failed to draw any comfort from Jewish or Christian approaches to the problem, not through any inherent inadequacy in them but simply because they were not *my* myth; I had never had them. I had grown up with a certain number of Jewish rituals, and with a great number of Jewish social attitudes, but with no myths (unless, of course, one were to count as myths Jewish jokes, which I had in abundance).

Perhaps I was unable to live the Jewish myths when I needed them because I had already unconsciously replaced them with the Hindu myths in which I had been steeped from the age of twelve, when my mother gave me a copy of E. M. Forster's *A Passage to India;* perhaps I simply had an innate affinity for the Hindu myths, an immediate individual response. In any case, I found that I could in fact make some sense of my father's death in terms of the Hindu mythology of death and evil—the subject of the book that I was working on at the time, and had begun some years before the onset of my father's illness.[20] In a certain sense, I had been experiencing, like a hunter, the same events that were narrated in the myth that I had been reading and writing about as a sage, though at first I did not realize that this was the myth that I was in, perhaps because I did not expect someone else's myth to be my myth.

But there was another good reason why I could not use Jewish myths to sustain me then, why, indeed, it would perhaps have been inappropriate to use them to understand my father's death: they had ceased to be his myths, too. The tendency to make use of other people's myths has long been a habit of the Jews, wandering or dispersed as they are.[21] Jews have always lived among Others—have always *been* the Others wherever they lived. Both of my parents were relentlessly assimilated, secularized, and Enlightened Jewish refugees, he from Poland (a small town not far from Cracow) and she from Vienna (she lived on the street where Sigmund Freud had lived). My father, whose father had been a Talmudic scholar, knew much of Frazer's *The Golden Bough* by heart and taught it to me. He had learned it at New York University, where he had worked his way through school as a stringer for the *New York Times,* going around to all the major churches in Manhattan every Sunday and summarizing the sermons; he was paid by the inch. Eventually it dawned on him that it might be profitable to serve as a kind of matchmaker between those ministers who yearned to see their sermons in print and those ministers who were eager to have at their disposal every week the sermons of the first sort of ministers. Thus he founded in the late 1930s, and published throughout his life, two magazines for the Protestant clergy, *Pulpit Digest* and *Pastoral Psychology*. And from time to time, when he was short of copy, he wrote, under various pseudonyms, sermons that were preached all over America by Protestant clergymen who little dreamed that their homilies had been composed by an East European Jew. Thus my father was a (Jewish) sage who entered the heads of others (Christians) but always managed to get out again.

In a similar way, I gradually came first to think with and then to feel with the karma theory. The karma theory *tells* us that we have lived other lives, that our souls have had other bodies. But how can we *feel*, as well as accept intellectually, the reality of those other lives if we cannot remember them? Plato constructed his own version of this theory in the myth of Er in the *Republic*,[22] but Plato was not a Neoplatonist and neither Platonism nor Neoplatonism became an integral part of Western thinking about death. It is easier for Hindus to *feel* the theory of rebirth, as they feel themselves to be a part of a larger human group in a way that we do not; they believe that they are joined in nature as well as in culture both with the other people with whom they have present contact and with the people in the past and future to whom they are related. But what about us who are not Hindus? For us, the previous incarnation unrecalled has no existence. For some things in life can be remembered in one's soul; but other things can only be remembered with one's body.

The body remembers some things, and the mind remembers others. But memory is not all there is; there is also a reality of unrecalled experience that gives a kind of validity to our connection with lives that we do not recall. The karma theory recognizes the parallelism between events forgotten within a single life—the events of early childhood, or the things that we repress or that (in Indian mythology) we forget as the result of a curse[23]—and the events forgotten from a previous life. It also recognizes a similarity in the ways in which we sometimes half-recall these various sorts of events, often with a sense of *déjà vu*. We remember something that we cannot remember, from a lost past, through the power of the invisible tracks or traces left behind on our souls by those events; these traces the Hindus call perfumes (*vasanas*).[24]

The karma theory tells us that we have lived lives that we cannot remember and hence cannot feel. Sages can imagine the lives of others, and so live them; and sages are rare. But for those of us who lack the imagination to perceive the infinity of our lives in time, it might be possible to perceive the infinity of our lives in human space. Again, the Indian texts tell us that we are karmically linked to all the other people in the world; they *are us*. I have known and respected this theory for a long time, though I have not always believed it.[25] But for one important moment, I did believe it. It was at a time when I was feeling rather sorry for myself for having only one child; I wished that I had had lots of children, and now it was too late. I felt that having six children would have meant having an entirely different life, not merely six times the life of a woman with one child, and I wanted that life as well as the life that I had. This thought was in my mind as I wandered on a beach in Ireland, and saw a woman with lots and lots of children, very nice children, too, and at their best, as young children often are on a beach. Normally, I would have envied her; but this time, I enjoyed her children. I was happy to watch them. And suddenly I felt that they were mine, that the woman on the beach had had them for me, so that they would be there for me to watch them as they played in the water. Her life was my life too; I felt it then, and I remember it now. What had been an idea to me until then, the idea of my karmic identity with other people, became an experience. I was able to live her life in my imagination.

One way of interpreting my epiphany of the woman on the beach was this realization that my connection to her—and, through her, to every other woman who had ever had or ever would have children—meant that my brief lifespan was expanded into the lifespans of all the other people in the world. This is a very Hindu way of looking at one's relationship with all other people. Woven through the series of individual lives, each consisting of a cluster of experiences, was the thread of the experience itself—in this case, motherhood. That experience would survive when her children and mine were long dead.

I felt then that all the things that one wanted to do and to be existed in eternity; they stood there forever, as long as there was human life on the planet Earth. They were like beautiful rooms that anyone could walk into; and when I could no longer walk into them, they would still be there. They were part of time, and though they could not go on being part of me for much longer, part of me would always be there in them. Something of me would still linger in those things that I had loved, like the perfume or pipe smoke that tells you that someone else has been in a room before you. This is the same "perfume," the same karmic trace of memory, that adheres to the transmigrating soul. And through my connection with the woman on the beach, I would be the people in the future who sensed in that room the perfume that I had left behind, though (unless I was a gifted sage) I would not recognize it as my perfume. Perhaps, since I am not a Hindu, that is as close as I can come to believing that I can remember my other lives: remembering other peoples' lives as my life. And perhaps it is close enough.

Fire and Ice

Scholars can learn to think with the myths of other cultures. More than that: they sometimes learn to *feel* with them. Thinking (with the head) and feeling (with the heart) when we confront other people's myths has serious implications. There are several things that it does *not* mean. It does not mean that a scholar of religion should become an apologist for another tradition, let alone convert to it; though conversions of this type do in fact occur from time to time, they are not the usual course of events, and they are hedged with problems. Nor does it mean that mythologists should proselytize for the texts that they study, using them in an attempt to cure the ills of a demythologized age. As we shall see, people other than mythologists certainly do take up foreign myths (just as they convert to foreign religions), but they do not take them up in the same way that the historian of religions takes them up, and in any case it is not the task of the historian of religions to facilitate such conversions. Nor does it imply that the way to study other people's myths is to take them into our own lives; the way to study them is to *study* them, learning the languages in which they were composed, finding all the other myths in the constellation of which they are a part, setting them in the context of the culture in which they were spawned—in short, trying to find out what they mean to the people who have created and sustained them, not what they mean to us. And this is hard enough to do.

But sometimes something happens to us when we study other peoples' myths; sometimes they enter our hearts as well as our heads. Some scholars have come to think and feel with other peoples' myths, an enterprise that always affects the construction of a scholar's personal worldview (one's life as a hunter) and may also affect one's professional scholarship (the life as a sage). What happens to the scholarship of sages who take seriously the myths that they study?

There is an entire continuum of ways of interpreting a myth. At one end of the spectrum is the scholarly attempt to find out what the myth meant to the people who created it: this is the method of learning the language and so forth that I have just described. It is also a method that takes serious account of the interpretations offered by believers within the tradition (though the hermeneutics of suspicion would also take into account other scholarly data that might contradict a statement from within the tradition). Such interpretations, based upon the unique characteristics of the particular culture that created this particular version of the myth, can be judged and criticized by the same criteria that would be applied to any academic enterprise. At the other end of the spectrum is the nonscholarly experience of the myth, which deals solely with the meaning that the myth has for the person who encounters it. Such an experience can only take place if the person who interprets the myth believes in certain universals of human experience and sees in the myth not merely a particular cultural version but also a universal theme that has some meaning beyond culture, across cultures. Such interpretations cannot be judged or criticized by any academic criteria; they are purely subjective, valuable only to the person who draws personal meaning from the myth.

But what of the middle ground between these extremes? What of scholars who see, as well as any good scholar can, what the myth means to its parent culture, and find that that interpretation also has meaning for them? Do we understand other peoples better if we *do* take their myths into our lives or if we do *not* take their myths into our lives? Do we understand other peoples' myths better if we like them, or if we hate them, or if we remain neutral?

Many scholars who have written great studies of religion have been motivated not by love of religion but by hatred of religion, or at least by anger directed against religion, or fear or loathing of religion. Freud and Marx are the most outstanding examples of brilliant haters of religion, but there are others.[26] Hate is, like love, fueled by the heart rather than the head, and emotional fuel has great staying power. Hunters *must* love and hate; ideally, sages do neither, if they remain in the cool realm of the head. But, as we have seen, they do *not* always remain in the realm of the head; they, too, hunt in the heart, and so they, too, may love and hate what they study with the head.

Robert Frost wrote of the power of hate compared with the power of desire (which is, of course, not precisely the same as love, but close enough for poetic license):

> Some say the world will end in fire,
> Some say in ice.
> From what I've tasted of desire
> I hold with those who favor fire.
> But if it had to perish twice,
> I think I know enough of hate
> To say that for destruction ice
> Is also great
> And would suffice.[27]

So hate, like desire, can destroy; and I think that, like desire, hate can create. The Hindus know that hate can even be a way of loving, particularly a way of loving a god: they speak of "hate-love" (*dvesha-bhakti*), a form of devotion in which by trying to destroy or resist a god one is drawn into an ultimately salvational intimate relationship with him. In chapter 5, we shall see some of the consequences of hating a god.

But hate may have been a more appropriate academic motivation in the salad days of the academic study of religion, when, like Shakespeare's Cleopatra, we were green in judgment, and trying to be cold in blood. Nowadays, when we can, and must, be more subtle in our criticisms of religion, hate has its limits. The attempt to sympathize is always interesting, perhaps because it is ultimately impossible; but the enterprise of killing is ultimately boring. It doesn't take very long to kill something academically—that is, to demonstrate how wrong or bad a religion, or a colleague in the study of religion, may be—but then you're finished; there is nothing left to do.[28] Killing may be amusing while it lasts, but it never lasts very long, and then you're back where you started from; there is nowhere to go *on* to. Hunters have to kill; sages do not. Sages have their opinions, of course, but they have learned to move with a careful tolerance in strange waters. Hate is creative but not generative; scholars who study what they hate go round and round, obsessively, ad infinitum, like an ouroboros biting its own tail forever—or until it burns out.

The issue of the legitimacy of affect (the heart) in the academic study of religion (a discipline of the head) has thus led us to the question of the relative validity of the two different sorts of affect, love and hate. Hate seems to provide an answer to the embarrassing problem of caring about what one teaches when what one teaches is religion. For though in the academy at large (if not in most divinity schools) it is regarded as wrong to care *for* religion, it is not wrong to care *against* religion. Criticism is more *wissenschaftlich* than praise in all academic disciplines, but particularly in religious studies. Since the Enlightenment, hatred of religion has been a more respectable scholarly emotion than love, particularly hatred for one's own religion.

The problem of affect is thornier when one is studying not the myths of others but one's own myths, a delicate enterprise that has been much discussed. If we teach what we believe in, our subconscious commitment to our own worldview may skew our supposedly innocent approach to the data; the heart may pollute the head. Teachers with such secret agendas (sometimes secret even to themselves) force their theories and their pupils onto a Procrustean Hide-a-Bed. Hunters lead dangerous lives; there are many traps that lie in wait for scholars who bring their lives into their work, who allow too many liberties to the hunters within themselves, who fall into the traps laid for them in the jungles of their unconscious assumptions.

The simultaneous use of heart and head seems to violate many of the unspoken canons of scholarship, particularly the rather nervous scholarship of those of us who study religion.[29] Scholars of religion tend to be particularly gun-shy when it comes to admitting to any sort of personal investment in the subject that they teach, and with good reason: the battle between those who believe that religion has a place in the academic curriculum and those who believe that it does not has had a long and ugly history, beginning from the time when the American Constitution banished the church from the state. Americans have generally assumed that one could not be both pious and educated; this formulation was challenged long ago by William Rainey Harper, the founder of the University of Chicago, but his challenge was never truly accepted, least of all at Chicago. The battle still rages today; die-hard creationists still rouse passions with their objection to Darwin, as do fundamentalists with their demands for prayers in schools and their claim that secular humanism is a religion. Religion remains the academic Scarlet Woman, pilloried primarily by those who react against the Reaction of the Moral Majority, but also by those who have always been, rightly, frightened by the power that religion has (like alcohol, sex, and nuclear energy—or drugs, sex, and rock 'n' roll) to do evil as well as good.

Though, still in the academy at large, the love of religion is never considered as academically legitimate as the hatred of religion, the love of *other* peoples' religions is regarded as at least less illegitimate than the love of one's own. In an attempt to undo the damage done by centuries of scholarship motivated by colonial and missionary hatred (or loathing) of non-Western religions, the scholarship of recent decades has leaned over backward and fallen into awkward postures of cultural relativism.[30] Many historians of religions hope that none of the othernesses of other religions will prove so overwhelming as to prevent us entirely from understanding them. In this, historians of religions endorse Terence's affirmation that "nothing human is alien to me" and Merleau-Ponty's assertion that ethnography is a way of knowing that allows us to see the alien as our own, and our own as the alien. But though many historians of religions acknowledge the ultimate inadequacy of cultural relativism and are willing to confront the ugly shadow side of religious phenomena, I think they still maintain a covert hope of learning to sympathize with, if not necessarily to approve of, that ugliness.[31] It is surely significant that the discipline of the history of religions was born and raised in the context of the World Parliament of Religions, which spawned the still operative optimism that the more you know about other people (even when you do not like what you know), the less likely you will be to kill them. One of the results of this position is that some historians of religions have let down their guard to such a point that they have made their own academic writings about other peoples' texts into sermons for the truth values of those texts. Such scholars are sometimes accused of committing the deadly academic sin of cryptotheologizing; this is sometimes said even of Mircea Eliade.

I do not think this accusation can be justly applied to all scholars who regard other peoples' myths as potential vehicles of meaning; I think that there are ways, scholarly ways, of saying that other peoples' myths may have meaning for us without preaching them. But this must be done with great self-awareness. For if they say that other peoples' myths are good, scholars are in danger of legitimating these myths just as priests do; and it is not the job of a scholar to replicate the claims of religious believers.

The other side of the coin of cultural relativism is equally slippery. For it is also dangerous for scholars to say that other peoples' myths are *not* good, to admit to hating aspects of other peoples' myths. Bigots, who hate other peoples' religions, are not a problem peculiar to the academy; bigots may be hunters or sages. But the problem of bigotry takes on an interesting twist when it comes to the study of religions. Relativists often assume that we may say that our own myths are evil, but they tell us that we must not say that other peoples' myths are evil. It is no longer legitimate to say in print (at least in a scholarly text) that one hates some aspect of other peoples' religions, that one thinks the Aztecs were nasty to massacre all those children, or the Hindus were/are wrong to burn their widows alive. If we were to make such Eurocentric judgements, it is feared, we would be no better than the Spanish under Cortés or (perish the thought) the British in India. Yet, as Edward Said has demonstrated, at bottom we *are*, and can be, no better (that is, no fairer) than the British;[32] and, as Allan Bloom has demonstrated, relativism when slavishly pursued has profoundly disturbing effects upon our own culture.[33]

Yet I think that if we are going to take other peoples' myths seriously, we must not feel constrained to love them, or, even if we do love them, to overlook their flaws. Indeed, as with the people that we love, to love deeply is to know deeply, and to know deeply is to be aware of the shadows too. And surely if scholars are to have the right to love other peoples' myths, they should have the right to hate them as well. There should be a place for honest affect—which must necessarily include the judgment that some myths are good and others are not—within the legitimate study of other peoples' religions, even for—or, rather, especially for—people who have made the initial judgment that mythology as a whole has meaning for us.

Thus, for instance, I find personally repugnant the Hindu tradition of *suttee* that theoretically exalts widows who burn themselves alive on their husbands' funeral pyres. But I hesitate to call the myth that establishes this tradition a bad myth, for it is a genuine expression of one aspect of a complex worldview that has complex meanings. Before making our judgments, we must first admit our personal revulsion and then attempt to transcend it. First we must find out what may be the Hindu widow's concept of what will happen to her after her death and what will happen to her if she continues to live, and her broader concept of the relationships between wives and husbands, between mothers and children, and between the living and those who have died and those who are yet to be born. Only then may we come to realize that for some women the act of *suttee* may have had a value not unlike the value that we would attribute to the self-sacrifices of heroes of the Resistance at the hands of the Nazis in World War II, or the self-sacrifices of the Christian martyrs: the willing death of the individual for a greater cause. At the same time, we must recognize that other women, who did not necessarily share this worldview, may have been forced, by moral or even physical pressure, to commit *suttee* unwillingly, and thus may have perceived it as we initially perceive it, as a murder. But so long as what the Hindu widow sees in *suttee* remains invisible to us, we have no choice but to view it as a murder; only when the broader context becomes visible are we able to choose to view it as a murder or not.

I myself find the Hindu worldview as a whole both beautiful and meaningful, and I have been able to make many Hindu myths my own myths, to use them to construct my own meanings. But my personal resistance to the institution of *suttee* means that I cannot use the myth of *suttee* as *my* myth. This poses a further limitation for the goal of "getting inside the head" of a Hindu: there are parts of that head that I don't want to be inside. Moreover, it is evident that the myth of *suttee* has several different meanings for the lives of the people who tell that story—some for those Hindus who approve of *suttee,* others for those who disapprove, and still others, perhaps, for the willing or unwilling widows. And if there are (and there are) Hindus, too, who have not taken *suttee* into their heads, I reserve the right to avoid that particular part of the Hindu head, myself.

The ambivalence that I and other Western historians of religions have experienced in confronting such phenomena as *suttee* is in part a reflection of the fact that it is harder to accept other peoples' rituals (*suttee*)—or, even more, other peoples' realities (the woman who is burned alive)—than to accept other peoples' myths (the story that tells how Sati, the wife of Shiva, established this custom; see chapter 5). In the first case, *moral* relativism would ultimately prevent us from making essential decisions about the one way in which we can act in a given situation (or, in its more extreme form, the way in which anyone should act in that situation). In the second case, *ontological* relativism, relativism about ideas, does not necessarily involve a yes/no decision about any particular action; it merely allows us to consider all the options. Moral relativism does expose us to serious dangers, but these dangers are not necessarily attached to ontological relativism. Ontological relativism is neither cowardly nor inconsistent with the pragmatist position: when forced to make a decision, one does so, but when not forced to do so (and one should not be forced to do so), one does not.

Within all the options that we may consider, we have the right to love some myths and to hate others. By and large, I regard the myths that I have told in this book as laden with perceptions that have meaning for me; this is why I have allowed them to speak for me, to express my opinions about the meaning and use of the telling of myths.

Academic Hardware and Religious Software

Thus historians of religions must fight a war on two fronts. The first battle is against the covert truth claims of theological approaches to religion that masquerade as nontheological approaches, whether these be self-justifying at the expense of other peoples' religions (bigotry) or self-denegrating at the expense of one's own religion (mindless moral relativism or promiscuous conversion). But the historian of religions must also be on guard against the overt objections of superrationalists, who oppose the study of religion in *any* form or would allow it to be studied only within the sterile confines of an objectivity that is in any case impossible and probably not even desirable. It is a razor's edge not at all easy to tread, but it is the Middle Way for the humanistic study of religion.

Scholars of religion are not unique in caring about the personal implications of what they teach, but their commitment is usually more vulnerable than that of many of their colleagues in other fields. For though the personal commitment of scholars engaged in the teaching of Marxism, women's studies, black studies, and even regional studies (Chinese, Middle Eastern) is often just as intense and just as potentially disruptive of academic objectivity, scholars of religion have made the most self-conscious effort to be more objective than the chemists, *plus royaliste que le roi*—or, in Martin E. Marty's formulation, "more secular than thou." This is all well and good; if one is going to teach a highly charged subject like religion, one must be more aware, not less aware, of the impossible goal of pure objectivity. It behooves us, even more, perhaps, than it behooves anthropologists or classicists, to play by the rules of the game of scholarship—to learn languages, read commentaries, examine firsthand reports, and take into consideration the various biases of the many people in the chain of transmission that ends with us. Clifford Geertz has stated the problem well: "I have never been impressed by the argument that, as complete objectivity is impossible in these matters (as, of course, it is), one might as well let one's sentiments run loose. As Robert Solow has remarked, that is like saying that as a perfectly aseptic environment is impossible, one might as well conduct surgery in a sewer."[34]

We tell ourselves (and others, particularly our colleagues in the "harder" disciplines) that we study our texts from the outside, in the approved manner of the head, like sages, cool and objective, while we deal with the religious affairs of the heart, if we deal with them at all, from the inside, like hunters, with passion and commitment. We maintain an objective interest in one sort of religion and a subjective faith in another. For historians of religions, the "objective" religion may be obviously other—Hinduism or Islam—, but even if we are dealing with our "own" tradition we are prey to a kind of schizophrenia in artificially defining it as "other" for the duration of the period in which we have it under the academic microscope. That our stock-in-trade is ideas about gods rather than ideas about electrons or phonemes is not supposed to bother anyone. The same basic rules should apply; the mental computer follows the same synapses, and we merely change the software to *very* soft software.

But in making such assertions, in attempting to play the game of objectivity with the Big Boys on the playing fields of the harder sciences, we often tend to play down the more subtle but equally genuine sort of objectivity that good scholars of religion can and do bring to their discipline, a critical judgment that allows them to be critical even of their own faith claims. And leaning over backward is not always the best posture in which to conduct a class; it is a posture in which one can easily be knocked over by any well-aimed blow from the opposition (indeed, from either of the two oppositions). Moreover, this pressure often makes scholars of religions deny that they care about religion, which is untrue; we do care, which is why we have chosen this profession, instead of becoming lawyers and making lots of money.

Some scholars—I think of Paul Ricoeur and David Tracy—do manage to accomplish the rapprochement from the heart to the head, using their own religious commitment in their academic study. But others take the safer path, using their academic study of other peoples' religions in their private religious understanding (the approach from the head to the heart). This latter approach, the way of the sympathetic sage, is, as we have seen, more easily achieved, though it is less often discussed. To write about a religion that one cares about may be academically unfashionable; but to let what one reads and writes affect one's personal religion is academically irrelevant. The assertion that critical objectivity makes it possible for a scholar to deal even with his or her own faith claims in an academic forum demands a far more delicate defense than the assertion that a scholar may derive new faith claims from the subject matter that is first taken up with critical objectivity.

A cynic might view this second process as merely a disguised form of the first, achieving the same end through a means less susceptible to criticism. I am reminded of the Jesuit who was informed that he was not permitted to smoke while he meditated. Quite right, the Jesuit replied; but surely no one would object if he were to meditate while he was smoking. In fact, I think the two procedures that I have outlined are truly distinct, though my justification for both admittedly rests upon my conviction that it is not necessary for the head and the heart of the scholar of religion to answer to two different masters, that the head and the heart can nourish rather than sabotage one another.

It sometimes seems to me that we arrange our talents and weaknesses like the foolish blind man and lame man in the old story: they agreed to team up, but the lame man carried the blind man on his shoulders. If the blind but physically whole man is the hunter, the experiencer, surely we should let him be led about by the lame sage, the *see-er,* the scholar. As we have seen, though a hunter is basically limited to one side of experience (the physical and emotional), a sage is not necessarily limited to only the other side of experience (the intellectual). In any case, since it is ultimately impossible for the sage to deny the hunter within him, it is best for him to come to terms with his hunter. But more than that; the sage who acknowledges his hunter aspect is a better sage, the sage whose heart melts (in the Indian example) rather than the one who is dried up by his books.

If we return now to the metaphor of "getting inside someone else's head," we realize its more complex implications. For me, it implies the (ultimately unreachable) goal of cross-cultural studies. In attempting to understand Hinduism, I would want to get inside the head of a Hindu, to become in a way a kind of ersatz Hindu. But then, one might say, why not just talk to a Hindu and find out what is inside his head? (This is the "Take-a-Buddhist-to-dinner" approach to the comparative study of world religions.) There are a number of reasons why this is not a satisfactory equivalent for getting inside the head of a Hindu oneself. (1) There are many Hindus, and the one that I talk to might be as ignorant of or mistaken about her own tradition as a Jew or Christian chosen at random might be wrong about her own tradition. (2) There are so many Hinduisms that no single Hindu could speak for the entire tradition. (3) In many ways, a Hindu is the very worst person to ask about Hinduism; he is so bound up in it that he is blind to many of its aspects that an outsider might see.[35] (4) A Hindu would not ask of Hinduism the sorts of questions that I might want to ask of it, might leave out of his necessarily selective summary precisely the sorts of things that I would want to know.

This last objection, in particular, reveals the fact that when I say that I want to get inside the head of a Hindu I really mean that I want to get inside it *but to remain, at the same time, inside my own head.* The sage, at a certain point, realized that he was a sage inside a hunter, that he was running both systems of perception at once. Thus, the ideal scholar at this point is two-headed: he has his own head and the head of the Other. But if we look closer, we see that such a scholar must, in fact, have more heads than the most capitally extravagant Hindu deity. For there are many heads of the Other (many different sorts of Hindus, all of whom one hopes to understand) and, of course, many heads of Us. For each scholar is not only simultaneously hunter and sage but often also simultaneously superstitious and a secular humanist, and many other things. Freud once remarked that when two people made love, there were four people in the bed (the two there, and the two being fantasized); in the study of comparative religion, when we attempt to penetrate not the body but the head of the other, there are always hundreds of people in the head.

Eclecticism in personal cosmologies may be too elusive and idiosyncratic to be subjected to the structures of a public, communal, academic discourse. But eclecticism does have a legitimate place in the evolution of private universes. Eclectics make better hunters, people who use their academic discoveries to enrich their personal worldviews; they embody the positive side of Socrates' famous dictum that the life that is unexamined is not worth living. And I think that they are better sages, too, scholars whose sympathy gives them greater understanding of the subject that they teach; for it is also true that the life that is not lived is not worth examining.[36]

Yet "eclecticism" may be too arrogant a word, implying, perhaps, that we decide what myths are true or make up gods that suit our moods. Perhaps we should find some more modest, passive word to describe what we do in receiving and accepting the myths from other peoples' religions. Perhaps our myths, like greatness in Shakespeare's formulation,[37] are not something that we are born with, or achieve, but something that we have thrust upon us, to confront not only with our heads but with our hearts.

Chapter 2

Other
Peoples'
Lies

The Cave of Echoes

I t is impossible to define a myth, but it is cowardly not to try.[1] For me, the best way to not-define a myth is to look at it in action, which is what I have tried to do throughout this book: to see what myth does, rather than what myth is. It seems to me that by the time you've defined your terms in an argument, you've lost interest in the problem. But at this point, as we begin to reexamine our own assumptions about myths, it might be useful to list some things that I think myths arc *not:* myths are not lies, or false statements to be contrasted with truth or reality.[2] This usage is, perhaps, the most common meaning of myth in casual parlance today.[3] Indeed, other cultures, too, call myths lies. The Malagasy end the recitation of any myth with a traditional tag-line: "It is not I that lie; this lie comes from olden times."[4] In our culture, in particular, myths are often given the shadowy status of what has been called an "inoperative truth,"[5] when in fact they might better be characterized as operative fictions. Picasso called art a lie that tells the truth, and the same might be said of myths.

What a Myth Is and Is Not

The desecration of the word "myth" to mean "lie" began with Plato, who contrasted the fabricated myth with the true history.[6] It is, I think, an irony that our word for myth in most European languages, together with our basic attitude to myths, comes from ancient Greece, one of the very few cultures

25

in the world from which we have almost no example of real, live myths, of myths as a part of a vital tradition; by the time most of the Greek myths reach us, they have been so thoroughly reworked in artistic and philosophical forms that they are mythological zombies, the walking dead.[7] Plato was, as Eliade pointed out long ago,[8] the first great demythologizer; he "deconstructed" the myths of Homer and Hesiod. It was Plato who challenged, successfully, the status of the poetic myth-carvers and myth collectors and banished them from his Republic. We can see in Plato a spectrum of mythmakers: at one end are anonymous wet nurses, who transmit the old myths to helpless infants;[9] at the other end are the poets, like Hesiod and Homer, the "mimetic clan" who cannot imitate the true forms since no one has ever seen the forms and the poets can only imitate what they have seen.[10]

Plato warns us that we must not tell these poetic myths about the gods even if they are true;[11] in this, I think, he affirms the power of myths to influence human life; for he fears that a bad myth will make a bad life. (We shall see, in chapter 6, other Greek arguments against the evil effects of the myths in Greek tragedies.) Moreover, it is hard to escape from this image of the bad life; the stories that we learn in childhood have a marvelous hold on our memory.[12]

Yet it is necessary for people to believe in *good* myths, even if they are false; this is the argument that Plato advances for the "noble lie" (*gennaion pseudos*) in the *Republic,* the statement that distorts an outside surface in order to convey an inner truth. Some of these good myths come from the old days; Plato distrusts this sort of "mythologizing," the stories about centaurs and Chimaeras and Pegasus and so forth, but he distrusts even more the people who analyze them away as metaphors for the North Wind and so forth (anticipating Friedrich Max Müller by some twenty-four hundred years); such analyses are altogether too clever and waste an awful lot of time.[13] People do have to have myths, Plato concedes; if they don't believe in the old ones, we must construct new ones for them, logically, and this is very difficult to do, for we must convince them, in the cold light of reason, of the truth of the myths in order to make them accept the laws that we wish to give them:

> How can one assert in cold blood that the gods exist? Because we must hate and find unbearable those who, today as in the past, due to having refused to allow themselves to be convinced by the myths related to them since earliest childhood by a mother or a nurse giving them the breast, have obliged us, and still do so, to develop the arguments which take up our time now.[14]

For this reason, despite his opposition to myths and mythmakers, Plato himself was also a great "*re*mythologizer" who invented the drama of the philosophical soul and made it a new kind of myth, a reasonable, logical, "likely" myth,[15] to challenge the old myths of centaurs and so forth. In this way, when it came to myth, Plato managed to hunt with the hounds and to run with the hare. As Marcel Detienne has put it: "Plato's work marks the time when philosophy, while censuring tales of the ancients as scandalous fictions, sets about telling its own *myths* in a discourse on the soul, on the origin of the world, and on life in the hereafter."[16] It was Plato who transformed ancient mythic themes to make the myth of Er,[17] the myth of Eros,[18] and the myth of the creation of the universe.[19] Though Plato's "likely or resembling story" can be a myth in the sense of a narrative (and in that sense is interchangeable with *logos* meaning "narrative"), it is *not* a myth in the negative sense of a bad copy, like the myths of Homer (which are negatively contrasted with *logos* meaning "reason").[20]

Yet Plato does apply the word "myth" (*muthos*) to the story of the world that he creates in the *Phaedo*,[21] a myth that he says is "worth hearing," though it is merely another "likely story":

> Now, to assert vehemently that things like this are really so as I've narrated them, doesn't befit any man of sense. But that this is so, or something pretty much like it, about our souls and their dwelling place, since it is clear that the soul is immortal—it is quite fitting that we say that.[22]

The likely story is not the truth; but it *resembles* the truth, and is as close as we can ever get to the truth about certain subjects.[23] Plato confesses that he resorts to telling myths, despite the fact that such stories are not literally true, because there is no other way of using words to produce even the effect of truth.[24]

Plato regards the myth that he constructs in the *Phaedo* as an essential vehicle for salvation, a kind of religious or magic charm:

> It is well worth running the risk that these things are so for anybody who thinks them so. (For it's a fair risk.) And he must recite these things over and over to himself like a magic charm, even as I at this moment and for a long time past have been drawing out this myth.[25]

Plato ends the *Republic* with his own myth, the myth of Er, which he certainly does not regard as a lie: "And so the myth was saved and was not lost, and it will save us, if we believe it, and we shall safely cross the river of Lethe and we will not sully the soul."[26]

For Plato admits that a myth says something that cannot be said in any other way, that cannot be translated into a logical or even a metaphysical statement. A myth says something that can only be said in a *story*.

Which brings me to what I think a myth is. Let me begin with a rather cumbersome and rather functional definition: A myth is a story that is sacred to and shared by a group of people who find their most important meanings in it; it is a story believed to have been composed in the past about an event in the past, or, more rarely, in the future, an event that continues to have meaning in the present because it is remembered; it is a story that is part of a larger group of stories.

The assertion that a myth is a story is basic to my argument; for I think that the myth is persuasive to us because the *action* itself is persuasive. Even when what happens in the myth is not physically possible in this world (as when, for instance, a man turns into a fish), when the event is described in detail, as something that happened, we can *see* it happening, and so it enlarges our sense of what might be possible. Only a story can do this.

Myth, then, is a story, or a narrative. How, then, is it different from other narratives, from the narratives of history or the narratives of legend? To say that a myth is a sacred story is to say that it must have religious meaning (though it need not be a story about gods). I do not wish to become embroiled here in the genuinely problematic argument surrounding the definition of religion and the sacred. Nor do I wish to take shelter in the perhaps valid, but unproductive, assertion that the sacred level of the myth is precisely the level that cannot be expressed in words, the ineffable. Let me merely say that the stories that I want to talk about as myths (and that I wish to distinguish from, for example, stories about George Washington or Paul Bunyan) are about the sorts of questions that religions ask, stories about such things as life after death, divine intervention in human lives, transformations, the creation of the world and of human nature and culture—and, basically, about meaning itself.

Not only is a myth shared by a group of people; each member of that group believes that the story is anonymous, the creation as well as the possession of the group rather than of an individual. This involves us in a series of paradoxes. Myths belong to a peculiar genre of texts that, after they come into being, seem to create their own authors. The myth must have been told originally by an individual, of course, but once it is accepted by the group it is regarded as having been created by the group, as being multiauthored.[27] In many cultures, a shaman may dream for the group as a whole; he is not, however, regarded as the creator of the myth, but merely as the medium of its transmission from a supernatural author. Claude Lévi-Strauss has described another consequence of this paradox:

> It is a consequence of the irrational relation between the circum-
> stances of the creation of the myth, which are collective, and the
> particular manner in which it is experienced by the individual. Myths
> are anonymous: from the moment they are seen as myths, and what-
> ever their real origins, they exist only as elements embodied in a
> tradition. When the myth is repeated, the individual listeners are re-
> ceiving a message that, properly speaking, is coming from nowhere;
> this is why it is credited with a supernatural origin.[28]

One is, therefore, in danger of commiting the basic sin of *hubris*—masquerading as a god—if one sets out to create a myth. Of course, this is a very common sin nowadays; many people seem to think that they can create new myths. But I don't think they can.[29]

Moreover, even the assertion that a myth, after its creation, comes to be shared by a group must be carefully qualified. Many myths are the official possessions of a group, officially defined from the inside of the tradition: "This is our myth," or, even, "We define ourselves as the people who have this myth." But we who are on the outside of other peoples' traditions may see myths in other places. With a kind of god's-eye view, we may find a story in complete isolation from any validating tradition—in a fragmented stone tablet of a lost civilization, for instance. To say that such a narrative is a myth is to say that it is the *sort* of story that has been shared by other people, even if we do not know that *this* story has been shared by other people.

It might be said that Plato's likely story is not, technically, a myth at all, since it is the conscious artistic creation of a single individual and never became canonical for the Greeks or anyone else. But Plato's myth of creation in the *Timaeus was* a cult for the elite, linked to Orphic and Pythagorean cults before him, and to Gnostics (not to mention Neoplatonists) after him.[30] Indeed, even in the *Laws,* the myth takes on a cult—the cult of the celestial bodies—with an ethical eschatology. And Plato himself seems to suggest that the good lie in the *Republic* might be used to provide a cult for the masses.

It is often asserted that a myth is about an event believed to have taken place in the past, but this is just one side of the situation. Though many myths are indeed set in the past, there are also myths about the future, millennial myths and eschatological myths, for instance; moreover, as Teilhard de Chardin has pointed out, even the myth of Eden and the myth of the Golden Age are myths not about the past but about the future. *Illud tempus,* as Mircea Eliade excavated it, exists in the future as much as in the past.

The assertion that the mythic story is believed to have existed for a long time has implications for the archaism of the stories themselves, in addition to the archaism of the events described in the stories. Myths are not necessarily atavistic holdovers from some primitive time or hand-me-down beliefs that are no longer believable. But tradition is, in Husserl's words, a "forgetting of the origin,"[31] which, as Mary Barnard has remarked, "means, of course, that we can never see a mythmaker in action. If we do, he is not making a myth, but a story, a dance, or a dramatic production, perhaps a ritual. Or are the mythmakers not the originators of the tale, but the almost equally invisible succeeding generations who have passed it along until by some process it became a myth?"[32]

Such a process of cultural amnesia (or "mystification") may be seen, for instance, in the way that many Americans now regard "Ol' Man River" not as the creation of Jerome Kern and Oscar Hammerstein II but as an anonymous folksong.[33] One has to drag the train of the past along with one in transmitting a myth. Woodrow Wilson, when he was president of Princeton, once remarked that changing the curriculum was like moving a graveyard: the dead have many friends. This is certainly true of any conscious attempt to "move" a myth.[34] Like a fine brandy, a myth needs to have been a myth since time immemorial.

In what sense, then, is a myth ever told for the first time? The answer to that paradox depends again upon one's point of view, from inside or outside the tradition. Within the logic of the tradition that regards the myth as a myth, there can be no beginning to the *tradition* of any myth. To be conscious of such a moment would be tantamount to calling World War I by that name before World War II. From inside the tradition, there can never be a first telling of a myth; "No Indian," as A. K. Ramanujan has remarked," ever hears the *Mahabharata* for the first time."[35] And Claude Lévi-Strauss has remarked of myths, "The original form (provided this notion means anything) is and remains forever elusive. However far back we may go, a myth is known only as something that has been heard and repeated."[36] Viewed from outside the tradition, however, with the same god's-eye view that allows us to see an individual myth outside of its group context, one might identify a particular story as a myth even upon a first hearing, by recognizing the qualities that it shares with other myths that one knows to have stood the test of time, and guessing that this one, too, will be taken up by the tradition. If the guess proves wrong, the story might be regarded in retrospect as a myth stillborn. Finally, from inside or outside the tradition, one might say that the tradition of a myth begins when it is heard for the *second* time—that is, when it is remembered for the first time. After World War II, we remember World War I.

Myths therefore strike a false note when we try to construct them or legislate them (rather than merely reinterpret them) to suit our momentary needs. Though it is true that mythmaking continues to go on in every culture, it is also true that we cannot recognize the myths of our culture as myths until later on, just as we may be happy at some moment in our lives but be too busy being happy to realize it; only later do we think, "How happy we were then." The myth cannot, by definition, be simultaneously new and true; the relationship between truth and novelty in myths is like the relationship between the two Soviet newspapers *Pravda* ("truth") and *Izvestiya* ("news"), as the Soviets cynically remark: "There is no truth in *Izvestiya* and no news in *Pravda.*"

The assertion that a myth must be part of an ancient tradition and a group tradition may seem to involve us in an awkward contradiction when we consider one particular subspecies of myth, what might be called the myth of the individual. For if the classic genre (to which, as we shall soon see, myth belongs) is what is shared and common, the myth of the individual celebrates what is particular and personal. How, then, are we to regard myths (and there are many of them) in which the hero is the only one who sees the truth, the only one who has the faith and courage to follow his particular and personal vision against the often deadly threats of the rest of society? Almost all myths of the foundation of religions are of this sort.

The answer lies in the transformation through time: what begins as an individual experience of rebellion against society (Jesus breaking away from the Judaism into which he had been born) becomes the new charter for a myth of a new society (Christianity); the individual who begins as a rebel becomes part of the establishment. Only when that transformation has taken place does the individualistic story become a classic myth—a shared, traditional myth *about* a personal, antitraditional individualism. Another paradox of a revolutionary myth was expressed by Voltaire, who was approached by a man who praised him and thanked him effusively for having destroyed the credibility of religion; the man then said that he himself wanted to found a new sort of religion, with none of the flaws that Voltaire had pointed out in the extant traditions, and he asked Voltaire's advice on how to go about this. "Simple enough," said Voltaire; "go get yourself crucified and rise from the dead."

The assertion that myth is a story about the past whose meaning is remembered in the present might lead us to ask precisely *why* myths are remembered. They are remembered because their form, the narrative, encodes meaning in a genre of discourse that people find natural, simple, and always fascinating; and also because their content deals with human questions of perennial importance. We always remember what we find easy, interesting, and important. Through an only apparently circular argument, I would say that myths are remembered precisely because they are about the sorts of events in the past that are not bound to the past, that continue to be given meaning in the present. Myths are, moreover, remembered because the need for them persists. Myths encode meanings in forms that permit the present to be construed as the fulfillment of a past from which we would wish to have been descended.

A final reason why myths are remembered (and another incidental factor mitigating against the conscious creation of a "new" myth) is expressed by my final criterion for a myth: a myth is part of a larger group of narratives, a mythology. A myth cannot function as a myth in isolation; it shares its themes, its cast of characters, even some of its events with other myths. This supporting corpus glosses any particular myth, frames it with invisible supplementary meanings, and provides partially repetitious multiforms that reinforce it in the memory of the group, as Claude Lévi-Strauss has demonstrated.[37] The broader context also supplies a partial corrective to the distortions produced by inevitable interpretation.

For the assertion that a myth is a story in which many people have come to find their meanings might be expanded to suggest that such a story is, in some sense, true. Indeed, I am inclined to say (only partly in order to infuriate the rationalists) that the best short definition of a myth is that it is a *true story*. But this statement must be immediately qualified: it is regarded as true not literally, but in its implicit meanings. This assertion has serious consequences for the interpretation of myths. It means that one cannot understand a myth merely by telling it, but only by interpreting it. In other words, there *is* no myth devoid of interpretation; the choice of the words in which to tell it begins the process of interpretation. We never really have the myth at all; we can only see the tracks that it leaves in our minds, like the visible trail of smoke left in the sky by a tiny, invisible plane. In this (as in some, though not all, other qualities), myths are like dreams: there can never be a dream entirely unpolluted by secondary elaboration; to tell the dream—even to *recall* the dream—is to interpret it.[38] As the culture retells the myth over time, it constantly reinterprets it, however much the culture may claim that the myth has been preserved intact. The myth provides a paradigm on which a number of meanings may be modeled.

Myths are perceived as true when the reality to which they point has "always" been perceived as true or becomes newly perceived as true. And a myth become newly perceived as true either by inspiring people to change the way things are or by enabling people to project their new view of reality over the world, even when that world remains the same. In fact, "true" and "false" are woefully inadequate words to apply to myths. Other cultures make other sorts of distinctions; they may contrast their "true" myths with various kinds of false stories, including what our culture would term history.[39] The Maring of New Guinea draw a contrast between stories that they call, on the one hand, *anchmal*, a category that would comprise both stories of literal fact ("I went to the field and planted a crop yesterday") and stories that we would call myths (stories about the descent of a god to give the tribe a plant or an animal to eat); and, by contrast, stories called *terum*, stories about something that could not or should not be true (such as a story in which men went to work on the lands owned by their wives, which is against all the principles of the tribe).[40]

This latter type of story is one that our culture has used, too, and classifies as a myth. A good example is the Grimms' fairy tale of the husband and wife who switched roles for a day (the woman working in the fields and the husband keeping house, each making a series of hilarious and costly mistakes); another example of this genre is the group of stories that imagine a world in which there is no death. But in the sense that I am trying to carve out, such stories carry a true meaning for us: they preserve for us the cultural "truth" that women should *not* work in the fields and men should *not* keep house, or the philosophical truth that we *must* die. To paraphrase the Italian saying, "If it's not true, it's been well invented." Thus words like "true" and "false," which are quite useful in the courtroom, are merely misleading when applied to myths.

When people assert that myths are true, do they say anything more than "Myths are about important things" or "I believe this, but you do not have to believe it"? I think that, although these implications may well be contained within such assertions, the truth claims made for myths say more. They aver not that great myths are literally true answers to certain great human questions, nor even that they carry such answers in symbolic transformation, but, at least, that they express a particular culture's best representations of those questions. And, as we shall see, several different representations of this type might all be regarded as "true."

Some scholars have argued that certain myths are true because everyone in the world has these same myths, myths that agree about certain essential human problems. This does not work. Though I am in fact inclined to agree that there *are* certain basic, universal human meanings encoded in myths, I will also argue that these meanings are not what keep myths alive in each culture, that what preserves myths is, rather, the individual details and the very different meanings that each culture brings to the basic myth. Moreover, even if all myths said the same thing (and they do not), this would constitute no proof that they were all telling the truth about that thing. Fifty million Frenchmen can, indeed, be wrong.

The problem of the truth of myth becomes even more irrelevant, I think, when we consider the fact that a major part of the impact of any myth lies not in its argument or *logos* (true or false) but in its imagery, its metaphor. The power of a myth is as much visual as verbal. The myth combines the functions of philosophy (the plot of the myth: what happens, and why) with the symbolism of ritual or cosmology (the actors in the myth: gods, animals, elemental powers). Myths are both events and images, both verbs and nouns. To analyze a myth in terms of either element alone (the verbal/philosophical event or the visual/symbolic image) is to reduce and distort it.[41]

If some myths are held by a culture to be true, are all myths regarded as true? Is there, then, no such thing as a myth that its own culture regards as false? I think there are not only false myths but pseudomyths and bad myths. A story is regarded as a pseudomyth by anyone who has a criterion or definition of myth that that story fails to satisfy. I would call a story a pseudomyth if it failed to satisfy my basic definition of a myth: for me, a pseudomyth would be a myth made up as a myth and disseminated as a myth, for some particular purpose, but not growing out of a tradition or taking its place within the context of other myths in that tradition. But a false myth might be something else. Since myths purport to tell us how things *are,* a myth might be falsified on that account by a demonstration that things are not, in fact, that way at all, that the myth in question has misrepresented the reality perceived by its own culture.

And there are, in addition to pseudomyths, not only false myths, but bad myths—though we may not all agree as to which these are. It might be argued that myths are bad when they are pernicious, when they support evil action. A bad myth in this context would be one that evoked an action regarded as unethical within its culture. But, just as I cannot see how to apply "true" and "false" usefully to myths, I cannot find a way to argue that some myths are "good" and others "bad" in any absolute sense (that is, in a sense that has meaning beyond the culture in which they occur). Since not all myths tell you explicitly what to do, myths are not so susceptible to moral criticism as are, say, philosophical arguments, and we may take refuge in ontological relativism. Yet some myths *do* tell us what to do, and many myths present a construction of the world that can easily imply an ethical stance that will drive the pragmatist into the swamps of moral relativism. We have already stumbled into these swamps in considering the myth of *suttee.*

The above discussion, convoluted though it may seem, merely scratches the surface of our own complex set of assumptions about what a myth is. But I hope that I have at least sketched the basic point: We may mean either that the myth tells us that things are not as they are, or that it tells us to do bad things, when we call other peoples' myths lies.

The Cave of Archetypes

Though it was Plato who taught us to call myths lies, it was Plato, too, who established the basic text on the value of myth, a text to which all subsequent analyses of myths were but footnotes. Plato's concept of eternal forms became reincarnate in what Adolf Bastian called the elementary ideas (*Elementargedanken*), which became manifest in the ideas of different peoples (*Völkergedanken*). Carl Gustav Jung refined this theory, referring to archetypes (shared by all human beings) and manifestations (appearing in each particular culture); and Mircea Eliade developed this theory into his own, far more subtle and complex theory of universal religious symbolism.

It may be that there is a universal truth, what Jung called the archetype, that speaks to us out of a foreign myth, but it is also true that what attracts us and fascinates us is not the archetype but the particular detail of that particular, foreign version of the archetype, what Jung called the manifestation. The archetype itself is so simple as to seem trite or obvious when we try to isolate it. This aspect of the archetype may have been what Leonard Meyer had in mind when he remarked, rather grumpily, that archetypes are "what children learn when they tediously reiterate nursery rhymes, intone tiresome chants, and make visual images that only fond parents delight in, psychiatrists regard as interesting, and Wordsworthian Romantics find profound."[42] The archetype itself is dead. It is like a coral reef: it supports life but is not itself alive. Or, rather, more precisely: the archetype, like the coral reef, consists almost entirely of the bones of once-living coral, of which only the thin edge of the surface is still alive.

It is, moreover, very difficult to isolate a pure archetype, or to see it when we have it. Like the Invisible Man in the old science fiction movie by that title, who could only be seen when he was wrapped in bandages or dressed in a hat and a coat, the archetype can only be "seen" when it is enveloped in the bandages that each cultural manifestation puts on it. Or, to update the image, the archetype is like a Barbie doll that you dress in different moral values; but the story itself has no moral values, it is just a narrative, an image of *what happens,* and it is up to the interpreter to ask *why* it happens. In turn, the nonexistent archetype lets us "see" the myth that is built around it, just as the hole in the doughnut is what lets us see the doughnut as a doughnut.

Jung himself acknowledged the transparency of the archetype:

> The archetypes . . . are eternally inherited forms and ideas which have at first no specific content. Their specific content only appears in the course of the individual's life, when personal experience is taken up in precisely these forms. . . . There are undoubtedly inherited archetypes which are, however, devoid of content, because, to begin with, they contain no personal experiences. They only emerge into consciousness when personal experiences have rendered them visible.[43]

We shall return to the importance of personal experiences in coloring in the archetype.

Archetypes are necessarily transmitted by manifestations. One might define an archetypal myth as what a story would be like if no one told it; but we cannot hear such a story. Moreover, the details lend the myths their verisimilitude. We believe other peoples' myths because we see in them the *details* of the fabric of their relationship with the human condition, in which we ourselves find a place; and, finally, the details lend the myths their beauty, and that, too, persuades us that they have meaning for us.

But it is in the very nature of archetypes to attract manifestational meanings to themselves. The phallus may well be archetypal (for Jungians as well as Freudians, let alone the rank and file), producing a universal, instinctive response in real life as well as in myth; but it is always *someone's* phallus, someone with manifestations (a tone of voice, a taste for a particular brand of Scotch) or (to switch from the Jungians to the structuralists) someone situated within a context (a past, a social role). These are the banal details that make the myth real and also our own.[44] On the other hand, the manifestation itself may sometimes be understood only in terms of the archetype. The great Vedantic sage Ramakrishna described what he called his madness: "When I experienced that divine madness, I used to worship my own sex-organ as the Siva-phallus" (the *lingam* of the god Shiva, venerated by many Hindus).[45]

Archetypes may or may not have inherent meanings, but they *find* meanings; they provide a blank check on which people cannot help writing meaning, a mold into which people are irresistibly driven to pour meaning; an archetype is a vacuum into which meaning keeps falling, which meaninglessness abhors. Like their archetypes, myths do not, strictly speaking, have meanings; they provide contexts in which meaning occurs. Like other religious symbols, in Clifford Geertz's formulation, myths "reek of meaning."[46] To this degree, a myth is not so much a true story as a story on which truth is based,[47] a story which people may infuse with their truth. As the shaman replied to the anthropologist who persisted in asking him, "What do the myths *mean?*": "The myths signify—nothing. They mean *themselves*."[48] More precisely, myths have been called "tautegorical" rather than "tautological": they do not *explain* themselves, but, rather, *symbolize* themselves.[49] Myths perform what has been called "a mating dance with meaning."[50]

Some people would reduce all myths to a colorless, minimal, universal form, a common denominator so common that it has no nobility left at all.[51] What happens to myths in the hands of such scholars is very much like what happens to sounds in the cave described by E. M. Forster in *A Passage to India.* In this cave, one that existed long before the emergence of either Hinduism or Islam in India, a peculiar echo is experienced by an elderly Englishwoman, Mrs. Moore, who wanders there in the heat:

> Professor Godbole had never mentioned an echo; it never impressed him, perhaps. There are some exquisite echoes in India; there is the whisper round the dome at Bijapur; there are the long solid sentences that voyage through the air at Mandu, and return unbroken to their creator. The echo in a Marabar cave is not like these, it is entirely devoid of distinction. Whatever is said, the same monotonous noise replies, and quivers up and down the walls until it is absorbed into the roof. "Boum" is the sound as far as the human al-

phabet can express it, or "bou-oum", or "ou-boum"—utterly dull. Hope, politeness, the blowing of a nose, the squeak of a boot, all produce "boum". . . . And if several people talk at once an overlapping howling noise begins, echoes generate echoes, and the cave is stuffed with a snake composed of small snakes, which writhe independently. . . . Suddenly, at the edge of [Mrs. Moore's] mind, Religion appeared, poor little talkative Christianity, and she knew that all its divine words from "Let there be light" to "It is finished" only amounted to "boum."[52]

In addition to the many profound things that this cave is about, the specific occasion that leads to this passage is a violent confrontation between two cultures. For Mrs. Moore, the cave is an answer to the sporadic, unsympathetic, and doomed attempts on the part of the British to sympathize with a culture as radically Other as it could be—India. It is significant that the Hindu, Godbole, is not bothered by the cave; and it is also significant that, after the experience of the cave has violently disrupted Mrs. Moore's sense of a possible harmony between India and England, it goes on to disrupt her sense of harmony even with her own religion, "poor little talkative Christianity." Reduced to its extreme, the ideal of empathy and harmony recoils and destroys itself. Boiled down to nothing but the coalesced archetype, the manifestations become meaningless. When the archetype is regarded as the sum total of all the manifestations, when everything is put in, the myth is enriched; when the archetype is regarded as what is left when all the manifestations are removed, when everything is taken out, the myth is impoverished.

Plato's cave was the reverse of the Marabar cave (as things Greek are so often the reverse of things Indian). The Platonic cave was the place of false images of transient diversity, mere shadows of the true, ideal forms, mere "likely stories" about the world outside the cave, which is the world of the eternal archetypes; the confusion inside the cave was the disorder produced by the intrusion of necessity into the purity and harmony of the eternal forms outside the cave.[53] In the *Phaedo,* Plato offers another variation upon the theme of the cave:

> We live in the hollows of this earth, and don't know it, and we think that we live on the earth's surface, as if a man were to live in the depths of the sea, and to think that he were living on the surface of the sea, and to look through the water at the sun and the other stars and think that the sea was actually heaven. . . . If one were to take wings and fly up, as he bobbed up, as fishes who bob up from the sea see our world here, so that man would see that other world there, and if his nature were sufficient to endure looking at it, he would know that this outer one is the true heaven, and the true light, and the true earth.[54]

We shall encounter, in chapter 4, the image of the fish used as a symbol of the inhabitant of a world that is entirely other. In Plato's myth, *we* are the fish, the ones who are entirely "other" from the standpoint of the true world of the forms.

The Greek cave is thus full of the confusion that results from mistaking many false images for the one true ideal, which is outside of the cave. The Indian cave, by contrast, is full of another kind of confusion, the confusion that represents the true nature of things, the chaos of primeval nature and ultimate reality before it has been artificially and falsely structured by individual cultural perceptions outside the cave. The multiple echoes—the detailed, "exquisite echoes"—in the Indian cave echo many things: they are the manifold manifestations of single archetypes, the many variants of each myth, the network of myths that are best understood as echoes of other myths. The single coalesced echo—the "boum"—is the archetype, the mythical Ur-myth, the stripped-down universal myth, the ideal form that only exists *outside* of Plato's cave. Nevertheless, Plato's advice remains valid for well-meaning mythologists who enter the Marabar cave of universal myths: Get out of the cave.

Myths and Classics

Myths are a species of the more general genus (or genre) of classics. For we might define a classic in a rather broad sense as a work of art (particularly but not necessarily a work of literature) that comes from the past and is accepted by a tradition over a great period of time as embodying what is good and important. In addition to this criterion of content, a classic is usually regarded as a paradigm of form: it is beautifully expressed. A myth, as I have just defined it, shares with a classic the first set of criteria: it comes from the past and is accepted by a tradition over a great period of time as embodying what is good and important. But myths have two qualities that other classics need not have: they are narratives, and they deal with religious questions. This final quality, the religious, supplies a support that serves instead of the second criterion of a classic, the criterion of form, that a myth does not necessarily have: a myth is not necessarily beautifully expressed. In the absence of this support of beauty, myths are sustained by being imbedded in a context of religious meaning. Thus not all classics are myths, nor are all variants of myths classics; but they intersect in important ways. A classic is not necessarily sacred and is not necessarily a narrative; a myth, on the other hand, need not satisfy the aesthetic criteria of a classic. Where the myth and the classic intersect is in the criterion that they must be accepted by tradition as embodying an important meaning.

Myths and classics resemble one another primarily in the way in which they are transmitted and received. One reason for the historical endurance of classics (as for the remembrance of myths) is that the theme(s) on which they are based may be redefined as models for the interpretation of experience. The connection between the myth and the classic is therefore hermeneutic; what they share is a way of interpreting things that turns out to have applicability to widely different historical and existential situations.

The myth, the core of meaning, may survive to some extent even without language; the myth can be recreated again and again, reinflated like a collapsible balloon. The story of the Trojan horse and the myth of Eden survive as myths, free-floating without words; the nonmythological classic, by contrast, survives only in language, despite the sustaining nature of the ancient core of meaning that it embodies. As Claude Lévi-Strauss has remarked, whereas poetry may be lost in translation, "the mythical value of myth remains preserved through the worst translation."[55]

Eliade has demonstrated how, even when myths become degraded, even when they lose their power and even, on an overt level, their meaning, they always retain something of their intrinsic value, however much this may be disguised or forgotten.[56] He applied this insight to the survival of mythic themes even in apparently nonmythic contexts, in rock 'n' roll music, novels, secret societies, and movies.[57] In these examples, the *content* is mythical even when the *form* is not. But the degradation of a myth can be of the opposite sort: the *form* may be mythical even when the *content* is not.[58] Either of these situations can produce what we might call mythological kitsch.

Myths can be impervious to kitsch. They survive in a ragbag of tawdry modern avatars: Hindi films, complete with rock 'n' roll choruses, depict the battles of gods and demons, and the Indian version of our own Classic Comics (*Amar Chitra Katha,* "Immortal Picture Stories") present the ancient Hindu classics in a strangely westernized but still recognizably Indian form. Though these comics are ostensibly written for children, many adults read them; and for some (as, indeed, for many of the Americans who read no fiction other than comics about superheroes, let alone Classic Comics), they provide the only remaining source of the classical mythology of India.

And there are other, even more unlikely cartoons in which the myths live on. Hindus may not know from the *Rig Veda* or the *Mahabharata* the story of the aged sage Chyavana, who was rejuvenated so that he could marry a beautiful young girl, Sukanya.[59] But they may know the story from another source: newspaper advertisements for a patent medicine called Chyavan-Pras. The ad begins with a Sanskrit verse, which can be translated thus: "This is the story of the Chyavana Food that the sage Chyavana ate; even though he was worn out with old age, he became a joy to the eyes of women." The verse is followed by a series of cartoon illustrations with descriptions below them, in English, telling the story of Chyavana, and ending:

> The pleased twins [the Ashvins, divine physicians] asked Sukanya what boon she wanted. She replied that her husband should retain his youth perpetually. The twins prescribed a rejuvenating tonic containing Amla (gooseberry), later on known as "Chyavan-Pras." Thus Chyavana was blessed with the special yoga and having consumed it he became a full-grown youth pleasing to the eyes of the women. And as the yoga was consumed by Chyavana it came to be known as Chyavan-Pras (Chyavana Food). Kottakkal Arya Vaidya Sala manufactures this potent tonic prescribed by the divine physicians in the traditional and conventional manner with scrupulous care and attention.

Thus the myth of Chyavana lives on, withered but still firm, even in an advertisement for a dubious rejuvenating medicine. And it is Western travelers, not Hindu worshipers, who are shocked by the apparent blasphemy in the Rishikesh "Zoo," where the gods are kept by the dozens in little plastic cages, embodied in mannequins that move like display-window models. Present-day Hindus devote themselves indiscriminately to some of the most beautiful sacred images ever created (such as the carvings on medieval temples still is use) and to garish, hideous, mass-produced idols and oleographic "calendar art" icons; to the devout Hindu, the archetype exists not only in a Chola bronze but also (if, perhaps, less compellingly) in a plastic Kewpie doll.[60] In one sense, this is a good thing; if myth could not survive kitsch, some myths would never have survived at all. Indeed, some myths begin as kitsch and eventually become classics; taste, after all, is often dependent on context, and new stories, from whatever source, *do* sometimes become genuine myths.

Nor is mythological kitsch limited to Hinduism; it is widespread in the West, particularly but not only in Catholicism, which places in the niches of great Gothic cathedrals plaster-of-paris images garishly painted like the modern Hindu idols; and these tawdry, funky icons are still infused with great power. The symbolism of the Eucharist survives no matter whether the cup holds wine or grape juice or South African sherry. When the archetype is truly powerful, it does not need a powerful manifestation to convey it.

Outside the realm of organized religion, too, myths often survive, at least in their crude outlines, in kitsch transformations. In the film *Never On Sunday,* a whore in the Athenian port of Piraeus retold all the Greek tragedies to her customers, but she always gave them a happy ending: everyone—Oedipus, Medea, everyone—went to the seashore. In America, a company called Impulse markets "Instant Mythology," a packet of small capsules that are literally *reduced* (and reinflatable) myths: "Drop capsule in warm/hot water and watch mythological characters appear! Fun—educational—non-toxic. For ages 5 years and above. Not to be taken internally. Capsules contain: centaur, dragon, Pegasus, unicorn, or mermaid." And finally, the metaphor of the reinflatable balloon comes to life in a series of patented Mythological Balloons that expand to reveal "Adam and Eve" and "Noah's Ark." Some archetypes seem to be able to exert at least a semblance of their power in almost *any* manifestation.

Soap operas and myths may sometimes appear to be about the same archetypal human problems; but soap operas do not ask the same questions about these problems that myths ask, nor do they ask them in the same words. Science fiction, too, often contains kitsch mythology. The myth of the incarnate god is reduced to the comic-book tale of Superman disguised as Clark Kent or Wonder Woman disguised as Diana Prince;[61] the evil look-alike or shadow double becomes a clone created by extraterrestrial invaders and bodysnatchers. The shaman's voyage to the gods has become a Star Trek, and the battle between gods and demons a Star War.[62] Creatures from outer space often pinch hit for the gods; after all, what could be more *other* than a Martian? In one science fiction film, *Chariot of the Gods,* the heroes of the classical Greek myths appear as aliens.

This paradigm began much earlier, in what might be called the Shazam syndrome.[63] The close kinship between religious mythology and the secular mythology of superheroes is apparent even to children. My son, Michael Lester O'Flaherty, who by the age of four had absorbed a considerable corpus of Hindu mythology and C. S. Lewis from me, and a lot of American mythology and science fiction from what is euphemistically referred to as "the street," spontaneously created (and dictated to me) the following myth, which he called "A Christmas Story":

> In the old days, no one got presents. There weren't any gods, just good monsters that made things happen. The wicked queen said no one could give presents. They stabbed the queen in the heart and she died. They fought with the king, and the monsters scratched the king, and out came a piece of paper, and it said, "You can have presents." And then they gave soldiers and things to the children, and the grown-ups gave each other jackets. The queen got alive, and she got good. Batman married her. The queen was dipped in cottage cheese and the devil ate her, but Batman saved her by punching the devil on the chin. And that's the story of Christmas.

Even children are able to synthesize the myths of their own culture with foreign mythologies, but the result is hardly a religious classic.

Indeed, even science fiction written by grown-ups usually lacks the rich texture of meanings of traditional mythology; students respond immediately to the quality of the bizarre in science fiction, but they must be taught to respond to the less immediately accessible meanings hidden behind the wilder bizarrerie of great religious fiction. Though some science fiction does deal with great cosmic and ethical questions, and even resorts to a transcendent element at times, it usually lacks the substance that traditional mythology draws from its tradition. The phenomena I have cited, many of which function in the manner of the more classic texts that Northrop Frye called "secular scriptures,"[64] are instances of what Eliade termed the degradation of symbols.

The archetypal charm of such stuff as soap operas and science fiction are made on was delightfully analyzed by George Orwell in his essay on Rudyard Kipling. Orwell argues that Kipling is "a good bad poet":

> Most of Kipling's verse is so horribly vulgar that it gives one the same sensation as one gets from watching a third-rate music-hall performer recite "The Pigtail of Wu Fang Fu" with the purple limelight on his face, *and yet* there is much of it that is capable of giving pleasure to people who know what poetry means. . . . Kipling is almost a shameful pleasure, like the taste for cheap sweets that some people secretly carry into middlelife. But even with his best passages one has the same sense of being seduced by something spurious, and yet unquestionably seduced.[65]

Thus, when Winston Churchill wished to move the British people during a wartime broadcast, he quoted not Shakespeare but a second-rate Victorian poet named Arthur Clough; as Orwell remarked of this broadcast, "Not even Churchill could have gotten away with it if he had quoted anything much better than this."[66] In a similar vein, Walt Whitman was once described as the literary equivalent of a Hawaiian shirt. And in his essay on "Good Bad Books," Orwell is willing to bet that *Uncle Tom's Cabin* will outlive the complete works of Virginia Woolf or George Moore.[67]

What is "good" about this bad poetry?

> A good bad poem is a graceful monument to the obvious. It records in memorable form . . . some emotion which very nearly every human being can share. . . . However sentimental it may be, its sentiment is "true" sentiment in the sense that you are bound to find yourself thinking the thought it expresses sooner or later, and then, if you happen to know the poem, it will come back into your mind and seem better than it did before.[68]

This is not at all a bad description of the kitsch charm of myth, of the depths (or, perhaps, the breadth) to which the language of myth can sink while the myth still bobs along blithely above it.

But kitsch can sometimes sink even a great myth, and some theologians have argued that because religious kitsch destroys religious feeling, it is the work of the devil.[69] As J. M. Cameron remarked,

> I set beside "I come to the garden alone" the noble hymns of Isaac Watts and Charles Wesley and the former simply falls away from the world of authentic religious discourse, as do the holy pictures that used to—perhaps still do—puncuate the lives of Catholic children. I think kitsch presents us with a serious theological problem and stands, far beyond the formal bounds of theology, for something amiss in our culture, as, for example, when well-washed fat babies or puppy dogs presented on the cinema screen evoke disproportionate cries of delight. Kitsch is a form of lying, and religious kitsch lies about what is, for the believer, the deepest reality.[70]

For myth, too, is carried on language as perfume is carried on a wind. Mary Douglas has challenged Lévi-Strauss's assertion that myth can be translated, and has pointed out the ways in which myth, like poetry, cannot be translated after all.[71] When a myth is translated, its classic component is somehow tarnished; this part of the Bible is invisibly lost to those who cannot read Hebrew or Greek and was visibly lost to many people when the King James translation was discarded. The Bible has crossed many linguistic borders in its journey from ancient Palestine to us, and a toll has been paid at every crossing. There is a loss of power in the myth when the Bible is translated from its magical language into our language; so, too, there is a loss of power in the ritual when the Latin Mass is translated into English.

These two losses reinforce one another when we speak in English the words that were first uttered in Greek to establish the ritual of the Eucharist, and then, again in English, the words of the Latin prayers that grew up around that ritual (themselves already preserving, archaically, bits of the older Greek in phrases such as *Kyrie eleison*). This is in part the result of the decision to open up the meaning to everyone, even at the cost of a loss of magic, rather than to preserve the magic of the ancient words of the ritual, even at the cost of a loss of comprehension. The loss of magic is also in part a reflection of the fact that by reading the text in the original we maintain the otherness of the text, which is, as we shall soon see, one of the sources of its mystery.

For even a myth needs *some* linguistic detail, some spark of originality, to ignite it for us; it must eventually be reinflated, re-tumesced, and if the language that attempts to do so is inadequate and unexciting, the myth will not rise again. This being so, Lévi-Strauss's assertion of the independence of myth from language is true only of a certain sort of myth, and then only partially true. Oral traditions—particularly more ritualistic traditions—maintain that their texts are untranslatable; people who feel that their sacred texts must be *heard* do not believe that the text will remain sacred in any language but the original. But people who feel that their sacred scriptures can be *read*—particularly people from more rationalistic and less ritualistic traditions—will usually allow them to be read in translation.

The myth itself needs to have some vehicle in which to survive between its incarnations. The reinflatable balloon must always leave behind its rubber shell even when it is emptied of meaning and language. Werner Heisenberg is said to have remarked that if he had never lived, someone else would have discovered the principle of indeterminacy, but if Beethoven had never lived, no one else would have written his symphonies.[72] This may or may not be a valid statement about the difference between science and art; but it is certainly true that, though *anyone* can discover an archetype, only an artist can produce a great manifestation.

The Kannada novelist Anantha Murthy has spoken of the way in which, as a child, he believed the myths and felt himself to be a part of them. Referring to the story of Chyavana and Sukanya, in which Sukanya first discovers the aged Chyavana when he is meditating inside an arthill (a not uncommon practice for sages in myths), Anantha Murthy remarked, "In my youth, every anthill had a sage inside it." As he grew up, and became debunked and demythologized, he became critical of these myths and ashamed of his belief in them. Yet he still felt the need to recreate them in his stories; and even now, he said, "When I write a poem about an anthill, there *is* a sage in it."[73] Sometimes it is art, and art alone, that can recreate the myth; and to do this the words must be the right words, the words of poetry. Some myths do not survive some translations.

When the myth and the classic overlap, we have a narrative that captures the content of a mythological core in the form of a beautifully expressed work of literature. These are the great artistic renditions of myths: Homer's *Odyssey* in Greek or in Chapman's translation, the Bible in Hebrew or in the King James translation, the *Mahabharata* in Sanskrit or in Tamil. We may stray farther from the traditional forms, too, without necessarily entering the cultural wastelands of kitsch. The literary classics of science fiction—Mary Shelley's *Frankenstein*, Robert Louis Stevenson's *Dr. Jekyll and Mr. Hyde*, Bram Stoker's *Dracula*—do raise religious questions within powerful myths. It may be that this tradition has been continued by writers such as Ray Bradbury, Isaac Asimov, and Ursula LeGuin.[74] But great works of art that express myths are the form of religious discourse that is most likely to survive the perilous journey from one culture to another.

Chapter 3

Other Peoples' Classics

Retelling the Mahabharata

W e in the West[1] tend to indulge in two different but related misconceptions about our own classics: we think that our classics are in a sense eternal—forever fixed, frozen in the amber of carefully preserved written documents—and that they provide a shared communal base for all educated members of our culture. But neither of these assumptions is true; our classics are not fixed and eternal, and all of us do not have access to them.

The Page and the Stage in the West

Let us begin by looking more closely at our first assumption about our own classics, and let us take the works of Shakespeare and Homer as our paradigmatic classics, which surely no one will object to. Shakespeare had such sources as Holinshed's *Histories,* Plutarch's *Lives,* and Homer (perhaps in the original Greek, perhaps in Chapman's translation), but he used these sources with great freedom. Whatever there may have been of myth in these sources, they were not myths for Shakespeare, not myths current in his culture; they were stories, from which he made his own stories, transforming them into his own creation, which was recorded in texts that were preserved and more or less fixed during his lifetime. But the Shakespearean classics changed through performance. A different Hamlet was reborn in David Garrick, in John Barrymore, in John Gielgud, in Laurence Olivier, to say nothing of the ways in which the play as a whole was transformed in the hands of each innovative director. Sometimes such transformations could be counterproductive. Dressing all the characters in *Hamlet* as Hell's Angels may prove initially useful for audiences who are unfamiliar with Shakespearean costume or, more important, unaccustomed to drawing parallels between historical or mythical situations and contemporary or actual situations. But such a transformation does not add to our original understanding of the play, for we already know that the human issues raised in *Hamlet* apply not merely to the Elizabethan world but to any world, including ours; and such gimmicks may actually detract from that understanding, by subtracting the particular Elizabethan manifestation of the general archetypal meanings.

There are, nevertheless, ways in which self-conscious contemporizations may tell us something new, not merely by making clearer the contemporary inflection of the ancient meaning of the classic, but by making explicit the relationship between the ancient form and the modern form of that meaning. A good example of such a transformation was Robert Fall's direction of *Hamlet* in Chicago in 1986. The play was visually translated into the present: Claudius was a successful politician in a three-piece suit, complete with PR men, bodyguards, and press conferences with television coverage. The final scene, however, the duel in which everyone is killed, was played in Elizabethan dress—doublets and hose and crowns and long trains—as if to remind the audience that this was, after all, a play about sixteenth-century politics rather than (or as well as?) about twentieth-century politics. But at the very end of this scene, when Fortinbras entered and viewed the dead bodies, the twentieth century reasserted itself; Fortinbras himself was in twentieth-century paramilitary dress and was accompanied by television cameras recording the bloody carnage, as television cameras do nowadays at disasters. His cameras pointed at the corpses—Hamlet, Laertes, Gertrude, Claudius—dressed in the Elizabethan costumes that they wore in that final scene. But what we the audience saw projected onto the television screens at the side of the stage, seen through the eyes of those twentieth-century machines, were those same figures, in precisely the same contortions of death, but wearing twentieth-century costumes as in the earlier scenes, and realistically covered with documentary blood that was not there on the stage. And when Fortinbras called for Hamlet to be borne out like a soldier, Hamlet's body (in Elizabethan dress) was lifted onto the shoulders of four ghosts who had died earlier in the play but who were silent witnesses to the fatal duel—the ghosts of Polonius, Rosenkrantz, Guildenstern, and Hamlet's father—still in their twentieth-century clothes. This was, for me, a brilliant metaphor for the simultaneous archaism and contemporaneity of Shakespeare.

It is also significant that when the Shakespearean classics are transformed in performance, we experience them as a group, sitting together in the darkened theater. This shared moment is an important source of our belief that the plays of Sophocles or those of Shakespeare or those of Tennessee Williams are our classics. Thus even our "written" classics are in fact experienced, in their most important form, orally.

Homer is a rather different sort of model of a classic. The stories that

Homer himself inherited were indeed myths to him, though he himself was
accused (by Herodotus) of having invented many of the specific features
of the Greek gods himself.[2] Homer, we now know, was one—perhaps the
last one—in a series of poets who improvised constantly in reworking the
great themes that they had inherited. Of course, Homer used these sources to
compose his *own* poem. As David Grene has said of the relationship between
Homer (in the *Odyssey*) and the stories that he inherited,

> These stories must have had overtones of meaning that contradicted
> his own vision. Which means that the poem he composed presents
> its truth in an almost but not quite self-conscious relation to an
> older world, now outmoded, the reality of which at any time is
> toyed with, doubted, held in suspense, and then in this ambiguous
> light made the substance of his created world of illusion . . . bred
> of conscious contrast with something else and original in its new
> infusion of meaning.[3]

What Homer produced may well have been, for a while, both a retelling
of an old myth—a religious narrative—and a newly created secular poem for
the culture in which he lived, but it soon became merely a poem. Once
Plato had given myth its bad name and exiled the poets from his republic,
Homer's work lost whatever religious element it may have had and remained
only a literary classic. But the retransformations that took place within the
Shakespearean classics through performance are minor compared to the major
transformations that took place in the Homeric classics through translation.
For the language of Homer soon became archaic even in Greece, and Homer
was then taken up as a classic by non-Greek-speaking European and English
cultures. Each generation has been inspired differently by these classics and
retranslated them: Homer became reincarnate in Virgil and Dante in one sense,
and in Chapman, Pope, and Lattimore in another.[4]

It may even be, as has been suggested, that the very defining characteristic
of a classic is that it is a work that must be retranslated by each new generation.
But we "retranslate" Shakespeare in a very different sense from the way
in which we retranslate Homer; we do, at least, have Shakespeare's words,
Shakespeare's poem, whether or not we really have his myth. With Homer,
we "have" neither the poem nor the myth, in the sense that we can never
have them in a language which is our mother tongue.

There is a paradox of otherness hidden in the mysterious process of
translation. To read a myth in an English translation makes it seem like an
English myth; it seems like other myths that we have read in English. But to
work at understanding it in the Sanskrit or Greek means, on the one hand, that
we come closer to understanding what it really says, but, on the other hand,
that it becomes even *more* other to us as we come to realize how very weird
its way of telling itself is, and how it thinks things that cannot be thought
in English. Thus reading it in the original does, at first, distance it from us,
does make it harder to understand than it was (or, rather, than it *seemed*)

in English. Yet when we do eventually break through the challenge of that otherness, we are in fact closer to the myth in every sense.

It might be argued that our classics are fixed in the sense that the core of meaning is preserved, even when the words of the translations change. Classics define themselves as being tied to a fixed core in the distant past. But this link is often rather weak. Our "tradition" of the classics, including Homer, was lost for centuries and only discovered, and self-consciously recreated, at the time of the Renaissance. As for the core of meaning, the literary classics from Homer on down have often been valued for meanings that are interpreted in diametrically opposed ways from one age to another. These texts have, moreover, from time to time been demoted as classics and then reinstated. How wrong we are when we think that we have "always" had our own fixed, written classics.

Let us turn now to our second major assumption: that what makes our classics our classics is the fact that they are shared by all educated members of our community. The shallowness of this assumption is revealed as soon as we ask who the "we" are who know our own classics. Even in the so-called good old days, when everyone who mattered was able not only to read Greek but to translate editorials from the *Times* of London into Greek prose—even then, the paradox of the classics was that they excluded rather than included people. The classics were the texts that *we* knew and *they* didn't. The classics defined a tiny elite who in turn defined the Community as consisting of themselves, the people who spouted Latin quotations in the House of Commons.

The classical education was designed primarily for the training of British civil servants, more precisely for the foreign service, the colonizers, the men sent out to rule the world, to rule India. They were stuffed, like so many Strasbourg geese, with the Greek and Latin classics that constituted a bulwark against the supreme danger of Going Native, like the garlic clove that was thought to protect people against vampires. The power of the classics enabled the colonizers to hang on to their own culture in the maelstrom of the temptations provided by the alternate cultures that they were to rule. The classics created a kind of force field around them, filled their ears with the wax of Homer so that they couldn't hear the siren song of the colonies.

It was another aspect of this same instinct that made the colonizers wear white dinner jackets in the tropics, to make sure that no one (least of all themselves) might mistake them for natives; that made the government send them home after five years, lest they actually get to like the place; and that posted them to Australia if they knew how to speak Chinese (a skill that might make them identify with the Chinese or get to like the Chinese).

There is an irony in the other side of the coin of the fate of the classics in India, the assimilation of the classics by those whom the British ruled. In the 1820s and 1830s, when students in Hindu College, Calcutta (later known as Presidency College) were first exposed to the full range of English and European literature, their first choice was Homer (read first in Greek, later in English and Bengali translations), and after Homer, Shakespeare. Tne unquenchable ability of these great works to breach cultural and linguistic boundaries ultimately transformed them from a barrier between the rulers and the ruled to a bridge between the rulers and the ruled, or at least those among the ruled who emulated their rulers.

But let us return to the problem posed by the so-called Community of the classics as it exists among us today. Nowadays, of course, the arrogant self-deception of that Community has been shattered. Only a tiny percentage of Americans read Homer even in English translation, let alone in Greek, and it is advertising jingles that constitute the basis of our shared culture, words that are a lie by the very definition of their function ("truth in advertising" being a ludicrous oxymoron). And as for narratives that have a universal franchise, we have Dick Tracy and "Dallas."[5]

The examples of Dick Tracy and "Dallas" are particularly apt, I think, because they belong to the genre of the serial, a genre that also includes more intellectual and less mainstream cartoons like "Doonesbury," "Bloom County," and Walt Kelly's "Pogo." Films, too, often perpetuate themselves in this way (like *The Return of the Son of Jaws, III*), as children's books used to do (like the multivolume adventures of the Hardy Boys, Tom Swift, the Rover Boys, Nancy Drew).[6] The serial is a Western parallel to the never-ending chain of stories that is taken up, link by link, night after night, by village storytellers in traditional societies like India. Indeed, the close kinship between the two forms has recently been demonstrated by the fact that the most popular show on Indian television today is a fifty-two-episode version of the Sanskrit epic, the *Ramayana;* its success has led to plans to begin a similar version of the other epic, the *Mahabharata.*[7]

When Charles Dickens published his novels in serial form (novels that, by the way, contained some of English literature's greatest studies of both children and strangers), the English-speaking world would hang upon the next installment. It is said that when a ship docked in New York carrying the latest chapters of *The Old Curiosity Shop,* the crowd on shore cried out to those on board, "Is Little Nell dead?"[8] Likening a contemporary American serial novel to Dickens's serials, one writer commented, "The experience of a serial is that of a common, contained world. It is a shared event. Everyone is reading or watching the same episode within the same time frame. No one can skip ahead until the next installment comes out. And that level of containment is important, for it provides the serial with its basic subtext: we are all in this together."[9] This is not at all a bad definition of one of the functions of myth.

But there are other functions that Dick Tracy, "Dallas," and other exploiters of the "subtext" in soap operas on television do not fulfill as the novels of Dickens did. Most of our Western myths now survive only on the level of kitsch; the real myths, in their classic forms, are no longer ours—if, indeed, they ever were. And kitsch mythology, as we saw in chapter 2, does not have the power of nonkitsch mythology. So much for the shared, communal base of our classics.

The loss of this community is much bemoaned by those who believe that they speak for it; most recently, it has been eloquently lamented by Allan Bloom.[10] I share his grief, but I do not share his belief that the way to repair the damage is to attempt to return, somehow, to the golden age in which we all had our classics. It wasn't golden; we didn't all have them; and there are better things, perhaps, to put into our heads now than our own lost classics.[11] I shall try later to suggest what these things are, and how we might get them. For now, let me try to say why I think we cannot get our own classics back.

The Otherness of the Classics

One reason why few of us can appreciate our classics is because they are, and have probably always been, archaic to most of us. Even Homer and Shakespeare chose (or were constrained) to base their own works on other works that they inherited from a generation that was to them already archaic. Indeed, it may well be that it is the very *nature* of classics to be other, to refer back to a lost golden age and to speak with an archaic diction that we must strain to understand. We sense instinctively that our classics were born long ago, in a galaxy far away. Even myths, the most accessible of classics, are subject to this distancing; a myth, it has been remarked, "is another culture even for those of its own culture, just as another culture is something of a myth for the anthropologist."[12]

Yet it is ultimately possible for us to possess our own classics, if by "possess" we mean to internalize, to experience as a familiar, non-other body of literature. On the one hand, there is within the great mythological classics a core of meaning that recalls us to our real world; and on the other hand there is an attraction that lies in the very otherness of the classic. This is true to some extent of Shakespeare, and even more true of Homer, who comes to us not only from another time but from another continent and in another language.

Homer is the mediating point, the classic that we regard as our own but that is in fact most dramatically other. We may have appropriated Homer, but only as an Other, now regarded as "our" Other, a stranger living inside our own culture. Once we admit this, we have admitted that what we find classic in Homer is classic to us not because it is familiar but because, even while it remains Greek to us, it has meaning for us who are not Greeks. Moreover, if we study it carefully, in the scholarly way that I have proposed, we may discover a great deal of the meaning that it had for the Greeks who first heard it. And once we have granted this, we can begin to realize that the classics of the rest of the world may also have meaning for us and may therefore also become ours. There are obstacles to be surmounted in comprehending strange myths, but they *are* to be surmounted. There are also, of course, people who have never had, and never will have, any need for classics, mythological or other; such people will neither notice the demise of our own mythological classics nor think to reach out for anyone else's. But there are also those who do feel a need for myths, people who may sense the loss of something that they may never in fact have had; and, as we shall see, foreign myths may have a special value and power for such people.

Moreover, once we are released from our expectation that it should be easy for us to understand "our" classics, we may be more willing to do the considerable hard work that is necessary to "translate" our own classics into our own language, instead of expecting them to be easy to read and discarding them in disappointment when the going gets rough. We may also be prepared to devote to other peoples' classics the additional hard work that is required to understand them. But the work may not be quite so hard when we deal with mythological classics rather than other sorts of classics. For, just as classics feel "other" to us even within our own traditions because of their archaism and intentional distancing, so myths feel less "other" to us even in foreign traditions, because we recognize the mythological core of human meaning. Nonmythological classics are also more difficult for us to understand because of the challenge inherent in the sophistication of their art forms; many myths, by contrast, are easier to understand at first because of their ability to ride in on waves of kitsch. Yet the myths that endure best, on any cultural level, are free of kitsch.

Our own imaginative faculty is a kind of magnet that draws to itself the reality inherent in the imaginative power of the myths and classics of other ages and other lands. And once we admit that our classics are not our own in the way that we used to believe that they were, that Homer is not "ours" in the way that we thought he was, we can begin to possess them in another way, a way that also makes it possible for us to possess a whole new world of classics, other peoples' classics, the *Mahabharata* as well as Homer.

For example, it may well be that if we were in fact only to reinstate the old Greek classics somehow, as Allan Bloom might wish, we would simply confine ourselves once more to the same old elite that owned them before. In India, by contrast, as we shall soon see, a mythological classic like the *Mahabharata* is experienced by the people as a whole, not by an elite; this might well make it ultimately more accessible to *our* people as a whole than Homer has ever been. In this way, by reapproaching our own classics as we simultaneously approach the classics of others for the first time, we may find ourselves creating a new humanism.

There are two complementary types of eclecticism that may enable us to assimilate both our own classics and the classics of others. Through the first of these methods, any one of us can make any single classic our own. At the end of Ray Bradbury's *Fahrenheit 451*, when all the books in the world have been burned, a group of people gather around a campfire. Each of them has memorized one of the classics and so thoroughly internalized it that when they are introduced to one another one can say, "Hello. I am Plato's *Republic*," while another identifies himself as the *Book of Ecclesiastes*.[13] This form of assimilation is very rare in our day; not many people do memorize, or even internalize, a whole book. But in ancient India, as we shall see, people really did memorize entire books of the Vedas and became known as the living incarnation of one particular school or branch (*shakha*) of the Vedic tree.

But just as an entire classic can become part of any one of us, so too, parts of the classics have become part of all of us. There is the old story of the woman who went to see *Hamlet* for the first time, and afterward was asked what she thought of it. "It was quite good," she said, "but it did have an awful lot of quotations in it." Many of the people who tell us that brevity is the soul of wit or that there is method in our madness do not know that they are quoting *Hamlet*. Indeed, the very fact that I am able to make this joke about *Hamlet* is evidence of its classic status.

A more poignant instance of this process of assimilation was noted by Hannah Arendt, who told of a concentration camp in World War II in which people got together and each tried to remember as much of Homer as he or she could, to piece together all the pieces that they knew. They did not manage to reconstruct all of Homer; and so their work did not keep Homer going, as it were (the way that the whole work was preserved in the fiction of *Fahrenheit 451*); but they did it because it "kept *them* going," she said.[14] The pieces of Homer in them were things that they clung to when all the rest of their civilization was destroyed.

Thus a classic may be preserved either through an individual eclecticism (the *Fahrenheit 451* model, each classic going into a fragment of society, a person), or through a cultural eclecticism (the *Hamlet* quotation model, the fragmentation of the classics, each piece going into all of us, into society as a whole). Claude Lévi-Strauss has used a similar metaphor to explain the process by which mythology fragments an inexpressible truth and then transmits the separate fragments, which the hearers must know as a group in order to understand the message as a whole.[15] These "hearers" may sometimes exist only in the world of scholarship, in the mind of the anthropologist who collects the myths from several different tribes, none of whom know "the myth" as a whole; but in a culture like that of India, there are many people, both scholars and illiterate people who like stories, who are able to put together all of the fragments.

The Bible, which may well be the only true classic that we have left, is the only one that is preserved in both of these ways to any significant degree. That is, almost all of us know some of the Bible by heart, and a few of us know almost all of it by heart. The pious hope that everyone should be able to understand the Bible in church led to the great translation into English under the sponsorship of King James I. Some people still internalize the Bible from their childhood, learning it from their parents, learning it as a myth in the strongest sense. But for others (those who know only some of it), the Bible as a whole functions only as a part of a ritual, in church. For such people, the ritual aspect of the Bible is preserved in what now appears to be an archaic form, the very King James translation that was meant *not* to be archaic.[16] The realization that we tend to confuse our favorite archaic version with the Ur-text was expressed by the man who is said to have remarked, "If the King James version was good enough for Jesus, it's good enough for me." A similar assumption about the special, if not supernatural, status of the author of the great translation underlies Rudyard Kipling's hilarious short story "Proofs of Holy Writ," in which a rather drunken William Shakespeare secretly ghostwrites the translation commissioned by King James from the bishops.[17]

And many people confer yet another divine sanction upon this text when they misname it the Saint James Bible.

When attempts are made to remove the archaism of the King James Bible, both because its diction is difficult for many Americans to understand and because we now know that much of it incorrectly translates the Hebrew and Greek, we are troubled. On the other hand, the very fact that most of us do not know the Bible thoroughly makes it possible for us to take the *text* of the Bible (that is, the Bible as myth, or sacred narrative, rather than as a piece of ecclesiastical ritual) and to redefine that text as a true classic, acknowledging its otherness. In this way we may begin to reapproach the Bible and to repossess its meanings outside of our own particular ritual context. We may be able to study it as humanists, as if it were someone else's religious classic, someone else's myth.

If the classic has not been entirely lost, and the audience can be expected to know the story, the storyteller is able to use the audience's assumptions and expectations to serve new purposes. We have already seen instances of one such purpose—making jokes about *Hamlet*—and there are many others. When Shakespeare reinterpreted Homer in *Troilus and Cressida,* or when Tom Stoppard in turn reinterpreted Shakespeare in *Rosencrantz and Guildenstern Are Dead,* even, perhaps, when James Joyce reinterpreted the *Odyssey* in *Ulysses,* they were doing what Homer and Shakespeare themselves were doing: using the classics both with and against themselves, simultaneously deconstructing and reconstructing the classics. For *Troilus and Cressida* is not a satire on Homer; it is an extraordinarily malignant interpretation of things that are buried in Homer. And even though the two bit-players in the Stoppard play provide a comic mockery of the nobility of the hero, Hamlet, they cannot help acting, nevertheless, as a foil for his tragic heroism. In a traditional society, each member of the audience would be running a replay of the *Iliad* or *Hamlet* in his or her head while watching the modern variant. Nowadays, when an audience can no longer be expected to know *Hamlet,* the Stoppard play may be produced in conjunction with a performance of *Hamlet,* either simultaneously (giving *Hamlet* and interpolating the Stoppard scenes at the appropriate points) or *seriatim* (*Hamlet* in the afternoon, *Rosencrantz . . .* at night).[18]

The modern variants of the two-tiered play within the play have many close ancient parallels in Asia, where the classics often exist simultaneously as archaic fossils—fixed texts—and as fluid modern re-incarnations (or *re-fleshings*) of those same fossils. In Indonesia and Bali, shadow puppets act out the ancient story of Rama in Sanskrit or a high dialect; the heroes are heroic, and the women who love them are above suspicion. But in front of the puppet theater stands a human figure—rather like Fran in the old *Kukla, Fran, and Ollie* show, or Leslie Caron in the movie of Paul Gallico's *Lili*—, a clown who speaks in the vernacular or in a low dialect. He mocks the hero and expresses the audience's cynical rejection of the noble ideal ("Rama, you ass, do you really believe that Sita lived for years in another man's palace and never slept with him? How dumb can anyone be . . .").

Sometimes the audience is disturbed by the discontinuity between the two levels and insists on going backstage to unmask the puppeteers, to show that there is, in fact, only one level, that the clown is also operating the puppets. In the Javanese *wayang* tradition, the image is twice removed from reality: the puppeteer (who is sometimes explicitly likened to a god) projects a shadow of the puppet. Yet the audience watches the puppeteer, too.[19] Similarly, in Japan the puppeteers wear black, to make themselves into shadows, but they, too, are clearly visible to the audience. The audiences in these performance traditions are thus self-consciously watching the illusion, in a manner that has been described (by Lawrence E. Sullivan) as "putting invisibility on display."

The two levels of reality exist simultaneously, like the physical embodiment of a Loeb Library text and translation, even when we read a written text. This split-level reality acknowledges the "otherness" of the classic—the fact that it no longer literally expresses the lives of the audience—even while it proves that the classic is, in fact, always relevant because, like Proteus, it always changes its shape to fit the needs of the moment.

Myth as Child's Play

Besides the Bible, there is one other body of literature that may still preserve our mythological classics, and that is the genre of children's literature. Images of children may come to embody what is quintessentially classic in any culture, what the tradition considers to be true and good and beautiful. In our culture, children are indeed connected with these classical values, but sometimes only in a pejorative way: they are generally regarded as the only people foolish enough to believe in fairy tales; they are the ones to whom we tell the hair-raising stories that the Grimm brothers collected from *adult* Germans. Children, too, are the ones for whom we continue to create superheroes, the last divine survivals in a kitsch mythology of atheism. A lot of science fiction kitsch was designed for children.

But children's literature is a genre of its own, not merely a reduced or second-rate version of another genre. C. S. Lewis chose this genre for his great Narnian epic of Platonic/Catholic theology and mythology; he said that the proper reason for writing a children's story is "because a children's story is the best art form for something you have to say."[20] Authors may use children's stories to write lightly about subjects that they fear may be too heavy to treat in adult literature without becoming maudlin; often this means that such authors resort to children's literature to write about what they care about most.

There is, I think, a touching instance of this phenomenon in the Soviet Union. The artisans of the village of Palekh were famous from ancient times for their painted icons; but, as a historian writing of Palekh observed with spectacular understatement, "After 1918, the demand for Icons stopped." No longer able to illustrate religious themes, the artisans began instead to illustrate fairy tales, *skazki:* the Little Humpbacked Horse, the Firebird, the

Frog Princess, the Snowmaiden, the Girl with the Golden Hair. There, as here, myths that had been plundered of their sacred meaning took refuge, and survived, behind the thin veils of children's stories.[21]

Many of our inherited classics of mythology (such as the works of Aesop, Hans Christian Andersen, Dickens, Edward Lear, A. A. Milne, Dr. Seuss, Maurice Sendak, Robert Louis Stevenson, and Mark Twain, along with the Grimms' *Fairy Tales, Peter Pan, The Wizard of Oz,* and my own particular favorite, Lewis Carroll's *Alice in Wonderland* and *Through the Looking Glass*) are regarded as children's books. And many of them have explicit or implicit mythological content; think of the evil apple and the resurrection of the dead in the story of Snow White. But as we read these stories to our children we see in them meanings we never saw when they were read to us as children. Even Plato grudgingly remarks, in the context of his argument against the telling of myths to children, "We begin by telling our children myths, and the myth is, taken as a whole, false, but there is truth in it also."[22]

As adults view their own children experiencing the events described in myths—seeing the ocean for the first time, falling in love—or hearing the myths that the adults loved when they were children, they experience a kind of temporal double-exposure: they feel the event as the first time for their children, and as the second time for themselves. This double exposure is closely akin to the sensation of *déjà vu:* what is a shocking surprise to the child is a familiar recollection to the adult. Being true mythologies, these stories change every time we encounter them, even while they retain their archaic essence. A great myth is, like Heraclitus's river, something that one cannot step into twice at the same place.

Some children's stories are classics, and some are not; the same criteria of greatness and kitsch that determine the classic status of works intended for adults also apply to works intended for children. But many children's books, regardless of their aesthetic quality, *function* as classics, or, rather, as the particular genre of classics that we call myths, in ways that no other works do. The archaism characteristic of all classics refers back, in the case of the classic children's story, to the past of the adult who is telling the story to the child. People tend to be reactionary about the myths and rituals of childhood; they want to give their children the books that they loved when they were children. The prestige of origins, that operates in so many myths, leads people to romanticize their own childhoods and to attempt to recreate many aspects of them for their children, including the stories that their parents told to them. To this extent it is an individual myth, not a group myth, that is recreated when a story is retold to a child.

But many of these stories are shared culturally far beyond the boundaries of our individual families, so that they form what Hindus call (in Sanskrit) a *param-para,* or unbroken lineage of transmission, within networks of families, just as in India (as we shall soon see) the Veda was handed down in several different interlocking *param-para*s of families of sages throughout India. Thus childrens' stories do provide a shared culture for many people in the West, if not for everyone.

And in addition to this shared content there is the shared form of the transmission, the ritual, the performance of the classics: people want to read these stories to their children as their parents read them to them. Reading aloud to children is, for most Americans, the only moment when the *oral* element of the mythological tradition is still actively preserved. In all other cases, we read our classics privately and passively; children's literature is the only one that an adult can share by participating in it, assuming the role of the singer of tales.

There are two other apparent exceptions to the general extinction of the oral performance of myths. The first is theatrical performances and movies, which do embody a significant aspect of adult mythology. But there people participate in the oral presentation only passively; they do not perform on the mythic stage. The second exception is psychoanalysis, which teaches us that sometimes the only answer to the question "Why am I suffering?" is the telling of a story about the past. But for the culture at large, storytelling to children is the main refuge of the oral tradition.

In India, too, children are the key to the preservation of the world of myth. For India is also under pressure from the mobs of rationalists and modernizers to demythologize. True, the plays that reenact the lives of the gods Krishna and Rama are still celebrated even in many highly urbanized communities, and people still travel from the cities to the country to see performances in their traditional settings. But as people move from the villages to the cities, the professional storytellers—those who present the dance dramas of the myths or recite the long epics, in Sanskrit or in the vernacular of the district—lose part of their audience. And even more threatening than the possibility that the particular craft of the storyteller may die out is the undeniable fact that, already, the *contexts* for storytelling are fast dying out—the occasions when stories are told, the moments of quiet work at the loom or the mending of nets, the long winter evenings around the fire.

But children are a safeguard against this loss, too. For however busy one may be, working in a factory or at an office desk, there still comes a moment when food is prepared and eaten, when children are washed and made ready for bed. And in India as in America, a small voice will say, "Tell me a story."[23]

Fluid and Fixed Texts in the East

Thus both the content and the form of children's stories make them good carriers for myths. Indeed, in a more general way, the question of the survival of the content of myth is inextricably related to the question of the form in which myth is preserved, as we saw in considering the question of religious kitsch. The forms taken by the classics of India challenge our Western assumptions about permanence and impermanence as well as the corollary distinctions that we make between written and oral texts.[24] In India, we encounter more oral traditions than written ones, and more fluid traditions than frozen ones. But more than that, we find a reversal of the link that we assume exists between what is written and fixed, on the one hand, and what is oral and fluid, on the other.

India has two sorts of Sanskrit classics, typified by two great texts, the *Rig Veda* and the *Mahabharata*. The *Rig Veda* is a massive collection of hymns, a text of over 350,000 words (as long as the *Iliad* and the *Odyssey* combined); it was preserved orally for over three thousand years. The *Mahabharata* is one of the two great Sanskrit epics (the other being the *Ramayana*), a text of over 100,000 verses, or three million words (almost ten times as long as the *Rig Veda*, and fifteen times the combined length of the Hebrew Bible and the New Testament); it was preserved both orally and in manuscript form for over two thousand years. The relationship between orality and fluidity in these texts is the reverse of what one would expect if one simply extrapolated from what we think we know of Western classics.

The *Rig Veda* was preserved orally even when the Indians had used writing for centuries, used it as the writers of Linear B used their script, for everyday things like laundry lists and IOU's. But they refused to preserve the *Rig Veda* in writing because it was a magic text, whose power must not fall into the wrong hands. Unbelievers and infidels, Untouchables and women were forbidden to learn Sanskrit, the sacred language, because they might defile or injure the magic power of these words.[25] If the sacred chants were to be spoken by such people, it was believed, the words would be polluted like milk contained in the skin of a dog.[26] Ancient Vedic texts state that "a pupil should not recite the Veda after he has eaten meat, seen blood or a dead body, had sexual intercourse, or engaged in writing."[27] People who read and recite (rather than memorize) the Veda are grouped with corruptors and sellers of the Veda as people heading for hell.[28] Centuries later, a story was told about the author of a famous commentary on Tulsidas's *Ramacaritamanasa:*

> The god Hanuman expressly forbade Ramgulam to compose any written *tika* [commentary]; the extraordinary *bhavas* [inspirations] were to come strictly "from his lips." Later, when Ramgulam discovered that some of his students were taking notes on his *katha* [recitation], he is said to have pronounced a curse on the writings, declaring that anyone who read them would go blind; some eighty years later, the great *vyasa* [expounder of epics] Ramkumar Misra, grand pupil of Ramgulam, would attribute his failing eyesight to the fact that, in his ceaseless quest for deeper insight into the *Manas,* he had dared to consult one of the forbidden notebooks.[29]

The text of the *Rig Veda* was, therefore, memorized in such a way that no physical traces of it could be found, much as a coded espionage message would be memorized and then destroyed (eaten, perhaps—orally destroyed) before it could fall into the hands of the enemy. And not only was it feared that misuse might injure the text; it was also feared that misuse might injure the person who used the text. Its exclusively oral preservation ensured that the *Rig Veda* could not be misused even in the right hands: you couldn't take the

Rig Veda down off the shelf in a library, for you had to read it in the company of a wise teacher or guru, who would make sure that you were not injured by its power as the sorcerer's apprentice was injured when he meddled with magic that he did not understand.

The oral nature of the *Rig Veda* (and of the other Vedas, too) was expressed in its name: it was called *shruti,* "what is heard," both because it was originally "heard" (*shruta*) by the human seers to whom the gods dictated it and because it continued to be transmitted not by being read or seen, but by being *heard* by the worshipers when the priests chanted it.[30] The oral metaphor is not the only one; ancient sages also "saw" the Vedic verses, and we call them "seers" (although the contrasting English term "revelation" has never prevented Christians from "hearing voices"). But it does reflect the dominant actual mode of transmission: orality.

Now, one might suppose that a text preserved orally in this way would be subject to steadily encroaching inaccuracy and unreliability, that the message would become increasingly garbled like the message in a game of Telephone; but one would be wrong.[31] For the very same sacredness that made it necessary to preserve the *Rig Veda* orally rather than in writing also demanded that it be preserved with meticulous accuracy. The *Rig Veda* is regarded as a revealed text, and one does not play fast and loose with revelation. It was memorized in a number of mutually reinforcing ways, including chanting in a group, which does much to obviate individual slippage. According to the myth preserved in the tradition of European Indology, when Max Müller finally edited and published the *Rig Veda* at the end of the nineteenth century, he asked a Brahmin in Calcutta to recite it for him in Sanskrit, and a Brahmin in Madras, and a Brahmin in Bombay (each of the three spoke a different vernacular language); and each of them said every syllable of the entire text exactly the same as the other two said it. In fact, this academic myth flies in the face of all the available evidence; Max Müller produced his edition from manuscripts, not from oral recitation.[32] Yet, like all myths, it does reflect a truth: the *Rig Veda* was orally preserved intact long before it came to be preserved intact in manuscript. There are no variant readings of the *Rig Veda,* no critical editions or textual apparatus. Just the *Rig Veda.* So much for the fluidity of oral texts.

Yet we, as Westerners, do not trust these fluid forms. When Frits Staal finally recorded the Vedic sacrifice of the fire-altar, he remarked with satisfaction, "Here was a unique opportunity, indeed a responsibility, to continue the oral tradition by means of a book,"[33] a remark that Richard Schechner rightly characterized as "magnificent, if unintentional, irony."[34] And when Penguin Classics published my translation of a selection of hymns from the *Rig Veda,* they themselves chose to put on the cover a Sanskrit manuscript, a most inappropriate visual image of a text that epitomized orality.

Correspondingly, the expected fixity of written texts dissolves when we look at the second sort of Indian classic, typified by the epic *Mahabharata.* In contrast with the divine *Rig Veda* that was "heard" (*shruti*), the *Mahabharata* is regarded as relatively man-made, "remembered" (*smriti*). Of course, since

smriti is based upon *shruti*, it, too, is canonical;[35] but at the same time
it is acknowledged to have been reconstructed very differently by all of
its many authors in the long line of literary descent from its first, human
author. Though the epic was preserved both orally and in manuscript, it is
so extremely fluid that there is no single *Mahabharata*; there are hundreds
of *Mahabharata*s, hundreds of different manuscripts and innumerable oral
versions. The *Mahabharata* is not contained in a text; the story is there to
be picked up and found, to be claimed like a piece of uncultivated land,
salvaged as anonymous treasure from the ocean of story. It is constantly retold
and rewritten both in Sanskrit and in vernacular dialects. Alf Hiltebeitel has
described it as "a work in progress",[36] and Milton Singer has seen it as a
literature that "does not belong in a book."[37] The *Mahabharata* describes
itself as unlimited in both time and space—eternal and infinite: "Poets have
told it before, and are telling it now, and will tell it again. What is here is
found elsewhere, but what is *not* here is found nowhere else."[38] As David
Shulman has put it,

> Vyāsa [the mythical author of the *Mahabharata*], it is said, left behind
> him [in his work] the entire world [*vyāsocchiṣṭam jagat sarvam*].[39]
> So the *Mahābhārata* is coterminous with the world—not a modest
> claim, perhaps, but one that does help to clarify the aims of this text.
> There is no escape built into it from its relentless, bleak vision. It
> presents itself not as a work of art but as reality itself. No boundary
> marks off this text from the rest of the world.[40]

One factor that abets this tendency of an Indian narrative to become
coterminous with the world itself is the text's anonymity, a quality that
belongs, by my definition, to all myths, and that is also characteristic of many
nonmythological Indian texts. Anonymity is in part the quality that allows us
to make a distinction between literature, or a literary classic, and myth. But it
is also a general distinction that may be made between Western classics like
Homer or Shakespeare and Indian classics like the *Mahabharata*. In Western
classics, the personality of the author stamps the work as something different
from the raw material on which it is based; the mind of the author is a pole
star by which the text orients and fixes itself.[41] In India, the anonymity of the
text makes it appear to be a part of communal experience, like a ritual, like
the whole sky; the author is as fluid as the text.[42]

There is a self-styled critical edition of the *Mahabharata*, with an apparatus of "interpolations" longer than the text itself, but it has not been able
to defend its claim to sit alone on the throne of the Ur-text.[43] For the *Mahabharata* grows out of the oral tradition and then grows back into the oral
tradition; it flickers back and forth between Sanskrit manuscripts and village
storytellers, each adding new bits to the old story, constantly reinterpreting
it. To attempt to pin down the *Mahabharata* in a critical edition is to attempt
to make a strobe photograph of a chameleon.

Traditional textual criticism in the West searches for the family tree of a text, the Ur-root, the main trunk, and the subsidiary branches. But the *Mahabharata* tradition is no ordinary tree. It grows like the Indian banyan tree: the (oral) root grows out of the ground, and puts out (written) branches; but these branches then grow back down into the soil and produce new roots and trunks, until one cannot tell where the original root was.

Bernard Faure has suggested another way of qualifying the botanical metaphor:

> We may say that orthodoxy takes its shape not from its kernel—a lineage,—but from its margins, the other trends against which it re-acts by rejecting or encompassing them. To account for this complex dialectical relationship, the "arborescent" or tree-shaped scheme used in traditional genealogies is obviously insufficient and even misleading. The "rhizom" metaphor of Gilles Deleuze and Felix Guattari seems more appropriate, and would at least allow scholars to avoid the pitfall of teleological concepts such as "origins," "degeneration" or "revival."[44]

Once we begin to distinguish between texts that were (or that we think may have been) *composed* orally (in contrast with those that may have been composed in writing), and those that were *preserved* orally (in contrast with those preserved in manuscript), and those that were traditionally *performed* orally, we begin to glimpse the complexity of the problem. For both oral and written texts have both fluid and fixed forms.[45] Indeed, it makes far more sense to mark the distinction between fluid texts, whether written or oral, and fixed texts, again whether written or oral, than to go on making adjustments to our basically misleading distinction between oral and written texts.

Our shifting textual sands shift still more when we distinguish between the use of the inside and the outside of written texts. To use the inside means to use the text in a fluid way, as we might use an oral text: to interrupt the recitation in order to ask about the meaning, to write a commentary, to choose only appropriate passages to recite on a particular occasion. But to use the outside of a text means to use it in a rigid way: to read or recite it without necessarily knowing its meaning at all, to recite it without any care for the choice of an appropriate message, or simply to refer to it as a whole ("It's in the Veda"). Since most Hindus do not read the *Rig Veda* at all, and no one, Hindu or otherwise, can understand all of it, it has become a canon so deified and reified that one can *have* it and *recite* it but seldom *think* with the inside of it. Yet the people for whom it is canonical use the outside of it (and some general structures of Vedic thought) as the most basic condition of their entire way of thinking. The arcane Veda has stamped its general worldview, its way of thinking in terms of resemblances and hierarchies, upon all subsequent Indian thought.[46]

Indeed, the "outside" of any text may be used even more rigidly. The book, the physical object, may be set down but never opened, making a silent statement about status or community; the whole text may be recited from beginning to end so fast that no one can possibly understand it, as a way of gaining merit; or one may throw it at unbelievers, as Luther threw his inkpot at Satan or a policeman may "throw the book" at a criminal. Upwardly mobile members of Western society, anxious to change caste, certainly use the *outside* of the book when they buy the twelve-foot shelf of Harvard Classics, bound in Moroccan leather, and display it in a prominent place—unread, often with the pages still uncut. The Constitution of the United States might be said to constitute a kind of classic of which the outside is used—certainly by everyone but lawyers and judges—far more often than the inside.

A fine example of the use of the outside of a text was told to me by a student who had worked in Japan. At a certain Buddhist temple in Kyoto, there was a woman who used to welcome pilgrims with cool water and so forth; and then she would hit them on the back with a copy of a sacred Buddhist text, the *Prajnaparamita Sutra*. The student thought this a most appropriate text, since it was, like the pilgrimage ceremony of which it was the culmination, a text about purification and absolution. One day he asked her why she hit the pilgrims with that book, and she replied, "I don't know. My father taught me to do it."

One can memorize the inside or the outside of a text. On the one hand, memorization is the basic Indian method not merely of preserving the outside of a text but of understanding its inside. Thus it is said that certain people were able to learn to understand Tulsi's *Ramacaritamanasa* by reciting it from beginning to end 108 times (an auspicious number)—even when they did not know a single word of Hindi, the language in which it is composed.[47] It is often argued, by Western Indologists (and by some late Indian texts), that ancient Vedic texts regarded it as not merely inevitable but actually desirable that people should cease to understand the meaning of the words *inside* the Vedas in order to preserve the outside of the text; the logic for this would be the assumption that if you *don't* understand the words you will be less likely to slip in paraphrases or synonyms and hence to dilute the power of the exact wording.[48] But in fact the tradition says something different. There is a hierarchy of desiderata, in which the highest achievement is that of the one who both knows and understands the text; much lower, though still valuable, is the memorization of the text without understanding it.[49] One ancient text states that "the knowledge drawn from the Veda is without fruit if the Veda has not been understood or rather if it has been learnt in writing."[50] This is a subtle acknowledgment of the twin beliefs that the existence of a written text is a barrier to understanding, and that only oral comprehension of the text is valid.

In India, it is often the very sanctity of the text that limits its use to the outside. Manuscripts of great importance are venerated like icons, and this veneration often takes the form of placing a daub of vermillion on the text; over the years, the wet heat of the atmosphere causes the vermillion to spread until the text becomes a mass of solid red, so that its sanctity makes it literally illegible. Its sanctity may also render it dangerous. Just as the magic contained in the *Rig Veda* contributed to the disinclination to commit it to writing, so, too, the *Mahabharata* has potentially inauspicious magic, particularly since it tells of a great holocaust and genocide, and for this reason to this day many people fear to keep written texts of it inside their houses.

The book itself becomes a physical object, a vehicle for meaning not through the decipherment of the individual syllables that it contains but through the vision of the thing that represents the deity. The Vedas are often placed in modern Hindu temples as the *murti,* the icon of the deity to which worship is offered. Ironically, this stratagem is usually resorted to by the most modern congregations, Neo-Vedantins and other groups of mixed caste and diverse sectarian backgrounds; they may wish to transcend (or avoid) sectarian arguments about the specific deity that should be enshrined or else simply to enshrine a nontheistic symbol. The Sikhs deified their book and called it the Guru Granth Sahib (Mr. Book, the Guru), and Hindus revere Tulsi's *Ramacaritamanasa* as an incarnation of the god Rama, offering it food, garlands, and other traditional elements of *puja* (though not, fortunately, bathing it as is done with other images of God).

Bernard Faure has described this process as it relates to the transmission of certain Buddhist texts:

> The text itself thus became a pure surface, an empty mirror whose content did not really matter, a sign of orthodoxy. Its semiotic value takes precedence over its meaning in the same way that, according to Valéry, the Latin sentence *quia nominor leo* does not really mean "Hence my name is lion" but "I am a grammatical example."[51]

Thus, just as the oral tradition of the *Rig Veda* is frozen, the so-called manuscript tradition of the *Mahabharata* is hopelessly fluid, in part because of the interaction in India between living oral variants and empty written variants. Indians have long been aware of the constant interaction between oral and written traditions of the *Mahabharata.* They explain that when Vyasa, the traditional author of the *Mahabharata,* was ready to fix it in writing, he summoned as his scribe the elephant-headed god Ganesha, patron of intellectuals and merchants. (In doing this, Vyasa was reversing the roles that were supposed to have been played by gods and men in the redaction of the *Rig Veda,* where gods had dictated the text to men, who inscribed it only in their memories). Ganesha agreed to take Vyasa's dictation, but only on the condition that Vyasa would not lag behind and keep Ganesha waiting for the next line; Vyasa in turn stipulated that Ganesha must not write down anything he did not understand. When, in the course of the work, the divine amanuensis seemed to be getting ahead of the mortal author, Vyasa would quickly throw in a "knot" that would make Ganesha pause for a moment. This story accounts for the many conceptual and linguistic stumbling blocks in the manuscript traditions of the great epic. The curse of Ganesha torments every scholar who works on a combined oral and written tradition. It is ironic, I think, that the passage narrating the dictation by Vyasa to Ganesha is the very first one that the critical edition relegates to an appendix—indeed, to an appendix to an appendix. Thus the passage that attributes the irregularities in the epic to its oral and/or written status is rejected as just such an irregularity or "knot."[52] So much for the inevitable fixity of the written tradition.[53]

The Hindus express their awareness of the relationship between *shruti* and *smriti* in another way, too. Beginning with the *Mahabharata,* various texts from the *smriti* tradition are called "the fifth Veda," a phrase that serves as "the proverbial Hindu euphemism for the text one actually knows and loves."[54] This means that the text that one knows with intimacy is regarded as an integral part of the text that one does not know but that one holds in awe. It means that the Veda becomes the ultimate orthodox authority for any post-Vedic text. It means that the fluid tradition (oral or written) is the child—the love child, perhaps—of the fixed tradition (also oral or written).

When literacy is not widespread, the written word is often the special privilege of an elite, while oral culture belongs to people in general. This was the situation in Europe for many centuries, and it is the one that has generally prevailed in India. The classic floats freely in India, and the Indian tradition was continuous, unbroken, for over three thousand years. Nevertheless, this continuous, free-floating Indian tradition was not always ubiquitous. In ancient India, as we have seen, the *Rig Veda* was kept within the oral tradition on purpose, precisely in order to limit it to an elite, exclusive group. Thus Sanskrit confined certain forms of the Indian classics (particularly sacred texts) to males of upper castes, and written literature even in the vernacular was similarly confined by the fact that many people in India were (and many still are) illiterate.

But we are certainly wrong if we assume that illiteracy is an indication of cultural deprivation. The oral tradition has made it possible for millions of illiterate Indian villagers to be richly, deeply familiar with their own classics. When printing began to make texts of the epic *Ramayana* widely available in India, both in Sanskrit and in vernacular translations, this did in fact lead to an increase in private study of the epic, but it also led to a great increase in the practice of public recitations of the *Ramayana,* attended by great crowds of literate people who experienced in the oral presentation something different from what they experienced in reading it silently at home.[55] One reason for this preference, in addition to the ones cited above—and a reason that applies to the persistence of our own traditions of oral storytelling, however truncated—may be that listening to the story frees the eye from the page and liberates it to wander imaginatively through the visual imagery that is an essential element of the myth. Moreover, in present-day India, even where literacy is growing steadily, low-caste women are more likely to attend group readings of fixed written texts than group recitations of fluid (sometime partially oral) commentaries on written texts, the latter demanding from them a level of knowledge and participation from which their background may have excluded them.[56]

Thus the Indian people as a whole have seldom had access to their fixed oral classics (such as the *Rig Veda*) and have recently gained access to their fluid written classics (printed texts of the *Mahabharata* and the *Ramayana,* in Sanskrit or a vernacular language). But they have always had access to their fluid oral classics (retellings of the epics and vernacular interpretations of the Veda). In our own culture, too, there are, as we have seen, some people who know the Bible by heart, and many of these people are otherwise illiterate or even entirely illiterate. Considerations such as these lead us to the surprising paradox that illiterate people often know their own classics, while we who are literate usually do not know ours.

Impermanence and Eternity in India

The fluidity of the Indian oral/written tradition is in part merely one aspect of the more general fluidity of Indian attitudes to *all* kinds of truth. This fluidity was eloquently described by E. M. Forster in *A Passage to India:* "Nothing in India is identifiable; the mere asking of a question causes it to disappear or to merge into something else."[57] In his notes on this novel, Forster himself succumbs to this fluidity in discussing Adela's accusation that Aziz had assaulted her in the cave:

> In the cave it is *either* a man, *or* the supernatural, *or* an illusion. If I say, it becomes whatever the answer a different book. And even if I know! My writing mind is therefore a blur here. . . . I wouldn't have attempted it in other countries, which though they contain mysteries or muddles, manage to draw rings around them.[58]

And in response to the suggestion that "the hallucination was not Adela's but Aziz's . . . but it communicated itself to Adela" (a process which occurs often in Indian philosophical narratives),[59] Forster remarked that "he had not thought of this explanation but that he liked it quite as well as any other."[60]

There is no Ur-text, for there is no Ur-reality. Like us, though more explicitly, Indians may maintain a belief in several different, contradictory answers to the same question; they alter their definitions of reality in order to let such contradictions survive.[61] All truths being multiple, it is not surprising that the true version of any story is also multiple. Lévi-Strauss has argued that all variants of a myth—Freud's Oedipus as well as Sophocles' Oedipus—are part of the myth.[62] It might be argued that not all variants are *equally* valid, but the basic maxim applies, I think, to our culture and even more dramatically to India.

In Sanskrit texts, the bard may recite a myth in a certain way, only to be interrupted by someone in the audience to whom the tale is being recited, who argues, "We heard it differently." When the person in the audience tells that second version, the bard replies, "That is true, too, but your version happened in a different world era"—or, in some stories, "in a different rebirth."[63] That is, the same event happens over and over again, but it may not happen in exactly the same way each time, and each happening is true. Moreover, what makes an event in India important is not that it happened at a particular time or place (which is what makes a historical event important in the West), but precisely the fact that it has multiplied, that it has happened many times in many places.[64] Marx remarked that history repeats itself, and that the first time is tragedy, the second time farce.[65] Myth repeats itself too, of course, but unlike history, it follows no evolutionary course; any of its countless retellings may be tragic or comic at random.

A wonderful example of the degree to which this sort of plurality is both a widely shared cultural assumption and a still debated open question is the manner in which the Jainas told the story of the end of the *Mahabharata:*

> The great Jaina sage Hemachandra went about lecturing to great crowds, telling them, among other things, that the Pandavas, the heroes of the *Mahabharata,* had become Jaina monks at the end of their lives. Upon learning of this, the Brahmins of that city complained to the king, pointing out that in Vyasa's *Mahabharata,* the Pandavas died in the Himalayas, after propitiating Shiva. "But these Jainas," they continued, "who are actually Shudras [low-caste servants], since they have abandoned the true words of the Puranas [mythological texts], in their own assemblies babble things about the Pandavas which are contrary to the *smritis.*"
>
> The king summoned Hemachandra and asked him, "Is it true that, according to the Scriptures, the Pandavas renounced the worlds according to Jaina rules [i.e., they became Jaina monks]?" The venerable acharya said, "This has been said by our ancient acharyas in our scriptures, and it is [equally] true that their sojourn in the Himalayas is described in the *Mahabharata.* But we do not know whether those [Pandavas] who are described in our scriptures are the same as those who are described in the work [*Mahabharata*] of the sage Vyasa, or yet by still other authors in different works.
>
> "Indeed, there is a story told in Vyasa's *Mahabharata,* that when Bhishma died, he wished to be cremated at a place where no one had ever been cremated before. His attendants took him to the top of the hill, but when they readied the body for cremation a divine voice spoke: 'A hundred Bhishmas have been cremated here, and three hundred Pandavas, and a thousand Dronacharyas. As for Karnas [cremated here], their number is beyond counting.' Knowledge can be obtained from any source. Like the River Ganges it cannot be claimed by anybody as his paternal property."
>
> When the king asked the Brahmins, "Is what the Jaina sage says true?" they remained silent, and the king praised the Jaina sage.[66]

"Knowledge"—that is, a true story—"can be obtained from any source." The Jaina sage wins on several counts. He outdoes the Brahmins by citing against them their own scripture, the *Mahabharata.* Though the story that he cites is not in the extant Hindu critical edition—for whatever that is worth—, it is a variant on another, well-known Hindu story: Once when Indra, the king of the gods, was puffed up with pride, he made Vishvakarman, the architect of the gods, build him a palace, to be the grandest palace ever built. But Vishvakarman humbled Indra by showing him a parade of ants and pointing out that every one of those ants had, in a former life, been an Indra.[67] The Jaina sage might also have had in mind a famous Buddhist parable, in which a woman whose son has died comes to the Buddha for consolation; he sends her to beg for a mustard seed from a house in which no one has died, and as she goes on this search, at first confidently and then with dawning awareness of its futility, she is humbled and consoled.[68] Thus Hemachandra reworks an old story to argue explicitly in favor of the reworking of old stories; and he maintains that even *that* story is not the only version of that event. The king, who keeps insisting on his duty to remain impartial, ends by praising the open-minded Jaina over the exclusivist Brahmins. The Jainas, moreover, have by their open-mindedness been able to assimilate into their own religion a great classic that belonged originally to another religion. This is a process that we might hope to emulate.

The *Mahabharata* continues to be reworked within the living experience of Hindus. The Baba of Sahawali, a contemporary sage with a local following, draws freely on epic themes and spontaneously identifies himself as a participant in the great *Mahabharata* battle of Kurukshetra—"as it continues in the realm of the spirits."[69] He maintains that his knowledge about all these things is the result of "a lot of 'research'" (here he uses the English word), and he uses his power to conjure up evil spirits, which he then employs to heal the sick; these evil spirits include the British (who belong to a particular category of ghouls called *rakshasas*) while the good spirits include Sir Edmund Hillary, Abraham Lincoln, and Jesus Christ.[70]

Baba also involves himself in a retelling of the other great epic, the *Ramayana*. But he differs from the Sanskrit text, which makes much of the celibacy of the monkey Hanuman, in arguing that Hanuman has a wife. He says:

> What a great falsehood that Hanuman is without a wife. All this has been mentioned in the texts. Hanuman-ji comes to my *havan* with his wife. This has not been mentioned in the Valmiki *Ramayana*. . . . I asked Tulsidas [the author of the Hindi version of the *Ramayana*] if it was true [that Hanuman had a wife]. He replied, 'Someone before me wrote it like that [that Hanuman had a wife].' Traditionally this [idea of Hanuman's wife] does not occur in Valmiki's *Ramayana*. This [idea of Hanuman's celibacy] has been added by high caste people . . . We are *Shudras* [servants, the lowest of the four classes of Hindu society], but we still have power.

Indeed, the fluidity of the epic tradition does give low-caste, non-Sanskrit-reading Hindus (like Shudras, or like the caste-less Jainas accused of being Shudras) power over the ancient epics.

In another part of the Himalayas, not far from where the Baba of Sahawali lives, the villagers argue just like the exclusive Brahmins, as the anthropologist William Sax testifies:

> I have seen heated arguments erupt when experts from different areas find that they differ with regard to some detail—a name in a lineage perhaps, or the manner of death of a minor character. Although they frequently witness such arguments, Garhwalis cling to the notion that the *Mahabharata* is an account of real historical events which is remembered correctly by some, and incorrectly by others. They are in fact laboring under an illusion that is precisely analogous to [that of] Western academics, who tend to believe that there is a single Sanskrit poem that is 'transformed' into inferior, vernacular versions. What is universal here, and ironically always convincing, is that it is always the 'other guy'—the bard from the next valley, or the illiterate and benighted peasant—who has got the story wrong. Garhwalis argue about which version is the 'correct' one because Pandavlila [their enactment of the *Mahabharata*] is important to them.[71]

Pluralism, it would seem, has its limits even in India. The Garhwalis are arguing about variant oral versions, and still they maintain in their songs that "man dies, but the story of the Pandavas remains." This is an idea that seems more Western than Indian.

In the West, we do tend to think of art as permanent, perhaps as the only permanent thing there is: *ars longa, vita brevis*. To some extent, this permanence is a part of the disembodied word, the oral tradition, as well as the physically preserved word, the book. Helen of Troy argues that the only purpose she can see in certain of her deeds (such as having run off with a no-good bum like Paris) is that people in the future will make songs about them.[72] After the Spanish Civil War, the woman known as La Passionara remarked, "They took the cities, but we had better songs." Storytelling is one of the best ways that we know to ward off death; if only we could tell stories forever, like Scheherezade, we might never die at all.

Western civilization tends to embalm the written word, rather than the oral, and to accord enduring status to other physical incarnations of art. Our libraries are full of books, our museums full of paintings, and these books and paintings are often the only surviving traces of lost civilizations. The nature of the physical incarnation of ideas in books and that in paintings are not the same, of course. As we have seen, it is possible for someone to memorize the entire content of a book so that what is lost when the manuscript or text is lost could be regarded as precious but inessential: the feel of the cover, the smell of the old paper, the look of the calligraphy or the typeface, the beauty of the illuminations or illustrations, the notes made in the margins by previous readers. By contrast, there are few people (if any) who could preserve in their mind's eye an exact replica of a painting if the painting itself were destroyed. Yet, to the extent that the *idea* of the painting can be preserved as a classic of which there may be variants (such as the archetype of the image of the Madonna and Child), while the *idea* of a book is also expressed in its incarnation (the "outside" use), there is a continuum of physical incarnation on which both books and paintings may be placed, though at the opposite ends of the spectrum. The tension between the body and soul of a work of art supplies not a solution but a parallel to the tension between the human body and soul.

In the contemporary West, certain antinomian artistic movements have attempted to establish a new kind of impermanent art. John Cage and others compose music that is different at every performance, eluding any full notation. Dada and Surrealism, hotly followed by Andy Warhol, make art out of objects that qualify as art only so long as we qualify them as art, and are then recycled, like Picasso's *Baboon and Child* made of toy cars.[73] Indeed, in a sense such strategies are responses to the threat of kitsch: where mass production made kitsch possible, Warhol turns the tables on mass-produced objects in order to turn them back again into art, which he nicely defined (summing up both kitsch and anti-kitsch) as "anything you can get away with." Between 1972 and 1976 the Bulgarian artist Christo constructed a work of art by stretching a sheet of white cloth for twenty-four miles along the California coast in Sonoma and Marin counties, and then took it down again (or let it be blown away; does it really matter which?). Subway art in Manhattan is valued in part because of the precarious and illegal nature of its composition and the inevitability of its destruction.[74]

The ironies of Soviet politics have produced yet another sort of ephemeral art, that is, like subway art, "underground" and precious because it is dangerous, illegal, and impermanent. Censorship has inspired "self-publication" (Samizdat): an illegal manuscript is taken at night to a room where people sit around a table. In silence, they read it page by page, passing each page on to the next person; at dawn, it is gathered up and taken away again, remaining only in their memories, not unlike the classics memorized under similar political oppression in *Fahrenheit 451*. This is a peculiar example of the communal sharing of a *written* text. An even more extreme form of Soviet ephemera was described by the dissident Irina Ratushinskaya, who wrote 350 poems during three and a half years in a Soviet prison: "I used what was left of a burned matchstick and wrote on a bar of soap in my cell. I would read it and read it until it was committed to memory. Then with one washing of my hands it would be gone."[75] She was allowed two hundred grams of soap a month. "Carefully, she sliced each bar in two. She gave back one half, following orders, then, using a matchstick, she wrote. With a finger, she wiped away words she didn't like, as other writers do with the flick of a computer key. Her storage area was her mind."[76] Nor was it her mind alone; she smuggled her poems out to her husband, who "also memorized her poems so that officials 'would have to break two heads to destroy them.'"[77] Stories like this force us to reshuffle our assumptions about the relative permanence and communality of oral and written texts.

Traditional Indian thought has expected neither books nor paintings to have the sort of permanence that they have traditionally had in the West. In India, where the neglect of all material objects is an article of Vedantic faith, all material art (including the physical texts of sacred literature and the stones of Hindu temples) is fluid. There, as we have seen, it is the spoken word, not the written word, that is sacred and eternal, in being handed down first from God to man and then from man to man (the infinite *param-para*), just as the individual soul survives in eternity by being handed over from one body to another.

This analogy has deep roots in Indian civilization. The authors of the *Rig Veda,* the invading Indo-Aryans, highly valued their freedom and abhored any constraint. Restlessly they wandered the wide open spaces like Texan cowboys, always in search of grazing land for their horses, never staying in one place long enough to build any lasting dwelling. Later they settled in the Ganges valley and built great cities, but the old resistance to being fenced in never left them. In time, perhaps inspired by the same, undying Indo-European *Wunderlust,* spiritual leaders, both Buddhist and Hindu, began to desert the cities and to abandon their material goods, to wander about as mendicants or to live in the forests, away from the constraints of civilization.[78] The city became a metaphor for the body, the perishable prison of the eternal soul, the trap laid by material life (*samsara,* the world of matter and marriage and mating); what the soul sought was freedom, *moksha.*[79]

Given this cultural background, it is not surprising that physical incarnations of art and literature are neither valued nor trusted in India; impermanence is the very nature of *samsara.* Books are eaten by the white ants or rotted away by the wet heat of the monsoon, and the secular literature that is preserved orally lasts no longer than the mind that knows it. But this may be a matter of choice, as well as of necessity—one may choose not to preserve physically something important. It is somewhat like the choice that one makes when viewing a beautiful scene in a foreign land: if one photographs it, one has preserved it (more or less) forever, but the act of photographing it may interfere not only with the full experience of it at the moment but with one's own power to preserve it in memory.[80]

This point is made in an argument by Plato against writing:

Socrates said to Phaedrus, "It was the Egyptian god Theuth [Thoth] who invented writing [letters, *grammata*] and went to King Ammon to show him his invention. . . . He said, 'O king, this learning will make the Egyptians wiser and more powerful in memory; for I have discovered a medicinal tonic [*pharmakon*] for memory and wisdom.' But the king replied, 'O Thoth, . . . as you are the father of letters and therefore well disposed toward them, you are saying the very opposite of what they are actually able to do. For this will produce forgetfulness in the minds of those who learn it, because of the lack of exercise of their memories, and their faith in writing which is entirely external to them will keep them from using their own memories that are within them. You have discovered a drug not of memory but of reminding [*hupomnesis*]'." . . . And Socrates said to Phaedrus: "Writing is a strange thing, Phaedrus, and is truly very like painting from life; for those who are created by this [painting] stand as if they were living, but if anyone asks them anything, they remain solemnly silent. And the same is true of written words [*logos*]: it might seem as if they speak with their own intelligence, but if one asks them anything, wishing to learn about what they are talking about, they always say one and the same thing."[81]

Socrates never did write. anything down; Plato, of course, wrote down even this statement, but Plato himself argued elsewhere that no book containing his philosophy was ever written down.[82]

Many people in India do not wish to be photographed for another, similar reason, a reason not unrelated to the old reluctance to put the *Rig Veda* into writing: they believe that the preserved image of themselves somehow drains a fraction of their lifeforce or soul. Lucien Lévy-Bruhl noted the same phenomenon long ago among his so-called "primitives."[83] Plotinus, too, would not allow an image of himself to be made, lest it take something away from his reality. Oscar Wilde toyed with this idea in his novel about Dorian Gray, the man whose portrait aged while he did not—until the portrait was destroyed. This sort of thinking may perhaps have contributed to the condemnation of graven images and general aniconic thrust of Judaism and Islam.

Nowadays, many Indian artists, both secular and religious, have caught our taste for preservation; they come to the United States to learn from our artists and conservators techniques to preserve their work. Indeed, there must have been Indian artists long ago who wished to preserve their work, for though the earliest religious monuments in India were carved in wood that decayed, sculptors very soon decided to build more lasting temples in stone. (Stone temples and stupas dating from the pre-Christian era imitate woodcarving techniques, transferred to the more enduring medium.) So, too, the existence of manuscripts in India is witness to a moment when the oral tradition decided to record itself for posterity. These permanent art forms, however, both sacred and secular, have existed side by side with the transient forms, just as frozen and fluid forms of the *Mahabharata* continued to exist side by side for centuries.

And not all physical art forms indicate a desire to preserve art. Painting in India is not always designed to be permanent. The women painters of Mithila use vivid natural dyes that soon fade.

> For the artists, this impermanence is unimportant—the paintings are not meant to last. The *act* of painting is seen as more important than the form it takes, and elaborately produced marriage sketches may be cast off after use, to be eaten by mice or even used to light fires. Frescoes on courtyard walls often fall victim to rain, whitewash, or the playing of children.[84]

To some extent, this is a concept common to many artists—they are interested in the act of creation, not in preserving the object that is created—but it may take on a more particular power in the realm of sacred art, and even more particularly in the sacred art of women, whose lives are primarily involved in producing human services that leave no permanent trace (with one great exception, of course: children).

In many domestic celebrations, women trace intricate designs in rice powder (called *kolams* in South India) on the immaculate floors and court-yards of houses, and after the ceremony these are blurred and smudged into oblivion by the bare feet of the family—or, as the women think of it, the feet of the family carry into the house, from the threshold, the sacred material of the design. As David Shulman has written,

> The *kolam* is a sign; also both less and more than a sign. As the day progresses, it will be worn away by the many feet entering or leaving the house. The rice powder mingles with the dust of the street; the sign fails to retain its true form. Nor is it intended to do so, any more than are the great stone temples which look so much more stable and enduring: they too will be abandoned when the moment of their usefulness has passed; they are built not to last but to capture the momentary, unpredictable reality of the unseen.[85]

The material traces of ritual art must vanish in order that the mental traces may remain intact forever. So, too, the smearing out of the *kolam* is a way of defacing order so that one has to recreate it; it is a fleeting stay against inevitable confusion.[86] The women who make these rice powder designs sometimes explicitly refer to them as their equivalent of a Vedic sacrificial hall (*yajnashala*). Their sketches are referred to as "writing"—often the only form of writing that, for many centuries, women were allowed to have—, and the designs are merely an *aide-mémoire* for the patterns that they carry in their heads, as men carry the Vedas. So, too, the visual abstraction of designs such as the South Indian *kolam* is the woman's equivalent of the abstraction of the Vedic literature, based as it is on geometry (the measurement of the sacrificial altar—one reason why mathematics developed so early in India) and grammar (the central paradigm of order out of which all commentary on Indian sacred texts develops). The rice powder designs are a woman's way of abstracting religious meanings; they are a woman's visual grammar.[87]

The explicit analogy between the *kolam* designs and the Vedic sacrificial hall has further implications of impermanence. For Indian sacred art is often purposely consigned to the realm of the ephemeral in order to prevent its profanation, again with much the same logic that prevented the preservation of the *Rig Veda* in writing. In many Vedic ceremonies, the stone altar (*vedi*) is abandoned, literally deconstructed, after the sacrifice, and the implements—which have become dangerously charged with sacred power—are thrown on the rubbish heap. What survives is the fire that was kindled in that altar, a fire that is used as the seed for the fire that is to be kindled in the new altar, the soul of the altar, that survives the destruction of the body. A more dramatic (though not traditional) expression of this custom was seen in the recent performance of the Agnichayana in Kerala. In the course of this ceremony, which involved many priests and lasted for many days, large and elaborate ritual enclosures were constructed of bamboo and thatch; at the end of the sacrifice, these enclosures were burnt to the ground.[88]

When enormous terra-cotta horses are constructed in South India, the choice of medium is not accidental. As Stephen Inglis writes, "Clay is the medium of the worship of the ephemeral. The horse, semi-mythical, temporary, fragile, cyclical (prematurely dying/transforming) fits snugly into the cyclical pattern of offering in village Hinduism. Power, especially 'outside' power, always advances and recedes."[89] Elsewhere, Inglis has described the work of the potters called the Velar:

> A key to the identification between the *camiyati* ["potter priests"] and the earthen image lies in their impermanent nature. By virtue of being made, of earth, the image is bound to disintegrate and to be reconstituted. By virtue of being human, with ordinary human needs and responsibilities, the *camiyati* . . . is also necessarily a temporary vessel of the divine, destined to be reactivated only periodically throughout a lifetime of service. . . . The potency of the craft of the Velar lies in impermanence and potential for deterioration, replacement, and reactivization of their services to the divine. . . . The Velar, and many other craftsmen who work with the immediate and everchanging, are . . . specialists of impermanence.[90]

There are other reasons for this emphasis on impermanence. The material traces of a powerful ritual must vanish in order that the power not remain casually at hand when the ritual awareness of it has ended. In Benares, life-sized clay images of Rama and Sita are made for the Ramlila festivals and then thrown away; the same is true of the images of Ganesha used in ceremonies in Maharashtra.[91] For the festival of Durgapuja in Bengal, hundreds of more than life-sized statues of the goddess Durga are made and beautifully decorated; at the end of the week-long celebration, the statues are carried down to the Ganges in torchlight parades at night and cast into the dark waters. The Bengali painter Jamini Roy once remarked that he felt that all his paintings should be thrown into the river after his death. He painted because he was meant to be a painter; his paintings were simply a part of his life and should die with him.[92]

The word used to describe this "dismissal" or "throwing out" of the statue is *visarjana,* cognate with *visarga,* the word used to describe the "emission" of the universe—that is, its creation—by Prajapati or Brahma.[93] In this sense, all fabricated things come into true existence only by being thrown out or thrown away; only when the body is shed is the soul set free. One word for "art" in India is *maya,* often translated as "illusion." The world of *maya* is the world of matter (*prakriti*), or rebirth (*samsara*), which is impermanent. Against it the Hindus contrast the world of truth, of ultimate reality (*brahman*), of spirit (*purusha*), of release (*moksha*), which is eternal.

What survives in the disembodied art-forms of India survives in the minds that hand it down one to another. A fixed canonical tradition survives like a thread (and is literally called a thread, a *sutra*) on which successive generations string their new interpretations and translations of the text. But a fluid tradition survives like a series of interlocking beads, one fitting into the next, which may or may not also have a connecting physical thread. This lack of a center corresponds to what has been observed of the concept of the self in India: whereas we in the West tend to think of a person on the analogy of an artichoke—peel away the leaves of the external, nonessential characteristics until you find the self at the center—, South Asians (particularly Buddhists) tend to think of a person on the analogy of an onion: peel away the leaves and at the center you find—nothing [94]

Children in India represent the only form of *physical* permanence. They are the links of the eternal chain of rebirths in an infinity of bodies (*samsara*), in contrast with (and often at the sacrifice of) the setting free or Release (*moksha*) of the eternal soul. We see our physical selves preserved in the bodies of our children; and we see our mythical selves preserved in their memories. For many—all but those who claim to have achieved Release—this is the only eternity there is. As the Hindu lawbook put it, "You beget children, and that's your immortality, O mortal."[95]

Thus we have seen that, on the one hand, Hindus have access to their own classics in ways that we do not and that, on the other hand, they have come to terms with the impermanence of their own classics. This glance at the Indian data simultaneously illuminates some of the reasons why we have lost touch with many of our own classics, both secular and religious, and points in the direction of a way in which we might compensate for that loss, through a new access to the religious classics of other people. The rest of this book will be devoted to an examination of the problems that stand in the way of such an enterprise and to an attempt to suggest some ways of transcending those problems.

Chapter 4

Other
People
as Animals

Rudra, Lord of Sacrificial Beasts

T here are enormous obstacles that challenge our understanding of the
myths of another culture—obstacles of translation, of unknown context,
of cultural relativity, of the incommensurability of an idea in one paradigm
with an idea in another paradigm.[1] It is often difficult for us to see, let alone
to accept, the treasure that is offered to us by other peoples' mythologies.
Laurens van der Post relates a story that I see as a parable of these difficulties.
It is an African version of the well-known story of a man who is visited by a
supernatural woman and falls in love with her; she agrees to stay with him
under certain conditions, and when he violates those conditions, she abandons
him.[2] In the version told by van der Post, the woman comes to him from the
stars, and she has a basket with her.

Before she would marry him his wife had made him promise her that
he would never lift the lid of the basket and look inside until she gave
him permission to do so. If he did a great disaster might overtake
them both. But as the months went by, the man began to forget his
promise. He became steadily more curious, seeing the basket so near
day after day, with the lid always firmly shut. One day when he was
alone he went into his wife's hut, saw the basket standing there in
the shadows, and could bear it no longer. Snatching off the lid, he
looked inside. For a moment he stood there unbelieving, then burst
out laughing. When his wife came back in the evening she knew at
once what had happened. She put her hand to her heart, and looking

at him with tears in her eyes, she said, "You've looked in the basket."
He admitted it with a laugh, saying, "You silly woman. You silly, silly
creature. Why have you made such a fuss about this basket? There's
nothing in it at all." "Nothing?" she said, hardly finding the strength to
speak. "Yes, nothing," he answered emphatically. At that she turned
her back on him, walked away straight into the sunset and vanished.
She was never seen on earth again. To this day I can hear the old
black servant woman saying to me, "And do you know why she went
away, my little master? Not because he had broken his promise but
because, looking into the basket, he had found it empty. She went
because the basket was not empty; it was full of beautiful things of
the sky she stored there for them both, and because he could not
seen them and just laughed, there was no use for her on earth any
more and she vanished."[3]

If I Were a Horse

How can we learn to see inside other peoples' baskets, other peoples' myths?
Or, rather, why do we often see nothing there when there is something there?
And even if we do look, are the myths the same once they have made the
perilous journey from their own baskets to our world?

An equine metaphor has been used, for several millennia, to express the
problems that we have in imagining people that we do not know—strangers,
or gods. Plato argued that just as no one could be familiar with the practical
realities of equine matters and not believe in the existence of horses, so too
no one could be acquainted with the practical realities of divine matters and
not believe in the existence of the gods.[4] The great British anthropologist E. E.
Evans-Pritchard, in criticizing the introspectionist psychologies of Spencer and
Tylor, warned that it was futile to try to imagine how it would feel "if I were a
horse."[5] Radcliffe-Brown, in conversation with Max Gluckman, had nicknamed
James George Frazer's mode of reasoning the "If-I-were-a-horse" argument,
from the story of the farmer in the Middle West whose horse had strayed
from its paddock. The farmer went into the paddock, chewed some grass, and
ruminated, "Now if I were a horse, which way would I go?"[6] Wittgenstein
would have been skeptical of this enterprise; he argued that "If a lion could
talk, we could not understand him."[7] Working the other side of the street, as
it were, Xenophanes said, "If cattle and horses or lions had hands, or could
draw with their feet, horses would draw the forms of god like horses."[8]

But it is the pious belief of many horsemen that they can think like horses.[9]
And maybe they can. If the farmer, after chewing grass, lopes off to a field
where the grass is much better than the field where he had been keeping his
horse, and finds his horse there, he *has* thought like a horse. On the other
hand, he does not have to eat the grass himself when he gets there; he does
not have to *feel* like a horse. Once again it is useful to distinguish between

the head and the heart, between ontological relativism and moral relativism. One need not adopt the morals of a horse to understand a horse.

In 1726, Jonathan Swift imagined how the Houyhnhnms, magic horses, spoke, and how Gulliver came to understand them. Anna Sewell's *Black Beauty*, sometimes subtitlted *The "Uncle Tom's Cabin" of the Horse* (1877), Rudyard Kipling's "The Maltese Cat" (1898; the Cat is actually a polo pony), and Leo Tolstoi's "Strider [Xolstomer]" (1894) are narrated by horses (the latter so vividly that it led Maxim Gorky to exclaim to Tolstoi, "You must have been a horse in a previous incarnation.") But we can never know if other people have really understood how horses think.

There is a justly famous Taoist parable to this effect:

> Chuang Tzu and Hui Tzu had strolled on to the bridge over the Hao, when the former observed, "See how the minnows are darting about! That is the pleasure of fishes." "You not being a fish yourself," said Hui Tzu, "how can you possibly know in what consists the pleasure of fishes?" "And you not being I," retorted Chuang Tzu, "how can you know that I do not know?" "If I, not being you, cannot know what you know," urged Hui Tzu, "it follows that you, not being a fish, cannot know in what consists the pleasure of fishes." "Let us go back," said Chuang Tzu, "to your original question. You asked me how I knew in what consists the pleasure of fishes. Your very question shows that you knew I knew. I knew it from my own feelings on the bridge."[10]

In addition to the obvious twists and turns of the epistemological argument, the Chinese text conceals yet another level. For the word "How?" in "How do you know?" also means "From what? From what position? Whence?" The answer "*From* my feelings on the bridge" suggests a metaphorical answer: we know because of the inexplicable bridge of emotion ("my feelings") that connects us with the fishes.

But the bridge is also a metaphor for all that *separates* us from the fishes. We never *can* be certain that we know how happy they are. In terms of our problem of confrontation, let us take this metaphor to represent the problems faced by scholars (Chinese philosophers) trying to understand people from other religious traditions (fish, or hunters)—and, indeed, to understand other scholars (other Chinese philosophers, or sages).[11]

It has been well argued that to study marine biology one does not need to become a fish; indeed, that one had better *not* be a fish (or even "committed to fish"). "We have learned, after all," says Frits Staal, "that it does not pay to ask elephants about zoology, or artists about the theory of art."[12] As Ernst Nagel put it, "Must a psychiatrist be at least partially demented to study successfully the mentally ill?"[13] Nor, of course, does one have to be old to be a historian, or gregarious to be a sociologist. Some have phrased the assertion even more strongly. One famous scholar of Turkish studies who had remarked, to an astonished inquirer, that he did not care for the Turks, justified himself by pointing out that a bacteriologist does not have to *like* bacteria. But I do think it *helps*. Years of encounter with my colleagues have led me to suspect that the scholars who come closest to the unreachable goal of knowing how fish think are those who are fond of fish, who are interested (like the Chinese sage) in whether fish are *happy,* not whether fish are sad or mad or bad. Such scholars, sympathetic sages, are piscophiles. And I think that some scholars may well know how happy the fish are. They understand fish not because they hate fish (as do many ex-fish, born-again piscophobes) but because they love fish (as another sort of ex-fish does). A few—I think of Mircea Eliade and Evans-Pritchard—have been able to use their own religious experience as a touchstone through which to understand the religious experience of others; they have had some experience of fish-hood, though not always experience of the particular species that they have studied. Such scholars are like sighted persons who become temporarily blind and then sighted again; not only will they have an unusual understanding of blindness, but they will also have an unusual understanding of what it means to see.[14] This double vision may have been what Herodotus had in mind when he noted that the Persians made it a point to debate every important point when they were drunk—and then again when they were sober; or else they debated the point first sober, and then drunk.[15] Plato, too, remarked that the liver is the source of inspiration—but that such hepetal inspirations must then be tested in the light of reason, a faculty that is situated in other organs.[16]

However, not all scholars are so amphibian as to walk the razor's edge between detachment and sympathy. Some fail to become true fish and become merely fishy, sitting like mugwumps on the boundary fence between us and the others. An anthropologist who attempts to live such a double life was described by Evans-Pritchard as being, at least during the period of his fieldwork, "a sort of double outsider alienated from both worlds."[17] And some people believe that this alienation may in fact become permanent; one may be caught not only between one's own culture and the other culture, but between the world of fish and the world of Chinese philosophers; one may be "forever excluded from the world of talking animals and from the world of talking anthropologists as well."[18] These talking animals, as we shall soon see, might be fish or horses—or lions. To be caught between them and the scholars who study them is to be stranded like Kipling's Mowgli in *The Jungle Books*—the boy who realized the deep human dream of learning the language of animals, breaking down the barrier between the wild and the tame, nature and culture, but who could neither become an animal nor remain merely a human.

Indian mythology assumes that we can know how happy the fish are, but that this very understanding may lead to a problem—not the problem of intellectual isolation but, on the contrary, the problem of human involvement:

> There was once a sage named Saubhari, who spent twelve years immersed in a pond. In that pond there lived a great fish who had many children and grandchildren. The young fish played around the

great fish all day, and he lived happily among them. Their games
began to disturb the sage's meditations; he noticed them and thought,
"How enviable is that fish, always playing so happily with his children.
He makes me want to taste that pleasure, too, and to play happily with
my own children." And so the sage got out of the water and went
to the king to demand a bride. He married the king's 50 daughters
and had 150 sons, but eventually he realized that his desires were
self-perpetuating and hence insatiable, and that he must return to the
meditations that the fish had disturbed. So he abandoned his children
and his wives and returned to the forest.[19]

The Hindu sage is not depicted as mistaken in his empathy: the fish *are* happy,
taking pleasure in the same thing that humans take pleasure in, playing with
their children. The sage understands the fish because he has become like a
fish himself: he lives underwater, in a transhuman condition made possible by
his extraordinary ascetic powers. But the sage is mistaken in believing that *he*
personally can be happy like a fish, or rather that such happiness is desirable
for *him:* he comes to learn that though other people may be like fish, he
himself is not like them, and hence not like a fish.

In several of the Buddhist *Jataka* stories, too, the Bodhisattva understands
the language of fish and/or becomes a fish. In one, an amorous fish, blinded by
passion, follows his wife right into a fisherman's net, which the wife cleverly
escapes. The Bodhisattva hears the fish lament: " 'Tis not the cold, the heat, or
wounding net;/ 'Tis but the fear my darling wife should think/ Another's love
has lured her spouse away."[20] (In another variant, the fish cries out: " 'Tis not
the fire that burns me, nor the spit that hurts me sore: /But the thought my
mate may call me a faithless paramour.")[21] The Bodhisattva buys the fish, tells
him, "Cease for the future to be the slave of passion," and throws him back
into the water. Here, as in the tale of Saubhari, the fish is embroiled in a fatal
passion (the net of emotion, including the worry that his wife will think that
he has been unfaithful) that separates him from the sage, not intellectually
but spiritually. When the Bodhisattva himself becomes a fish,[22] he remains
a bachelor, speaks with a human voice, and saves his fellow fishes from a
drought. In other words, when he becomes a fish, he doesn't become a fish.

Another Indian text tells of a person who is bothered by fish that get
literally into his head. It seems that King Bhoja decided to perform the ritual
of "purifying the skull" (i.e., washing out all the orifices of the head), which
he had not performed since he was a child. But when he did this ritual, a
tiny fish got into his head and began to drive him crazy, swimming around in
his brain. Bhoja tried in vain to find a doctor to cure him, and in a rage he
exiled all the doctors in the land and threw all the medical textbooks in the
river. In order to save the medical tradition, Indra, the king of the gods, sent
the divine twin physicians, the half-horse Ashvins, to Bhoja. They performed
surgery on him, cutting open his head and taking out the fish, which they
presented to him in a little pot.[23] Bhoja's problem (getting a fish out of his
head) is a curious inversion of the problem faced by the Chinese and Indian

philosophers—the problem of getting inside the heads of the fish (and of one another). King Bhoja cannot stand having other peoples' ideas inside his own head.

A striking parallel to the story of king Bhoja, combined with transformations of the themes of the infinitely expanding fish and of fish who enter the head of someone with a Chinese name, may be found in a story told by a five year old child. This story is, among other things, a superb parable of the academic life:

> There was a boy named Johnny Hong Kong and finally he grew up and went to school and after that all he did was sit all day and think. He hardly even went to the bathroom. And he thought every day and every thought he thought up his head got bigger and bigger. One day it got so big he had to go live up in the attic with the trunks and winter clothes. So his mother bought some goldfish and let them live in his head—he swallowed them—and every time he thought, a fish would eat it up until he was even so he never thought again, and he felt much better.[24]

These fish are a kind of antidote to thought, an antirational force; the child swallows them, as the antirational flappers swallowed goldfish in the 1920s, and they save him from the potentially infinite expansion of his own self-enclosed thoughts.

The sage who denies his physical nature is like Johnny Hong Kong, who lives alone in an attic: when the fish get into his head, all they do is destroy his own thoughts. But the sympathetic scholar is like the Chinese philosopher, who tried to get out of his own head and into the head of the fish. In these very different ways, the Indian sages and the Chinese sages discover that the insides of their heads are not, after all, like the inside of the head of a fish. For us, as for the Indian and Chinese sages, the question remains: how *can* we learn to think like horses or fish—or like any of the other Others, like Chinese or Hindus?[25]

Though animals may express the most intimate and primal sides of our own natures, what is most deeply *us*,[26] they may also represent the extremes of otherness, human strangers (barbarians and foreigners) or gods. What problems arise when we attempt to understand the thoughts (i.e., the myths) of animals who symbolize people far different from us? What problems arise when we attempt to understand the thoughts (i.e., the plans for the world, including us) of animals who symbolize gods?

The metaphor of animals in myths often provides a bridge between what we think we know (the nature of certain common animals) and what we think other people imagine ("fantastic" qualities attributed to certain common animals).[27] Animals are indeed "good to think" as well as "good to eat."[28] For although it is no longer believed, as it once was, that all mythology is somehow connected with totemism, it is certainly still true that divine animals and theriomorphic gods pervade most mythologies.[29] Animals and gods are two closely related communities poised like guardians on the threshold of either side of our human community, two Others by which we define ourselves. Aristotle remarked that a man who could not live in society was either a beast or a god.[30] Of course, these two extreme groups are in many ways as other to one another as they are other to us; just on the most obvious level, we have immediate and constant physical access to animals, but not to gods. Yet animals and gods are often *structurally* opposed like bookends around myths that attempt to define the boundaries of the human.

To the extent that animals are Other, the ways in which people think about themselves in relation to animals both reflect and are reflected by the ways in which they think about themselves in relation to the gods. The process works in two opposite directions at once. The observation of the local fauna provides images with which people may think of their gods; where there are lions, the gods tend to be leonine. On the other hand, the ideas that people have about the nature of the gods, and the nature of the world, and of themselves, will lead them to project onto animals certain anthropomorphic features, features that may seem entirely erroneous to someone from another culture observing the same animal (or, perhaps, the same god). The first of these two processes—imagining gods as animals—will be the primary focus of this chapter, though it can never be entirely separated from the second process—imagining animals as people.

All animals can be mythical beasts, though certain animals tend to be more universally mythical than others, more archetypal, if you will. But even when an animal appears in several different religions, it may turn out, on closer inspection, to play very different roles in different contexts. The fish is such an animal. Christianity and Hinduism share the same image of the ever-expanding divine fish; the fish eating the fish, ad infinitum, together with its variant, the fish biting its tail (the tautological fish, like the whitings that Alice encounters in Wonderland) is a form of the ouroboros, the snake biting its own tale,[31] a symbol of infinity. The fish that swallows the ring or the cast-off child (or Jonah or Pinocchio), only to reveal it again years later, becomes a symbol of memory, of the persistence of the past, perhaps of the unconscious. This symbolism is widespread, perhaps indeed archetypal. When the Chinese sages speak of fish, therefore, they are not only communicating with fish from the bridge (between two different species) but communicating with one another through fish, through the deep level of memory from which we fish things up into our conscious thought. The lost child who is saved by the fish is a variant of the lost child who is raised by wild animals, the Mowgli syndrome, to which we shall return.

The fish takes on very different forms in specific manifestations. Plato saw us as fish unable to see out of the water that was our imprisoning element. Nietzsche, who (as we shall see) made new use of Plato's image of the cave, also made his own use of the image of the fish:

Into your eyes I looked recently, O life! And into the unfathomable
I then seemed to be sinking. But you pulled me out with a golden

fishing rod; and you laughed mockingly when I called you unfathomable. "Thus runs the speech of all fish," you said; "what *they* do not fathom is unfathomable."[32]

Jesus promised his disciples that he would make them fishers of men; he also fed the multitudes with fishes that magically expanded.[33] In Hinduism, it is God himself (Vishnu) who becomes the fish,[34] and Man (called Manu) who fishes Him out of the water—not to kill him, but, on the contrary, to save him, for the fish is so little that he is in danger of being eaten by all the bigger fish. When the fish grows bigger and bigger, Manu puts him in bigger and bigger vessels, finally setting him free in the ocean (where he is now big enough to eat all the *other* fish); and, when the great flood arises, the Fish fishes Manu out of the water and saves him.[35] Thus where Christianity sees God as the fisherman, Hinduism sees God as the fish—but a fish that fishes.

The permeable boundary that demarcates humans from animals (sacred or profane) may be crossed in either direction: humans may become animals, and animals may become human. Both situations occur widely in mythology, but it is the former—the transformation of people into animals—that allows us to expand our mythic imagination of what it might be like to be an animal.

Humans as Sacrificial Animals

An important cycle of Indian myths begins in the Brahmanas, Sanskrit texts composed in about 900 B.C., and tells how humans came to be regarded as sacrificial animals. This cycle concerns the Vedic god Rudra, who is a god of the wilderness, a god of mountains and jungles, a wild animal; the adjective derived from his name, *raudra,* comes to mean "violent," "savage," or "wild," in contrast with "tame." Rudra in the *Rig Veda* is a wild beast who slays tame cattle and men; the worshiper prays to him, "Do not kill those of us who go on two feet, or those of us who go on four feet."[36] He lives on the margin of the civilized world as one who comes from the outside, an intruder. He is a hunter. He stands for what is violent, cruel, and impure in the society of gods or at the edge of the divine world.[37]

Rudra is both a hunter of wild game and a herdsman of domestic and sacrificial animals. In the *Atharva Veda,* Rudra is said to be lord of both wild animals (*mriga*s) and sacrificial animals (*pashu*s).[38] *Pashu* (cognate with Latin *pecus,* "cattle" [as in Pecos Bill or *impecunious*—meaning having no cattle, no bread, no money]) designates sacrificial and domestic animals, animals that we keep until we slaughter them, either in ritual or for food, or both. These are the animals that we own and measure ourselves by; they are the animals that are us. *Mriga,* related to the verb "to hunt" (*margayati,* which is also related to the noun *marga,* "a trail or path"), designates any animal that we hunt, in particular a deer. But just as "deer" in English comes from the German *Tier,* meaning any wild animal, a meaning that persisted in English for some time (Shakespeare used the phrase "small deer" in this sense), so too in

Sanskrit the paradigmatic *mriga,* the wild animal *par excellence,* is the deer, just as the paradigmatic *pashu* is the cow (or, more precisely, the bull). But *mriga* is also the general term for any wild animal in contrast with any tame beast or *pashu. Pashu*s are the animals that get sacrificed, whatever their origins; *mriga*s are the animals that get hunted. In both cases, the ancient Indians defined animals according to the manner in which they killed them.

The Vedas and Brahmanas often list five basic kinds of sacrificial animal, or *pashu:* bull (*go,* which can also mean "cow"),[39] horse, billygoat, ram, and human being (person, particularly male person or man).[40] Sometimes the horses are subdivided into horses and asses (and mules).[41] The great Sanskrit epic the *Mahabharata* puts the finishing touches on the scheme by saying that there are seven wild *pashu*s (lion, tiger, boar, monkey, bear, elephant, and buffalo), and seven domestic *pashu*s (the usual five—man, ram, bull, billygoat and horse—plus the donkey and the mule, both variants of the horse).[42] The *Book of the Laws of Manu,* on the other hand, lists *pashu*s, *mriga*s, and humans as three separate groups—though one Hindu commentator glosses this by saying that, even though humans are in fact *pashu*s, they are mentioned separately because of their special preeminence.[43] Clearly, even the theoretical classification of humans as sacrificial animals became a problem in India.

Hundreds of years after the time of Vedic sacrifice, the *Mahabharata* leans over backward to deny human sacrifice. Krishna says to Jarasandha, "You have captured kings and you want to sacrifice them to Rudra. . . . No one has ever seen a sacrifice of men. So how can you intend to sacrifice men to the god Shankara (Shiva)? How can you give the title of sacrificial beasts to men of the same species as yourself?"[44]

But were human sacrifices actually performed in ancient India? There is a certain amount of textual and physical evidence that suggests an answer in the affirmative. Though human sacrifice may not have been a part of extant Vedic ritual, the texts tell you how to perform a human sacrifice,[45] and there is actual physical evidence that it preceded and continued to cast its shadow upon that ritual.[46] Whenever a Vedic ritual fire-altar (*agnichayana*) made of bricks was consecrated, there were placed within it five golden images of the five *pashu*s, including a golden man. And archaeological evidence of human skulls and other human bones at the site of such fire-altars, together with the bones of other animals, both wild and tame (horses, tortoises, pigs, elephants, bovines, goats, and buffaloes), indicates that humans were once actually sacrificed in these rituals. The golden man replaced a man of flesh and blood.[47] It is also possible that the ceremony known in the Vedas as the horse sacrifice originally involved the sacrifice of a man as well as a horse.[48]

Certainly it is significant that humans were, at least theoretically, among the beasts who were "kept" by God. This identification was naturally supported by the symbolic connection (explicit in many sacrifices, and perhaps implicit in all of them) between the human sacrificer and the animal victim. When the ancient Indian sacrificer was initiated he was consecrated as the victim in the animal sacrifice: "When he performs the animal sacrifice he ransoms himself, a male by means of a male. For the sacrificial victim is a male, and the sacrificer is a male. And this, this flesh, is the best food to eat, and that is how he becomes an eater of the best food to eat."[49]

One Brahmana text arranges the five victims in what seems to be a chronological order:

> In the beginning, the gods used a man [*purusha*] as their sacrificial beast; when he was used, his sacrificial quality went out of him and entered a horse. They used the horse for their sacrifice; when he was used, his sacrificial quality went out of him and entered a bull [*go,* also ox or cow]. They used the bull for their sacrifice; when he was used, his sacrificial quality went out of him and entered a ram. They used the ram for their sacrifice; when he was used, his sacrificial quality went out of him and entered a goat. They used the goat for their sacrifice; when he was used, his sacrificial quality went out of him and entered this earth. The gods searched for [the sacrificial quality] by digging, and they found it: it was this rice and barley. And that is why people even now find these two [rice and barley] by digging. And as much virile power as these sacrificial beasts would have for him, that very same amount of virile power is in this oblation [of rice] for him. And that is how the oblation [of rice] has the completeness that the fivefold animal sacrifice has.[50]

This text explains how "sacrificeability" travels down the line from man through the other *pashu*s until it lodges in vegetables, each substituting for the one above it. As Eggeling glosses this text, "The sacrificial cake is a substitute or symbol (*pratima*) for the animal sacrifice (as this it would seem was originally a substitute for the human sacrifice) by which the sacrificer redeems himself from the gods."[51]

So, too, the myths of Dadhyanch and Shunahshepa[52] depict complex sets of substitutions, in which one human (Dadhyanch with the head of an animal, a horse, and Shunahshepa with the name of an animal, a dog) substitutes for another human (or god: Dadhyanch substituting for the horse-headed Ashvins, and Shunahshepa for the king's son, Rohita) in a sacrificial beheading or immolation. These myths are not historical, Euhemeristic explanations of a transition from human sacrifice to animal and vegetable sacrifice; they are about the nature of ritual symbolism, explaining how it is that the animal stands as a substitute for the human in the sacrifice. They demonstrate that human beings are, like all other animals, fit to be sacrificed to the gods; that they are, as it were, the livestock of the gods.[53] What animals are to us, we are to the gods.[54]

The malevolent implications of the inclusion of humans as sacrificial victims were spelled out in the Upanishads, shortly after the composition of the Brahmanas:

> Whoever among gods, sages, or men became enlightened became the very self of the gods, and the gods have no power to prevent him. But

whoever worships a divinity as other than himself is like a sacrificial animal [*pashu*] for the gods, and each person is of use to the gods just as many animals would be of use to a man. Therefore it is not pleasing to those [gods] that men should become enlightened.[55]

On the other hand, both *mriga*s and *pashu*s are associated with different classes of society at the time of initiation.[56] The Brahmin is the hunted wild animal (the antelope), the Kshatriya the hunting wild animal (the tiger, which is said to be the embodiment of courage), and the Vaishya the sacrificial beast or domesticated animal (the goat or a cow, said to be the symbol of food).

Thus *pashu*s usually include humans, at least in theory, in contrast with *mriga*s, though some texts regard humans as a third group. But the term *pashu* can also designate animals in general, both wild and tame, in contrast with humans. Some texts distinguish between two sorts of *pashu*s, those of the village and those of the forest, more properly the jungle, the latter including what might otherwise be called *mriga*s. The *Shatapatha Brahmana* instructs the sacrificer to offer cups of milk, which are village animals, and cups of wine (*sura*), which are jungle animals, in order to obtain both domestic and wild animals; but they must be kept separate:

> People say, "These jungle animals are the form of that evil god [Rudra]. If one were to mix the cups of milk with the hairs of those animals, he would put the animals into the mouth of Rudra; and the sacrificer would have no animals. For Rudra rules over animals." He mixes only the cups of wine with the hairs of those animals, thus putting into the wine what belongs to Rudra [or what is violent, *raudra*]; and that is why, when one drinks wine, one's mind [*manas*] becomes violent. And in this way he directs the spear of Rudra against only the jungle animals, and makes sure that the village animals will have safety [*ahimsa*].[57]

This same text further makes an explicit correlation between jungle animals and gods, on the one hand, and village animals and men, on the other:[58]

> Prajapati [the Lord of Creatures, the Creator God] desired, "Let me conquer both worlds, the world of the gods and the world of men." He saw these animals, those of the jungle and those of the village; he took them [for sacrifice], and by means of them he acquired both worlds. By means of the village animals he took possession of this world [of men], and by means of the jungle animals he took possession of that world [of gods]. This world is the world of men and that world is the world of gods. When he takes village animals, the sacrificer acquires this world with them; when [he takes] wild animals, [he acquires] that world.
>
> If he [the Adhvaryu priest, acting for the sacrificer] were to complete [the sacrifice] with village animals [only, i.e., without jungle

animals], the roads would run together; the two village boundaries of two villages would be [too] close; and bears, man-tigers, thieves, murderers, and robbers would not be in the jungles [but would be in the village].[59]

If he were to complete the sacrifice with jungle animals [only, i.e. without village animals],[60] the roads would run [too far] apart, the village boundaries of two villages would be [too] distant, and bears, man-tigers, thieves, murderers, and robbers would be in the jungles.

Some people say, "Surely the jungle animal is not a sacrificial beast, and one should not make an offering of it; if one were to make an offering of it, soon they [that is, the wild animals] would carry the sacrificer to the jungle, dead; for the beasts of the jungle have the jungle as their share. But if he does *not* make an offering of that [jungle animal], there would be a shortcoming in the sacrifice." Now, they set [the jungle animals] free after they have been carried around the fire, and in that way it is neither offered nor not offered. Thus they do not carry the sacrificer dead to the jungle, nor is there any shortcoming in the sacrifice.

So one completes the sacrifice with village animals.[61] Father and son go apart; the roads run together; the two village boundaries of two villages become close together, and bears, man-tigers, thieves, murderers, and robbers are not in the jungles [nor in the villages].[62]

The text plays upon the ways in which animals of the village and of the jungle—like the ways of men and the ways of the gods—may be too close (the roads running together, the boundaries merging) or, on the other hand, too distant. This is an underlying contrast in Indian thought.[63] But here it is significant to note that the wild animals, being divine, are not sacrificed—except by the god who himself partakes of the world of wildness and freedom. So too, another text of this period notes that, of the several victims in the horse sacrifice, "They bind the village animals at the stakes, but they hold the jungle animals in the open spaces [between the posts]. They use the village animals for sacrifice, but they set free the jungle animals."[64]

The Brahmanas tell how Rudra came to rule over the sacrificial beasts:

Prajapati approached his daughter; some say he was the sky, others that she was the dawn. He became a stag and approached her, as she had taken the form of a red doe. The gods saw him and said, "Prajapati is now doing what is not done." They assembled in one place the most fearful forms, and these, assembled, became the deity Rudra. The gods said to him, "Prajapati is now doing what is not done. Hunt him [*vyadh*]." "So be it," he replied, "and let me choose a boon from you." "Choose." He chose as his boon the overlordship of *pashus*.

[Rudra] took aim and hunted [Prajapati]; when he was hunted

he flew upwards; they call him "The Wild Animal" [*mriga*, the constellation Capricorn, also called "Head of the Wild Animal", or "Having the Head of a Wild Animal," *mrigashiras*]. The hunter of the wild animal is called by that name [the hunter, Sirius], and the red doe is [called the constellation] Rohini ["red cow," alpha in Taurus]. The arrow, made in three parts, became the Tripartite Arrow [the belt of Orion].[65]

Rudra is created to become the hunter, and he hunts a god who has already become a male wild animal in pursuit of a female wild animal. She had become a wild animal to flee, in part because that is the defining trait of a wild animal (to flee from attack) and in part because by committing the act of incest, her father had moved from the world of domestication to the world of uncivilized savagery.[66] By becoming a wild animal, Prajapati ceases to be a normal sacrificial victim and enters a realm that is beyond the control of the gods, who must resort to Rudra, the game hunter. The paradox of this text is that, as a result of punishing a wild animal, Rudra is given the power over sacrificial animals. Prajapati, too, straddles the worlds of the wild and the tame: though he himself is a wild animal, the text goes on to say that the seed that he sheds becomes various domestic cattle,[67] and his daughter the female deer is translated into a female cow—the quintessential *pashu* of later Hinduism.

This movement toward *pashu*s is greatly increased in a slightly later variant of this same myth, a century later, in an Upanishad that expands upon this theme, making a significant change: the two central protagonists now no longer transform themselves into wild animals, but become sacrificial animals:

> In the beginning, this universe was Self in the form of Man. He looked around and saw nothing other than himself. . . . He caused himself to fall into two pieces, and from him a husband and a wife were born. . . . He united with her, and from this mankind was born. She reflected, "How can he unite with me after engendering me from himself? For shame! I will conceal myself." She became a cow; he became a bull and united with her, and from this all the cattle were born. She became a mare, he became a stallion. She became a female ass; he became a male ass and united with her, and from this all whole-hooved animals were born. She became a she-goat; he became a billy-goat; she became a ewe; he became a ram and united with her, and from this goats and sheep were born. Thus he created all the pairs, even down to the ants.[68]

The myth thus accounts for the origin of the main sacrificial animals; after the original act, there are five transformations that produce four groups: humans, cattle, horses and asses, and goats and sheep. There is a fine symmetry to this list, in the context of Indian attitudes to categories of animals. At the two ends of the spectrum are humans and "ants and everything," the two animal categories that frame the rank-and-file *pashu*s. From our standpoint, humans and "ants and everything else" are equally remote from this central group, but in the Indian view the humans, at least, are a part of it.

The Upanishadic variant mentions no avenging god; but the Brahmana uses the myth to explain why it is that Rudra is called Pashupati, the Lord of (Sacrificial) Beasts. The first element of the epithet, *pashu*, I have just glossed. The second element, *pati*, literally "protector" or "lord," is ambiguous; it means both lord in the sense of guardian of others (guardian of animals, or herdsman—a human) and lord in the sense of king over his own kind (king of beasts, like a lion—an animal).

At the end of the myth of Rudra and Prajapati, it is said that the gods gave Rudra power over sacrificial animals. But though he is frequently called Pashupati, Rudra is often said to have no share in the sacrifice. As a wild creature, Rudra was originally an outsider; some texts of this period tell about this otherness and imply that he forcibly obtained his share of the sacrifice:

> No offerings were made to Rudra in the Vedic sacrifice, and the other gods divided among themselves the portions of the sacrificial animals [the *pashu*s]; Rudra cast his evil eye on them.[69]

> The gods rose to heaven by means of the sacrifice, but the Lord of Sacrificial Beasts [Pashupati] was left behind. Seeing that he was excluded from the sacrifice, he pursued the other gods and threatened them with his brandished weapon, saying, "Reserve a share of the oblation for me!" The gods agreed and assigned to him what was left over from the sacrificial offerings.[70]

Here the share is simply the leftovers (the portion usually assigned to Rudra, and laden with important symbolic values). But later texts expand upon this incident and make Rudra's portion, once again, the *pashu*s:

> Infuriated by the denial of his worship in a sacrifice, Rudra came to the Vedic sacrifice and killed and mutilated all the gods until they gave him a portion of the sacrifice and proclaimed him Lord of Beasts [Pashupati]. The gods who had been mutilated at the sacrifice said that they had been reduced to the condition of beasts; when they humbled themselves before Rudra, and agreed to be his beasts [*pashu*s] and to make him their Lord [*pati*], he agreed to restore them all.[71] . . . He reminded them that he had deformed them because they were like beasts in failing to acknowledge his divinity.[72]

Thus the other gods became tame beasts (*pashu*s) in the power of the god who was a wild beast, the Lord of Beasts.

In another late variant, to which we will return in chapter five, the sacrificer, named Daksha, is a descendant of the incestuous creator; he is beheaded still in anthropomorphic form, but Rudra (now called Shiva) replaces the lost head not with the head of a wild beast (*mriga*) but with the head of a goat, the most common sacrificial animal.[73] Yet Shiva himself by this time is known not as a wild beast but as the god who rides on a bull, Nandi, a *pashu* and indeed the most mild-mannered of bovines. Thus the myths themselves make the transition from a story about hunting a wild animal to a story about the sacrificial slaughter of a domesticated animal.[74]

These Sanskrit texts are not descriptions of sacrifices or abstract theories of sacrifice (though such texts do indeed exist, in abundance, from a very early period);[75] they are narrative myths about sacrifices. That is, they are imaginative fantasies arising out of the sacrifice, and may well, therefore, express a situation that is the polar opposite of the situation in an actual sacrifice. Indeed, I think this is precisely what many of these myths are: nightmares of human and animal sacrifice.[76] The patterns within these stories are mythic patterns—more precisely, mythic patterns about ritual patterns.

Carnivorous Hunters and Vegetarian Sages

The Vedic myths of sacrifice thus begin by narrowing the gap between humans and animals: they join humans with animals as sacrificial beasts. The later Vedic tradition then widens the gap by distinguishing humans from animals in sacrificing only the latter. But Hinduism then develops a myth of sacrifice that once again narrows the gap between humans and animals: this mythology joins humans and animals together as creatures *not* to be sacrificed, in contrast with vegetables (which remain other, and even in the Vedic texts came to replace the animal victim that was once a surrogate for a human).

In the Vedic myths, there are many substitutions (as when "sacrificeability" travels down the line), but they may be justified in two basic ways. First, Vedic texts describe substitutions of a most practical sort: if one could not for some reason obtain a certain substance, another could be used in its place, so that rice and barley are as "complete" as a goat.[77] Similarly, as we saw in chapter 3, the text of the Veda itself may stand as a substitute for the image of a particular Hindu god, and in later Hinduism the recitation of the Veda is regarded as the equivalent of a sacrifice. But where in Vedism *all* sacrificial substitution is justified on the grounds of necessity, in Hinduism at least *some* substitutions are rationalized on an ethical basis: rice and barley are *better* than the animal sacrifice, because they avoid the sin of killing.

The special emphasis that Hinduism places upon the cow, the totem of *ahimsa* (noninjury), may be seen as a result of the fact that the cow is a transformation of the sacrificed *pashu:* the cow generously gives her milk and survives, in contrast with the deer or other wild animal (or, later, the usual *pashu,* the goat) that is killed. The transition from eating the cow's flesh (as was done in the Vedas) to drinking the cow's milk alone (in Hinduism) is described in a myth in which the cow comes to symbolize the bloodless culture of the sage in contrast with the bloody nature of the hunter:

> Prithu the son of Vena milked the cow of plenty, using Manu [man] as the calf; and from her he milked cultivation and grain. She was then similarly milked by demons, who milked illusion out of her; . . . by the gods, who milked strength out of her; and by the serpents, who milked poison out of her.[78]

The cow thus yields in place of her mere flesh the milk that becomes whatever one desires; for mankind, it is cultivated grain, agriculture. Later Hindu texts explain how Prithu came to milk the cow:

> King Vena was evil; he went hunting and killed all the poor wild animals; as a child, he would violently strangle children of his own age at play as if they were beasts [pashus]. Finally, he neglected to perform Vedic sacrifices or to pay the traditional fees to the Brahmins. The Brahmins killed him; but then they were faced with a terrible famine as a result of Vena's misrule and with the even more terrible threat of anarchy, since Vena had died without leaving an heir. The priests churned the body of Vena and churned out of him a black creature, a tribal hunter [Nishada] who went away into the mountains, taking Vena's evil with him. Then the priests churned Vena again; this time they churned out of him Prithu, the good king and the founder of the lunar dynasty of kings. Prithu set out to end the famine; he attacked the earth-cow with his bow and arrow, but she begged him to spare her life. He spared her on condition that she promise to allow him to milk her of whatever his people needed, and she agreed to this. Using Manu as his calf, Prithu milked the earth-cow of all the plants.[79]

In this later version of the myth of Prithu, Vena, the evil father, kills children as if they were sacrificial animals (that are always strangled), but he is also said to be evil for killing wild animals as if they were animals. He is an evil hunter, and it is an evil tribal hunter, a Nishada (one of the paradigmatic others on the borders of the Hindu world), who is exorcised out of him. Kings who hunted were often closely associated in Hindu mythology with outcastes and Untouchables; and Vena's connection with the Nishada is an expression of this relationship.[80] Yet Vena's greatest sin consists in *not* killing domestic animals (in Vedic sacrifices). Prithu is good, but he, too, begins as a hunter: he sets out to attack the earth-cow, presumably to slaughter her for beef. In the course of the myth, however, he is transformed into a herdsman and a farmer: he learns to use not only milk but the crops of a stable civilization—to make bread instead of beef. Here, as in the Brahmana myth about "sacrificial quality," vegetables are the ultimate surrogate for the human victim. And, in the earliest variant of the myth, these are not merely edible raw vegetables, but inedible raw grains, which require work—the work of culture, the transformation from the raw to the cooked—to make them into food.

Like Vena, the hunters that we encountered in chapter 1 are carnivorous killers; they must destroy one body (their last) in order to cannibalize it as fuel for their next body. That is, hunters forget the past and do not learn from it. Like Prithu, sages are vegetarian shepherds; they can milk another living body of what they need without destroying it; they are historians. The lives and myths of hunters are violent; those of sages are gentle.

David Shulman has noted certain telling parallels between the myth of Prithu and the myth of Rudra Pashupati:

> Pṛthu performs the sacrifice within his more limited role of patron and warrior-king, but also as the successor to Rudra in the ancient agonistic model of the rite. . . . Pṛthu . . . opens up the doors that his father had sealed. He remains, it is true, closely linked to the sacrifice: even this ideal king has a violent bent to his nature, as we learn also from the explicit comparison of Prthu to Śiva. Indeed, this comparison is used to underline an action—Pṛthu's pursuit of thc Earth-cow—that implicitly suggests one of the basic myths of Rudra-Śiva, the Vedic tale of Rudra's pursuit of the incestuous Prajāpati (who has the form of a stag). Pṛthu's milking of the earth thus seems to express the terrifying [*raudra*] side of the king's nature.[81]

Both Rudra and Prithu perform sacrifices of their parents: Rudra hunts his incestuous father,[82] while Prithu hunts his non-nourishing mother, the earth-cow. Both of them begin by hunting, though Rudra hunts a wild animal and Prithu a domestic or sacrificial animal, a *pashu*. Both of these myths end by transcending their own paradigms, depicting a sacrifice which is no longer aggressive and martial, performed by hunters, but has become pacific, performed by sages.

Some scholars have suggested that sacrifice is the central ritual of hunting societies.[83] Others have asserted that animal sacrifice is *never* a feature of hunting societies, and has nothing to do with hunting, but is a feature only of agricultural and pastoral societies.[84] Without passing judgment on the question of whether or not hunting societies ever perform sacrifices (though the evidence indicates that they do), I would point out that animal sacrifice has many different meanings in different societies. But I would also suggest a middle ground by arguing that sacrifice is indeed characteristic of pastoral societies, precisely because it is a feature of *ex*-hunting societies, reformed hunting societies.

The uneasiness associated with the ritual slaughter of animals may be traced back to the Vedic texts themselves, but it comes out of the ritual closet only when Hinduism is in full spate, in the Puranic period. At that time, it takes the form of a corpus of myths about Vedic sacrifice, myths that simultaneously legitimate Hindu practices by presenting them in the guise of Vedic paradigms while they undercut, often by quite sharp satire, the entire rationale for one of the pillars of the Vedic sacrifice: the killing of animals. The myth of Prithu is one such myth; we shall encounter others in chapter 5.

In the myth of Prithu, the sacrifice of the cow expresses the ritualization of the paradox of hunting the tame animal, which is the riddle of the sacrifice. This paradox may be designed to restore to the grim and often guilt-laden butchery of tame animals some of the glamor and martial eroticism characteristic of hunting. It is by no means clear that all sacrificers experience guilt or regret at the death of the animal. But some evidently do have misgivings, by their own testimony (or at least the testimony of their priests). The sacrificial experts of ancient India included a rationale of ritual killing specifically aimed at obviating such guilt: a young boy who traveled to the other world saw people being eaten, soundlessly screaming; they were eaten both by animals and by rice and barley (the surrogates for the animal victim), which they had improperly killed and eaten in life. The way to avoid such a fate, he was told, was to perform the correct ritual before eating such an animal or vegetable.[85]

Another common ploy was to say that the animal willingly sacrificed itself.[86] On yet other occasions an attempt was made to convince the animal that it was not in fact killed. Thus, in the hymn of the horse sacrifice in the *Rig Veda,* the priest says to the horse, "You do not really die through this, nor are you harmed. You go on paths pleasant to go on."[87] The cow that generously gives her milk becomes the image of the ideal devotee; the myths of the transition from hunting to farming, from killing to milking, from blood sacrifice to vegetable sacrifice, explain the evolution of the Hindu concept of the good person, the devotional or Tantric worshiper, as the *pashu.* But all the Hindu gods do not evolve; some of them continue to demand blood sacrifice. For the dominant Hindu image of God is not the passive cow; it is the active wild animal, the *mriga,* who hunts down the cow-human.[88]

Each of the three great Hindu gods—Shiva, Vishnu, and the Goddess—is closely associated with the image of a wild animal. Like Rudra, Shiva—the Hindu descendant of the Vedic Rudra—is a lion: he is said to be called by the euphemism *shiva* ("auspicious") as an inversion of *vashi* ("controller"), since he controls everyone and no one controls him, just as the lion (*simha*) is so named as an inversion of the word for injury (*himsa*), because the lion kills all animals but cannot be killed by any of them.[89] And at Daksha's sacrifice, Shiva's demonic minion drives ten thousand lions in place of horses.[90] Vishnu in the *Rig Veda* is described as lurking in the mountains in the form of a ferocious wild beast, identified by the commentator as a lion.[91] In later Hindu mythology, Vishnu becomes the man-lion, Narasimha, who disembowels a heretical demon. And even a human avatar of Vishnu, the self-controlled and overrefined Rama of the *Ramayana,* is said to be a lion who hunts demons as if they were deer (*mrigas*).[92] Indeed, the monkey Hanuman says that he will offer the demon Ravana to Rama as one would offer a beast to Pashupati.[93] And the most notorious Hindu lion of all is the mount of the blood-thirsty goddess Durga; this lion attacks the theriomorphic form of the buffalo demon Mahisha—who assumes the stance of the devotee and loves the goddess—while the anthropomorphic form of the goddess attacks Mahisha's anthropomorphic form.

Not only are these three Hindu gods wild beasts (or associated with wild beasts). Each dominates a bovine devotee: Vishnu as Krishna protects the cows and calves; Shiva rides on the docile little bull Nandi; and Durga destroys the buffalo. In this, as in so many other aspects, the leonine god with his bovine familiar expresses what Eliade called the *coincidentia oppositorum*.

Although lions are animals that are hunted by men, they are, within the animal kingdom that they rule, hunters, not hunted. It is a general zoological rule of thumb that animals that hunt have their eyes facing forward out of the front of their head, while those that are hunted have their eyes facing backward out of the sides of their head. Cats (including lions) look forward; deer (and horses) look back. The gods are the big cats, and we the small deer—though with a difference: we, too, are hunters, with our eyes gazing forward, like the eyes of cats. Thus, just as sheep and goats are sacrificial animals for us who are in turn sacrificial animals for the gods, so too deer are prey for us who are in turn prey for the gods.[94]

Animals as Non-Others

To imply that humans are sacrificial victims just like other animals, or to imply that neither humans nor animals should be sacrificial victims, is, in part, to imply the belief that animals are non-other: that we are like them. The decision not to kill and/or eat animals reflects, in part, the belief that animals are non-other and that to eat them is, therefore, a kind of cannibalism. The belief that animals are *so* other as to be gods, on the other hand, gives yet another swing to the pendulum, and produces a reason to eat such animals after all—to eat them ritually.

It is useful to arrange animals along a continuum of otherness; in any culture, different stories will be told about animals on different levels. In our culture, first come horses and dogs, the animals closest to us, with whom we have developed fairly elaborate systems of communication that tempt us to believe that we can think like horses. Next come wild animals that seem to be very much like us, like the bears and monkeys in the *Ramayana* who speak a human language and stand erect. After them come the wild animals unlike us, but still mammals, such as lions; and at the far end of the spectrum are animals that we regard as totally unlike us, such as fish.[95]

Now we know that dolphins and whales can talk not only to one another but to us. This knowledge brings to life the myth of the fish and the bridge, and makes us wonder if perhaps someday dolphins will tell us their myths. But since dolphins are not fish but look like fish, and since they are animals but they talk to us as other animals cannot, they doubly straddle the boundary between our own categories of mammals and fish and thereby threaten our definition of what it is to be human. This accounts, in part, for some peoples' reluctance to call what dolphins do "speech." And in fact the language that people use to talk to dolphins is neither the language in which dolphins talk to one another nor the language in which we talk to one another—it is a Rosetta stone language. Yet it is a language, and it joins us with the fish.

The belief that all animals may be in some sense less other than they seem to be is the source of the ever-enchanting myth of a magic time or place or person that erases the boundary between humans and animals. The time of this animal paradise finds a close parallel in the myth that tells of the time when gods walked among people or people walked among gods. The place, like the magic place in the Looking-Glass forest where things have no names, where Alice could walk with her arms around the neck of a fawn, is like the high mountains where people mingle with the gods. And the particular individual with these special powers finds a parallel in the myth of a particular person (often a shaman or a priest) who has the special ability to traffic with the gods.

Famous examples of such people who live at peace among animals would include Enkidu in the epic of *Gilgamesh,* Francis of Assisi, and the many mythical children who are raised as cubs by wild animals, like Romulus and Remus, Mowgli, and Tarzan, like Pecos Bill (suckled by a puma) and Davy Crockett (raised among mountain lions). It might be extended to include children born and raised among domestic animals: Oedipus, raised among sheep, and Jesus, born in a manger. T. H. White (who once translated a medieval bestiary) imagined the young King Arthur's education by Merlin the magician as taking place among ants and geese and owls and badgers, whose language Arthur understood.[96] Our list might also include a group of women that we will soon encounter, the Bacchae, who suckle at their breasts fawns or wolfcubs, while snakes lick their cheeks.[97] It is significant that the Bacchae abandon their own nursing children and dismember tame cattle; it is only in the wild that they are at home. The myths in which we speak the language of animals are myths about friendships with the wild animals that we normally hunt, not with the tame animals that we sacrifice.

In the parallels to these stories in which we commune with gods rather than animals, the gods do not become human; a human becomes one of the gods. So, too, the ideal state of humans among animals is not one in which wild animals become tame (as they often do in reality, like Elsa the lioness in Joy Davidson's *Born Free,* as well as in myths such as the myth of Prithu). It is a state in which a human becomes one of the animals. Or rather, more precisely, a human becomes part of the society of the animals, but usually remains a human; the adopted child must eventually return to the human world. Nietzsche's Zarathustra encountered a sage in the forest who urged him, "Do not go to man. Stay in the forest! Go rather even to the animals! Why do you not want to be as I am—a bear among bears, a bird among birds?" But Zarathustra rejected the "saint" and mocked him for not knowing that God was dead.[98]

For the way to learn about others is not to become a fish forever (to convert, to become a Hindu) but to remain yourself as you get inside a fish for a little while or live among the fish, a Jew or Christian among the Hindus. To attempt to do this is to attempt to become a living Rosetta stone, not half one thing and half another, half human and half fish, a monstrosity, like the violent, bestial Bacchae, but *both* things at once, taking a fish or a Hindu into your head while maintaining it as your head at the same time.

A mediating form of the myth of the human among animals is provided by Gulliver's voyage to the Houyhnhnms, magic horses. Since horses are, even in our world, tame rather than wild animals, the magic reversal here consists not in taming their wildness, but, on the contrary, in reversing the relationship of dominance between them and humans: the horses become masters of the barbaric humanoid Yahoos who pull their carriages. To this extent, the animals move toward the world of humans. But they do not speak a human language; Gulliver learns their equine tongue. To this extent, the human moves into their world.[99]

The strongest form of the myth is the one in which wild animals are wild and speak their own language, and humans are also wild, innocent of civilization, and can speak with fish and lions. It is a world where wild and tame have not yet come to have, or have ceased to have, any meaning for people, or therefore for animals. The Garden of Eden is such a paradise in the past, and another is described in the Hebrew Bible, in *Isaiah,* as existing in the apocalyptic future:

> The wolf shall also dwell with the lamb, and the leopard shall lie down with the kid; and the calf and the young lion and the fatling together; and a little child shall lead them. And the cow and the bear shall feed; their young ones shall lie down together; and the lion shall eat straw like the ox. And the sucking child shall play on the hole of the asp, and the weaned child shall put his hand on the cockatrice's den.[100]

In this magic time, the only companions of the animals are *innocent* human beings, children, still wild, still unpolluted by civilization.

The nervousness with which our culture confronts this idyll (or, if you prefer, the stubbornness with which reality resists this particular myth) is revealed by a Soviet anecdote that I heard in Moscow in 1970. It seems that the Russians, who are justly famous for their animal-taming, decided to present the citizens of Warsaw with a zoo, in order to demonstrate their paternal regard for the Poles. The central exhibit was a cage in which a lion lived with a lamb. A Pole asked the Soviet zoo director how he managed this miracle. "Simple," came the reply; "every day, a new lamb."

Many mythologies of animals are haunted by the lost or unattainable paradise in which the lion does not eat the lamb. To be with the animals (or the gods) in this way would be to transcend our human condition entirely, to rise above it or to fall from it, depending upon one's point of view. In contrast with the rituals of cultural transformation, in which we cease to eat flesh by becoming quintessentially cultural and eating bread or rice instead, these are myths of natural transformation, in which we become quintessentially natural and eat what animals eat (food that may in fact include other animals). In the mediating myth of Gulliver among the Houyhnhnms, the hero finds that he is unable to live on their vegetarian fare; but after living among them he is also unable to eat the flesh that is the food of the horrid Yahoos, the deformed humans that are the beasts of the civilized equine Houyhnhnms. The solution appears: "I observed a cow passing by; whereupon I pointed to her, and expressed a desire to let me go and milk her." Henceforth Gulliver survives, in perfect health, on a diet of milk and a bread made of oats—two civilized alternatives to the two natural extremes of raw flesh and grass.

In Hindu myths of this genre, the humans among the animals eat "fruits and roots"; in the Buddhist variants, they eat nothing at all (not being true humans yet) or they eat the earth itself, which is delicious and nourishing—the antecedent of the earth-cow that Prithu milks.[101] These two strategies, one realistic and one fantastic, provide natural alternatives to the food that men do in fact share with *unmythical* animals: meat. Often, the myth does not tell us what the people and animals eat (though the author of the passage in *Isaiah* goes out of his way to assure us that those lions are no longer carnivorous). Nietzsche's Zarathustra, who refused to become a bear, was nevertheless befriended by a dove and by a lion who "acted like a dog that finds its old master." In this variant, though the lion laughs at the dove and Zarathustra says, "My children are near," the human and the animal do not talk together.[102] Yet such myths often tell us how they manage to speak to one another, and how they manage not to attack one another (two closely related problems). It is language, not food, that ultimately separates us from the animals, even in myths. Only by speaking their language—learning their myths—would we really be able to know how we would think if we were a fish or a horse or a lion.

Chapter 5

Other Peoples' Rituals

Daksha, Pentheus, and Jesus

The myth of Rudra and Prajapati is a myth about a ritual. Now let us go one step further, and consider myths about such myths about rituals. These myths ask, What happens to people who realize that they are part of other peoples' myths, especially when those myths involve them in rituals? What happens when they resist? How does the myth-and-ritual force itself upon them? What are the dangers of converting, and the dangers of not converting, to a strange myth-and-ritual? These questions are not easily answered, nor ever, I think, directly answered; but I will tell some stories that do at least suggest some answers. These answers bear upon both the form and the content of the problem: the question of form concerns the use that we may make of myths about myths about rituals, and the question of content concerns conversion to other peoples' myths and rituals.

There are many myths about people who become, often unwillingly, caught up in other peoples' myths and inspired to perform other peoples' rituals. There are also many myths about people who actively resist the temptation to believe in other peoples' myths or to perform other peoples' rituals. These myths pose warning signs: whether the people in such stories accept or reject the foreign myths and rituals, there is trouble; they are damned if they do, and damned if they don't. Or, as René Girard has put it, in discussing the myth of Dionysus and Pentheus, "The sacrificial crisis makes no distinction between those who submit to its demands out of prudence or opportunism . . . and the only man who has the boldness to reject it—the unfortunate Pentheus. Whether one chooses to fight or to submit, violence triumphs."[1]

Daksha and Shiva

One Hindu myth of this genre, about a god who comes from outside to impose his cult upon the people who do not believe in him, is the myth of Daksha, who refuses to offer the head of a sacrificial beast to the god Shiva:

> Daksha had unwillingly given his daughter Sati in marriage to the god Shiva. One day, Daksha performed a sacrifice to which he invited all his daughters and sons-in-law and grandchildren, but he did not invite Shiva, for Shiva, he said, was a Skull-bearer, nor did he invite Sati. When Shiva refused to attend the sacrifice, since he had not been invited, Sati insisted on going there without him. After she arrived, she rebuked the sages who were there, but Daksha continued to revile Shiva and to look upon Sati with hate. In anger and humiliation, Sati killed herself by burning her body in the fire of her own power of yoga.
>
> When Shiva learned of this, he tore out a clump of his matted hair, from which a horrible demon was born. He instructed the demon to burn up the sacrifice of Daksha and all who were there. The demon and his demonic throng seized the sacrifice, which had taken the form of a wild animal [*mriga*] to flee, and beheaded it. They mutilated the other gods, desecrated the goddesses, and polluted the sacrificial fire with excrement and filth. Then the demon found Daksha hiding in terror behind the altar; he dragged him out, tore off his head, and cast it into the fire into which oblations were placed.
>
> The gods went to Shiva and praised him, begging him to restore Daksha and all the others, and promising to give him a share in the sacrifice. Shiva restored them all, giving Daksha the head of a goat, the sacrificial animal. Daksha arose and rejoiced. Though he had hated Shiva in the past, his mind was now clear. He praised Shiva, who gave Daksha permission to complete his sacrifice, in which a full share was given to Shiva.[2]

This is a variant of the myth related in chapter 4, in which Rudra hunts Prajapati, who has taken the form of a wild animal like himself (a *mriga*), while he makes all the other gods into sacrificial animals (*pashus*) like the goat that he uses here for Daksha's head. Where Prajapati lusted incestuously for his daughter, Daksha (who is explicitly said to be a descendant of Prajapati) merely develops a hatred for his daughter's husband. Shiva is at first excluded from the sacrifice because he is the outsider, the other, the god to whom Vedic sacrifice is not offered.[3] The earlier myths of Rudra established this otherness but modified it so that Rudra was, in fact, given a limited share in some sacrifices. In the course of this later myth (recorded in a text composed well after the sixth century of the common era), Shiva is at first denied and then given a full share.

For Rudra is now identified with the later Hindu god Shiva, through the usual Hindu habit (which we saw in chapter 3) of grafting ancient Vedic pedigrees onto gods from the later Puranic traditions. And though Shiva is still not part of the Vedic world, the worlds of the Vedas and the Puranas become confounded in later Hinduism, and Shiva is the supreme god of the post-Vedic world, at least in the eyes of the Shaivas who tell this myth. In this regard, it is interesting to note that it is now not Shiva himself but his demonic minion who commits the act of aggression, thereby splitting off the benevolent god ("Shiva," the auspicious)[4] who gives Daksha a goat's head, from the demonic god who beheads him.

But there is a temporal paradox hidden in this myth. Daksha says that he is excluding Shiva in the first place because Shiva is a Skull-bearer. In another variant of this myth,[5] as soon as Daksha calls Shiva a Skull-bearer the narrator explains the origin of that epithet: Once upon a time, Shiva had cut off the head of the creator god Brahma, and Brahma's skull had stuck to Shiva's hand, forcing Shiva to wander the earth as an outcaste until he had finally expiated his crime and established for all times the sect of Skull-bearers and the ritual of expiation for murder.[6]

Now, this latter myth is, like the myth of Daksha's sacrifice, a variant of the Vedic myth of Rudra and Prajapati. The explicit reference to (or citation of) the myth of the beheading of Brahma forms a narrative bridge that brings the myth of Rudra and Prajapati forward into the present moment for Daksha. Daksha thinks that Shiva bears the skull of Prajapati/Brahma, from the past; but in fact Shiva is about to bear the skull of Daksha himself, now.

The "theoretical" identification of the sacrificer and the victim that is hypothesized by many theorists, and the all-too-demanding expectation, discussed in the Vedic ritual texts, that the sacrificer will offer himself are literally realized and enacted in this myth. Because Daksha is both the victim and the sacrificer, when Shiva beheads Daksha he simultaneously ruins the sacrifice (by injuring the sacrificer) and accomplishes the sacrifice (by injuring the victim). Moreover, the oft-postulated identity of the priest and the god is also actualized literally here: Shiva himself (or, rather, his surrogate, the demon) performs the act of immolation.

The "sacrifice of Daksha" is a theological pun (in English as in Sanskrit: *dakshayajna*), a sacrifice that Daksha thinks is "by" Daksha, but that he comes to learn is "made of" Daksha, when he substitutes for the sacrificial beast. The animal head that Daksha is given at the end is his true head, the head with which he can at last see clearly, as he confesses. The anthropomorphic head was a mistake, an illusion that he arrogantly accepted as reality. In getting the goat's head, Daksha comes home at last to his true nature as a sacrificial beast for Shiva. He has acted out our metaphor of "getting into someone else's head" in a most literal way. He has gotten into the head of the animal that is his own true self.

The myth of Daksha enacts a new fantasy of animal sacrifice. The Brahmanas contain many myths of the so-called social charter type, myths that establish a paradigm of behavior ("This is how the gods performed the sacrifice *in illo tempore,* and how we perform it now");[7] in one instance, the gods perform the sacrifice *incorrectly,* and humans who emulate those gods also do the sacrifice wrong, and fail, as the gods at first failed, to become immortal.[8] The myth of Rudra and Prajapati follows the general format of a myth of social charter: This is how the gods came to give Rudra a share, and why we now give him a share. Some myths, such as the myth of Shunahshepa or the biblical story of Abraham and Isaac, establish the paradigm of the sacrifice of an animal or a vegetable through the rejection of human sacrifice: a human is slated to be sacrificed as a surrogate for the animal victim (which is in itself a surrogate for the human sacrificer), and this sacrifice is at the last minute prevented by the introduction of a new animal/vegetable surrogate.

The myth of Daksha is an inversion of such a myth. In chapter 4 certain texts expressed misgivings about the killing of animals in sacrifice. These minor tremors, tiny faults in the Vedic ritual armor, eventually gave way to a major Hindu earthquake. Not only was the sacrifice of animals discontinued in Hindu temples; the entire mythology supporting that ritual was inverted. The epics and Puranas began to tell Hindu myths explicitly about the Vedic sacrifice, myths in which the concept of the sacrificial victim as symbolic of the sacrificer, or of the god, or of both, was not ignored but, on the contrary, was made so literal that it called the Vedic hand, as it were, and revealed the hidden deception inherent in the symbolic identifications. It is in this context that we must view the myth of Daksha.

Since the sacrifice is already established when the myth begins, this is not a myth about the origin of animal (or human) sacrifice. Rather, it is about the denial of the myth of animal sacrifice (the myth that created Rudra, gave him a share and made him Lord of Sacrificial Beasts). It begins with what is now the inversion of the extant social charter (the denial of the sanctioned inclusion of Shiva) but ends by establishing that paradigm after all.[9] Its narrative time begins at a time when animal sacrifice had long been established, and then moves back to a primitive time (which might never have really existed at all) when human sacrifice had not yet come to be replaced by animal sacrifice; or, rather, the myth moves behind the symbolic sacrifice of a goat to the actual sacrifice of the sacrificer.

What happens to Daksha is not what happens to the ordinary worshiper or what has to happen in order for the ritual to be established. It is what happens to people who deny the ritual or what has to happen in order for the ritual to assert itself against its enemies. The myth within the myth is the story of the origin of sacrifice and the origin of Rudra. But in the Puranic story of Daksha, that older myth is encompassed within another myth, the story of the denial of sacrifice and the ultimate acceptance of Shiva.

Thus the Daksha myth is not merely a myth about a ritual, but a myth about a myth, a kind of metamyth, a text that reflects self-consciously on another myth. We have already seen another sort of metamyth, in chapter 3:

myths that play explicitly against earlier variants of the classic story, as Tom Stoppard played against *Hamlet*. (Of course, all variants of myths, and all commentaries, do in fact refract the earlier variants, but it is the self-conscious or explicit contrast with the earlier myth, indeed, the actual citation of the earlier myth, that makes it "meta.") The myth of Daksha reflects self-consciously upon the earlier myth of Rudra and Prajapati and explicitly quotes that myth. In the present instance, that quotation takes the form first of the reference to the unglossed epithet of the Skull-bearer and then of the echoing of the central episode, which appears both in its archaic, hunting variant and its later, domesticated variant: first the sacrifice takes the form of a *mriga* and is beheaded, and then Daksha himself is beheaded and ultimately given the head of a *pashu*.

The texts that we are dealing with here are, more particularly, myths about myths about rituals. They are meta-metamyths, twice framed: for such a myth reflects upon a myth about a ritual, or, in another sense, it reflects upon the relationship between a ritual and the real life of the person who performs that ritual. In addition to placing the myth in the context of history, situating the myth within another myth in the past (as a metamyth does), a meta-metamyth moves the myth into the present and, indeed, into the future, by situating it within the life, or the ritual, or both, of the sacrificer (Daksha) or, as we shall see in chapter 7, within the life of the storyteller.

More than that, the myth of Daksha demystifies the mystification of the Vedic sacrificial ritual; it lifts the curtain of liturgy to expose the trick trap doors and two-way mirrors of the enacted metaphor. For when the sacrificer identifies himself with the victim, as he does explicitly here as in many sacrifices, he does not mean that he is *really* the victim; after all, the victim gets killed, but he doesn't. By actually sacrificing Daksha, Shiva reminds him (and the hearer/reader of the myth) that the victim in the ritual is merely a surrogate for the sacrificer. Unlike the ordinary worshiper, Daksha gets caught up in the literal enactment of the metaphor, or rather the collapse of the metaphor, in a ritual that entirely deconstructs its own symbolism: in Daksha's sacrifice, the victim does not "stand for" the sacrificer; he *is* the sacrificer.

By making the ritual literal rather than symbolic, the metamyth inverts it entirely; what happens here is what is always supposed to happen but never does happen, never should happen, and never can happen in the actual ritual. Only at the end, when the goat's head is used in place of Daksha's head, does the myth reapproach what happens in an actual ritual. In this way, the myth of Daksha demythologizes the ritual.

There are other examples of this demystification of the sacrificial ritual in Indian mythology. In one of these, the myth collapses together not the victim and the sacrificer but the victim and the recipient of the sacrifice, the god. That is, it explores what happens when the sacrificial ideal becomes real. In the ancient horse sacrifice, the chief queen pantomimed copulation with the slaughtered stallion, who was said to "be" both the sacrificing king (to whom he transferred his powers) and the god Prajapati. In Hindu mythology, Indra, the king of the gods, is one of several gods designated as the recipients of the horse sacrifice, but he is unique in that he is himself a performer of horse sacrifices, famed for having performed more horse sacrifices than anyone else and jealous of this pre-eminence.[10] He thus (unlike the usual human worshiper) normally combines the roles of sacrificer and recipient. In one text, the *Harivamsha,* an appendix to the *Mahabharata,* he adds to these roles that of the victim:

> Janamejaya was consecrated for the sacrifice, and his queen, Vapush-tama, approached the designated stallion and lay down beside him, according to the rules of the ritual. But Indra saw the woman, whose limbs were flawless, and desired her. He himself entered the desig-nated stallion and mingled with the queen. And when this transfor-mation had taken place, Indra said to the priest in charge of the sacrifice, "This is not the horse you designated. Scram."
>
> The priest, who understood the matter, told the king what Indra had done, and the king cursed Indra, saying, "From today, Kshatriyas will no longer offer the horse sacrifice to this king of the gods, who is fickle and cannot control his senses." And he fired the priests and banished Vapushtama. But then Vishvavasu, the king of the Gandharvas, calmed him down by explaining that Indra had wanted to obstruct the sacrifice because he was afraid that the king would surpass him with the merits obtained from it. To this end, Indra had seized upon an opportunity when he saw the designated horse, and had entered the horse. But the woman with whom he had made love in that way was actually Rambha, a celestial nymph; Indra had used his special magic to make the king think that it was his wife, Vapushtama. The king of the Gandharvas persuaded the king that this was what had happened.[11]

Janamejaya is already familiar with shadow sacrifices, nightmare sacrifices; it was he who had performed the surreal sacrifice of snakes, instead of horses (to avenge the death of his father, from snakebite), at the very beginning of the *Mahabharata.*[12] Here, at the very end of the epic, his sacrifice goes wrong in yet another way: he defies Indra implicitly simply by doing the extravagant sacrifice at all, which makes him the object of the envy of the god,[13] and then at the end he defies him explicitly, by excluding Indra from the sacrifice because the god has spoiled it by taking the form of the animal.

The story of Janamejaya, which *ends* with an exclusion of the deity and a refusal to worship him, is thus in many ways an inversion of the story of Daksha, which *begins* with the exclusion of the god Shiva and ends with the promise that Daksha will in fact sacrifice to Shiva, after Shiva has both spoiled and accomplished the sacrifice by making the sacrificer take the form of the animal. This inversion is made possible in part because Indra is in many ways the opposite of Shiva: Indra is the god of conventional Vedic religion, the most orthodox of gods, while Shiva is the unconventional outsider.[14]

In the epilogue of the Janamejaya story, the king is persuaded (by an appropriately equine figure, a Gandharva, related to the centaurs) that it was all an illusion. This is a common device used to undo what has been done in a myth, a kind of godhead *ex machina*. But here it is also a recapitulation of precisely what the central episode of the myth has just done: it has revealed the illusion implicit in the sacrifice, the illusion that the sacrificial horse is in fact the god Indra and not merely a horse. Where the myth of Daksha reminds us that we would not like it if the sacrificer really did become the sacrificial animal, as the ritual texts say he does, the story of Janamejaya reminds us that we would not like it if the *god* really did become the sacrificial animal, as the ritual texts also say he does.

These myths are hard-hitting exposes of substitution in the sacrifice, de-mythologizing within the structure of mythical discourse the ritual assumption that the sacrificial animal is a surrogate for the worshiper (Daksha) or the god (Indra). It may appear paradoxical that myths, which live in the realm of the imagination, should provide the tools to expose the illusory nature of rituals, which actually happen. But of course it is all taking place in the imagination: the Hindu myths are not actually doing anything at all to the Vedic ritual, but merely imagining mythically what ritual ideology would be like if it were realized. Here, as so often, the myth tells the truth about a paradox that other social forms—in this case, rituals—have kept in the dark.

Pentheus and Dionysus

But we may go even farther afield to find illuminating parallels to the myth of Daksha. There are striking similarities between the myth of Daksha and the tale of Pentheus in the *Bacchae* of Euripides,[15] which might be summarized as follows:

> Semele, the daughter of Cadmus, had given birth to Dionysus, whose father, she said, was Zeus. Her sisters denied this story and, hence, denied the divinity of Dionysus. Semele had died, struck by a thunderbolt sent by a jealous Hera, when Dionysus was born. Agaue, another daughter of Cadmus, had married Echion, one of the dragon brood sown by Cadmus, and given birth to Pentheus. Pentheus, now king of Thebes, denied Dionysus and forbade his worship in Thebes, but Dionysus came to Thebes disguised as a mortal and inspired the daughters of Cadmus to worship him, dancing in ecstasy on the mountains. When Pentheus opposed Dionysus, attempting to imprison him, mocking him for his effeminate dress, and insinuating that the mountain dances were orgies, Dionysus mesmerized Pentheus, enticing him to spy upon the women and to wear the Bacchic women's costume himself. In their frenzy, the women, led by Agaue, tore Pentheus to pieces, and Agaue carried back his head, which she believed to be the head of a lion. As Cadmus brought her to her senses, she realized what she had done and accepted Diony-

sus' sentence: that she and her sisters should wander in exile from
Thebes. Dionysus changed Cadmus and his wife into serpents.[16]

Pentheus denies the truth of the myth of Dionysus, the truth that the god
is a wild beast who possesses women and drives them to disembowel and
devour their living victims. Pentheus rejects the god by steadfastly refusing
to acknowledge the way in which the myth has taken over his own reality.
Dionysus proves his existence to the skeptical Pentheus by using him as the
sacrificial victim in place of the usual animal victim. The god draws Pentheus
helplessly and hypnotically into the whirlpool of the myth that he denies, by
transposing the ritual from the ancient past (*illud tempus*), where Pentheus
thinks it belongs, into the present moment, collapsing profane and mythic
time together, as ritual so often does. As Pentheus sets up the machinery of
the anti-ritual, he loses his balance and is sucked into it himself and crushed
in it. Pentheus is killed because he resists the worship of Dionysus, a god
full of otherness and ambivalence even for the Greeks who worshiped him:
Dionysus is both an old god and a young god, both a Greek god and a foreign
god.[17] Above all, Dionysus is bestial, sexual, and ecstatic—in a word, Dionysian.
Rudra, too, it will be recalled, is associated with wine, wild animals, and
violence.[18]

Dionysus in this play takes the form of a bull and is said to be a lion,[19]
forms which he also assumes elsewhere in Greek literature: he is invoked as a
bull, "raging with bestial hoof," as Dodds translates it, in the ancient hymn of
the women of Elis,[20] and as a lion in the Homeric hymn (7.44). Dionysus is
thus both a domestic, sacrificial animal, a *pashu*, and a wild animal, a hunted
(and hunting) animal. Pentheus hunts Dionysus, but Dionysus is himself the
greater hunter, the leonine hunter who traps Pentheus. Pentheus is thus made
to recognize the theriomorphic god, and to admit to his own bestial nature,
by becoming transformed into an animal himself and by being beheaded like
an animal.

René Girard comments upon the animals in the *Bacchae:*

We also find in *The Bacchae* reference to that loss of distinction
between man and beast that is always linked to violence. The bacchantes hurl themselves on a herd of cattle, which they mistake for
prying men, and tear them apart with their bare hands. And Pentheus,
mad with rage, imprisons a bull in his stable in the belief that he has
captured Dionysus himself. Agaue commits the inverse error: when
the bacchantes discover her son Pentheus spying on them, she mistakes him for a "young lion" and strikes the first blow to kill him.[21]

Pentheus was a human surrogate for an animal victim of the god. In this
regard, Euripides' version of the myth of Dionysus differs significantly from the
myth of Prajapati (and, to a lesser extent, that of Daksha), in which it is a god
who is sacrificed. But a significant parallelism between the roles of Pentheus
and Daksha exists if we define the role of Daksha, at least, as that of a person

who is in the myth clearly subservient in status to the destructive god, Shiva (though all of them are technically gods, the whole point of the myth is to establish the fact that they are not all *equally* divine), who comes to offer sacrifice to the god, and in fact himself becomes the victim of the god.

The *Bacchae* is not just a myth about sacrifice; it is another meta-metamyth, a myth about a myth about sacrifice. In the course of the myth told in the *Bacchae,* several characters refer to other myths behind the present myth, such as the story of the surrogate birth of Dionysus, which Pentheus has refused to believe. When Pentheus challenges the story of Dionysus's birth from the thigh of Zeus, the seer Teiresias tells him another version of the story of that birth, a striking instance of the Greek rationalization of an irrational myth: Zeus (to escape Hera's wrath) made a surrogate for Dionysus out of a piece (*meros*) of air, which was later mistakenly taken to be a thigh (*mēros*), and used it as a hostage (*hōmēreuse*).[22]

Can this myth be related to the Dionysian ritual in which a beast is torn apart? Is that beast, like the "piece of air," a substitute for Dionysus? This is a much-vexed question but one that cannot be ignored.[23]

Now, we do know of other Greek myths that speak of the god himself, Dionysus, as the divine victim, the god who is sacrificed by his worshipers and ritually eaten. Unfortunately, all of these texts were composed after the *Bacchae* and can, therefore, hardly be used as evidence that these ideas are implicit in that text. But it is clear that some sort of myth of Dionysus was known to the audience of the *Bacchae,* and the extant variants, however late, are worth looking at, if only because of the importance of the relationship between the myth of Dionysus and the still later myth of the Christian Eucharist.[24]

Later Greek texts[25] tell how Dionysus was dismembered by the Titans and then revived by Rhea, how he was transformed into a kid or a ram during his youth, and so on. Variants of the myth of Dionysus, later adopted by the Orphics, tell us that when Orpheus refused to honor Dionysus, Dionysus caused him to be dismembered by the Bacchae.[26] And when the Titans tore Zagreus apart and devoured him, Zeus struck the Titans dead with his thunderbolt.[27] The Orphics went on to say that when the Titans had dismembered Dionysus, roasted him, and eaten him, and Zeus had struck them with his thunderbolt, the human race arose from a combination of the ashes of the Titans and the portion of Dionysus that they had eaten (a fact that accounts for the combination of demonic and divine in our nature).[28]

That this myth did exist in Greek culture is as clear as anything is clear about Greek culture. What is not clear, however, is whether or not there was, before or at the time of Euripides (or even after), an actual ritual reenactment of that myth in which the victim was regarded as Dionysus. This uncertainty makes it unwise to view Dionysus as that victim in the *Bacchae.*

Yet many good scholars have taken this leap, and interpreted the Orphic variants of the myth of Dionysus as indications that there was an actual Dionysian ritual (the *sparagmos*) in which an animal was torn apart and eaten raw, and, further, that the animal represented the god himself. Freud referred to "the divine goat, Dionysus."[29] The belief that Dionysus was in fact ritually dismembered by the members of his cult has been passionately argued by James George Frazer, E. R. Dodds, Robert Graves, and others, in the context of other Greek (and non-Greek) cults of gods who are killed (sometimes dismembered and/or eaten) and resurrected. This school compares Dionysus with such gods as Osiris, Attis, and Adonis and argues that he is symbolized by the animal victim that is killed and eaten by his worshipers.

Dodds points out[30] that the eating of raw flesh (*omophagia*) is a frequent accompaniment of the ritual dismemberment of the victim (*sparagmos*) in descriptions of Dionysian rituals; and it occurs in the *Bacchae* (139). The eating of raw meat is, as we saw in chapter 4, paradigmatic for the earlier form of animal sacrifice that is then self-consciously transformed into a ritual of cooked food. Yet Dodds also notes that the *sparagmos* was regarded, like the Christian communion, as a commemorative rite, "in memory of the day when the infant Dionysus was himself torn to pieces and devoured."[31] And he goes on to explain it:

> The practice seems to rest in fact on a very simple piece of savage logic. The homoeopathic effects of a flesh diet[32] are known all over the world. If you want to be lion-hearted, you must eat lion; if you want to be subtle, you must eat snake.[33] . . . By parity of reasoning, if you want to be like god you must eat god (or at any rate something which is *theion*). And you must eat him quick and raw, before the blood has oozed from him.[34]

Dionysus is thus eaten in many forms, as bull or goat or fawn or viper. "Since in all these we may with greater or less probability recognize embodiments of the god, I incline to accept Gruppe's view that the *omophagia* was a sacrament in which God was present in his beast-vehicle and was torn and eaten in that shape by his people."[35]

But Dodds did not merely discuss the possibility of a Dionysian ritual of such a sort; he discussed it in the context of the *Bacchae*. Thus he implies that, when Pentheus dies—disemboweled and disembodied in the ritual *sparagmos*—he has unknowingly become not only the surrogate for the victim of the god he had denied, but, perhaps, a surrogate for the god himself. The fact that it is a human, Pentheus, rather than an animal that replaces the theriomorphic god, has convoluted implications that Dodds points out:

> Did the cult once admit—as the Pentheus story suggests—a still more potent, because more dreadful, form of communion—the rending, even the rending and eating, of God in the shape of man? We cannot be sure, and some scholars deny it. There are, however, scattered indications which point that way.[36]

Indeed, if one takes the Orphic myth as the text for this ritual, the animal for whom Pentheus was substituted would represent not Dionysus but the Titans whom he destroyed (in retribution for their attempt to dismember and kill him). This would make it a ritual of hatred of the demonic enemy, not a ritual of consummation of the beloved god. The overdetermination and multivalence of the nature of the victim (as sacrificer and recipient) and the conflation of the categories of humans, animals, and gods in the sacrifice facilitates this further identification of the victim with the demonic enemy.

In the *Bacchae,* however, there is no direct evidence that anyone but Pentheus is the victim. René Girard sees this as irrelevant:

> From the viewpoint of the sacrificial crisis, the relationship between the *doubles,* Dionysus and Pentheus, is reciprocal in a double sense. There is no reason why it should be Dionysus rather than Pentheus who sacrifices his companion. Yet from the viewpoint of established religion, even if this reciprocity is at one level acknowledged and the sacrificer and his victim are recognized as *doubles,* on another and more basic level this same reciprocity is abolished.[37]

Later, he states more clearly the nature and the significance of this lack of reciprocity:

> In *The Bacchae,* Dionysus plays the role not of victim, but of executioner. This difference, which may at first seem crucial, is in fact of no consequence for the religious implications of the work. As we have already remarked, the mythic or divine creature who appears as the incarnation of violence is not restricted to the role of surrogate victim. . . . Thus there are moments in Dionysus's career when he relinquishes the role of executioner to assume that of victim of the *diasparagmos.* In one episode of his myth, for instance, he is torn limb from limb by a raging mob of Titans: a mythic creature [Zagreus or Dionysus] is sacrificed to other mythic creatures.[38]

But none of this happens in the *Bacchae.* Instead, the Bacchae disembowel a herd of cattle and hunt down a "lion" (Pentheus, whom they mistake for a lion).[39] Only to this rather limited degree, it may be said that the god—who appears as a bull and a lion—is killed ritually and mythically, and that when Pentheus is killed literally, he substitutes for the surrogate god by becoming a human surrogate for the animal surrogate of a god.

But in place of a god who dies to give his loving worshipers immortality, Euripides gives us a god who kills his unwilling worshiper, incorporating him into the ritual in order to prove his own, the god's own, immortality.[40] Euripides may well be undercutting and inverting an inherited myth of Dionysus, using the myth simultaneously with itself and against itself, in ways similar to those that I discussed in chapter 3. For the *Bacchae* is a most peculiar text, different from all other Euripidean plays, perhaps reflecting a change of heart, even a conversion, perhaps reflecting a most cold-blooded, even manipulative use of a myth simply to write a sensational play. It may even be a satire on a sacrifice, a rather sick joke. Indeed, the death of Pentheus may best be viewed not as a sacrifice at all but as a mockery of a sacrifice. The Greek tragedies in general turn the Greek notion of sacrifice into a tragicomedy, as David Tracy has put it: three tragedies and a satyr play. By contrast, the texts that tell the tale of Daksha, the *Mahabharata* and the Puranas, are far more devout, far less ambitious in the literary liberties that they take with the myth. The Indian texts are pared down closer to the mythic core and clothed in minimal literary details; the Greek texts dress up the myths far more elaborately.[41]

The Greek text deals with the myth of the Bacchic rites; the Sanskrit texts deal with the Brahmana myth of the Vedic sacrifice and the epic and Puranic myth of the worship of Shiva. In both cases, there are disquieting transitions from life to ritual and back; the mortal opposes the god on an official ritual level, but the god then uses his ritual in a personal and sadistic way, until the mortal is catapulted back into the public ritual. The self-awareness of the myth produces a kind of play within a play. The texts demonstrate how Dionysus and Shiva lure Pentheus and Daksha into participating not only in the ritual but in the myth about the ritual, the myth that they do not believe in. They enact the web of triple skeins that entangle the sacrificer: the myth (the tale of Dionysus or Rudra), the ritual (the Bacchic ecstasy or the Vedic sacrifice), and the life (the sacrificer's antagonistic relationship with his mother—Agaue—or his daughter—Sati).

These two myths, Greek and Indian, are part of a larger corpus of stories in which ecstatic and charismatic deities who are resisted punish those who do not believe in them. This corpus can be traced in Stith Thompson's *Motif-Index of Folk Literature:* C. 57, "Neglect of service to Deity," subdivided into "Neglect of sacrifice to Deity" and "Fraudulent sacrifice." There is also an entire Tale Type, "The Offended Deity" (TT 939). Throughout Indo-European mythology we encounter the story of the intrusion of a charismatic god into a routinized cult. The *Bacchae* is an instance of one variant of this general theme that appears in the Stith Thompson index as "Punishment for having refused to take part in Bacchic rites" (oddly enough, attested only in Greece). Still other motifs seem to be distributed beyond Indo-European bounds: see, for example, Q 552.1.8, "Infidel defies god to strike him with lightning. God does."[42]

But what is peculiar to the Dionysus/Shiva corpus is the complex pattern of interaction between the mortal, the god, and the animals, and the subtle interpenetration of the myth, the ritual, and the reality. This pattern is, among other things, yet another exploration of the relationship between a human and a god who is simultaneously a wild animal and a tame animal, a sacrificer and a victim, and a hunter and a sage.

Another Indian myth of this genre is even more self-conscious about the complex relationship between the myth and the ritual:

> A Brahmin refused to worship Matangi [a low-caste South Indian goddess]. All kinds of evils came upon his household. When he enquired the reason, he was informed that it was because of his

refusal to worship Matangi. He was ordered to take the part of the storyteller in the buffalo sacrifice to the goddess, and then, later in the ceremony, to take the part of the buffalo, while his wife would play the part of Matangi. So he was killed, his membrane made into drums, his arms cut off and placed in his mouth, his fat spread over his eyes, and all the other things done to him that were customarily done to the buffalo. Then all the castes worshiped Matangi, and the Brahmin was brought back to life. Then all these things were done to a buffalo, and this was the origin of the buffalo sacrifice.[43]

In a jumble of time spans, the story of the buffalo sacrifice is told before it takes place; so too, the ritual is done with a man taking the place of a buffalo before it is done with the buffalo himself, forever after. The man and the buffalo become mutual surrogates for one another. The story of Matangi is about myths about the sacrifice of animals and humans, as well as about the sacrifices themselves. The Brahmin first tells the sacrifice, then is the sacrifice, then does the sacrifice; he moves from myth to reality to ritual. As A. K. Ramanujan comments on this text, "This myth is about myth itself, about how myth generates ritual; how men re-enact myth in ritual, and how 'Art imitates life, and life imitates art,' as Wilde would say. In this story, the storyteller's life enacts and becomes the story. And the story enters the life of the listeners. Stories are scenarios."[44] Myths are sometimes scenarios for rituals; but they are also sometimes scenarios for our own lives.

A brilliant example of the way in which the myth-and-ritual of the unwilling worshiper can enter real life is provided by two events that were said to have taken place recently in a village in the Himalayas.[45] On one occasion, a man whom we shall call Ramprasad decided to put an end to buffalo sacrifice among a group of villages. This is how another villager who knew Ramprasad told the story:

> It was an old tradition there. . . . I myself saw fifty or sixty buffaloes sacrificed there at one time, and as for the goats, well, you couldn't even count them. . . . Ramprasad wanted to close down the sacrifice. . . . The ones opposed to stopping the sacrifice had a lot at stake—they collected the offerings from the sacrifice or were too poor and uneducated to understand why things should be changed. . . .
>
> When the festival came, we were there in force, to make sure that those who had brought animals anyway would not be allowed to sacrifice them. The ones who still insisted on the ritual were there with their swords and axes. Ramprasad was a small man, just a sack of bones,. . . but even though he looked frail, he didn't lack energy. He jumped right in the middle of them and stuck out his neck, shouting, "Cut their heads off if you must, but first cut my head off! Go on, cut it off!" They all stopped. Someone from the back shouted, "Do it! Cut off his head!" But no one went to do it. With great difficulty he made them stop. He was like a wildman.

But then he was stuck with seventy male buffaloes. What to do with them? They won't take a plough, they don't give milk, they're only kept for the sacrifice. And seventy buffaloes eat a lot of grass. He managed to parcel most of them out to each of the local village councils, but he was still left with fifteen of them, and for quite a while after that he could be seen up on the mountainside, cutting grass and hauling it back down to feed the buffaloes he had saved.

After the high drama of the myth-ritual, in which the human is a surrogate for the animal surrogate, the myth moves bathetically into the profane world, where (against the usual form of the myth) the animal is *not* sacrificed but the hero suffers the practical consequences of his heroism.

The myth played out its basic course, however, in a similar confrontation in the same part of the Himalayas. This time, a man attempted to put a stop to the sacrifice of a ram to the goddess Kali by offering himself as a victim in place of the ram. He managed to prevent the sacrifice as long as he remained there in the temple all night; but after he departed, the ram was sacrificed according to custom.[46] In the myth, and sometimes in life, too, the Goddess always gets her ram.

The myths of Daksha and Pentheus teach us that, as we are animals, we are sacrificed to the gods; and as we are unbelievers, the gods draw us into their sacrificial rituals. Other peoples' myths teach us that people who do not believe in myths are caught up in the rituals that enact those myths just like (and sometimes even more than) the people who *do* believe in them. And these myths also tell us of the dangers that come to us from any association, whether it be resistance or acceptance, with the dangerous gods of otherness, both those from other civilizations or those whose very essence is that they are opposed to *any* civilization, that they are by definition other, by definition wild animals that prey on us who are their sacrificial beasts.

But what happens to people who do not resist conversion, who welcome it? Herodotus tells of a man who was killed because he *did* convert to the worship of Dionysus:

Ariapithes, the king of Scythia, had among other sons, Scyles. But he was born of a woman of Istria, not a native-born Scythian at all. His mother taught him Greek speech and letters. . . . Later Scyles took over the throne of the Scythians and also his father's wife, whose name was Opoea. This Opoea was a native Scythian, and Ariapithes had had by her a son, Oricus. Though Scyles became king of Scythia, he was not pleased with the Scythian manner of life but was far more given to Greek ways, from the training he had had. So this is what he did: . . . He would take off his Scythian clothes and take on Greek clothes and in that shape would go and walk about in the marketplace, with no bodyguards or indeed anyone else. They guarded the gates so that no Scythian might see him wearing Greek dress. He followed a Greek way of life, and, in especial, he made offerings to the gods in the Greek fashion. When he had spent a month or more like this, he would put on his Scythian clothes and go back. He did this very often. . . .

Now he was destined to end ill, and this ill overtook him in the following instance. He was eager to be initiated in the rites of the Bacchic Dionysus, and when he had this project in hand, a very great portent occurred, for all to see. Upon [his house] the god hurled his thunderbolt. Though it burned down entirely, Scyles nonetheless completed his initiation. Now, the Scythians taunt the Greeks about the Bacchic rites; they say that the Greeks, against all reason, discover a god who sets men on to madness. . . . When Scyles appeared with his band of devotees and the Scythians saw him in Bacchic frenzy, they were furious at it and went and told the whole army what they had seen. When, after that, Scyles went back to his own country, the Scythians rebelled against him and set up in his stead his brother, Octamasades. . . . Octamasades beheaded Scyles on the spot. So careful are the Scythians to guard their own customs, and such are the penalties that they impose on those who take to foreign customs over and above their own.[47]

A number of points in this story bear upon the myth of Pentheus. It is Scyles' *mother* who—like Agaue, the mother of Pentheus—draws him into the strange cult. (It is interesting to note, in this connection, that where the Indian myths of Prajapati and Daksha speak of a father's incestuous relationship with his daughter, the dominant form of incest in Indian mythology,[48] the Greek texts speak of a mother's power over her son, the problematic relationship in Greek mythology.)[49] The lightning strikes Scyles' house as it strikes Semele dead and later strikes her grave in Euripides' play; and Scyles is beheaded, like Pentheus—a fitting punishment for a victim of Dionysus. Scyles dresses up in Greek clothes as Pentheus dresses in Bacchic dress, and with much of the same secrecy and perversity.

Jesus: Myth with Ritual

And there are other myths that tell of the danger of converting to a new ritual. The founding myths of many religions are necessarily about gods who are other before they become our gods. Jesus combined in himself certain aspects of the roles of both Dionysus and Pentheus when he came to be seen as a divine/human surrogate for an animal surrogate (the Paschal lamb) even while he retained his role as the divine shepherd. For though Dionysus in the *Bacchae* of Euripides is not the victim of the sacrificial dismemberment, there is, as we have seen, considerable evidence that he did play this role in other Greek myths, if not in other Greek rituals. And though Pentheus resists and rejects the cult, he is, *volens nolens,* sacrificed (and perhaps eaten) in it. To this limited extent, then, Jesus is both the divine victim like Dionysus in the

Orphic myth (and Prajapati in the Brahmana myth) and the human surrogate for the animal surrogate for that victim, like Pentheus in Euripides' play (and Daksha in the Puranas). This combination is a new religious paradigm.

The significance of the Pentheus connection, that distinguishes Jesus from Dionysus, was emphasized by Nietzsche, whose first book (*The Birth of Tragedy*, 1872) was about Dionysus and whose last published words were: "Have I been understood? *Dionysus versus the Crucified.*"[50] But the Dionysus connection provided a more useful metaphor for the early Christians who created a myth about the origin of the ritual of the Eucharist. They tell us of someone who realized that he was part of a myth, one that others did not at first recognize or accept. In their retelling, when Jesus at the Last Supper ate of the Passover Lamb and then instructed his disciples to drink his blood in the form of wine, he knew, though the others did not, that he was to become that lamb, whose blood was to be painted on the doorposts so that death would pass over us.[51] In the Gospels, Jesus *predicted* that he would become such a god; in the myth, he knew (with the god's-eye view that I posited in chapter 2) that his own myth and ritual were taking place for the first time. Jesus is depicted as having established the ritual of his own myth when he taught his worshipers to drink his blood and eat his flesh. He reestablished the old ritual so that people would remember the new myth: "Do this in memory of me."

This text raises the myth to the level of a metamyth, a transformation of an old myth, and indeed a meta-metamyth, a transformation of an old myth about an old ritual. Jesus is depicted as speaking with the vision of one who realizes that he is situated in the encompassing frame of a new myth of denial and resistance, the myth of a man who is sacrificed in hate, crucified. But from that frame he sees the inner myth, the old myth of origins and acceptance, the myth of a god who sacrifices himself in love. With one exception, the first myth provides a parallel to the myth of Daksha, and the second a parallel to the myth of Prajapati/Purusha. That exception is in the contrast between love and hate, a contrast that is irrelevant in the Hindu context and is an important innovation in Christianity.[52]

In the narratives told by Luke, Matthew, and Mark, the sacrifice of the Paschal lamb directly precedes Jesus's injunction to his disciples to eat his own body and blood; they may well have been making an implicit connection between Jesus and the lamb. John alone explicitly refers to Jesus as the Lamb of God, not at the time of the Passover or the crucifixion (which are for John alone simultaneous) but in the very first chapter of his gospel, when Jesus first appears, to be baptized by John the Baptist (1:29). And it is only in the *Epistle to the Hebrews*, several steps distant from the original narrative, that the theory of the crucifixion as a sacrifice is explicitly expressed:[53]

> Neither by the blood of goats and calves, but by his own blood, he entered in once into the holy place, having obtained eternal redemption for us. For if the blood of bulls and of goats, and the ashes of an heifer sprinkling the unclean, sanctifieth to the purifying

of the flesh; how much more shall the blood of Christ, who through
the eternal Spirit offered himself without spot to God, purge your
conscience from dead works to serve the living God?[54]

In this metamyth, the text reflects upon its own history, upon the transition
from the story told in the Hebrew Bible to the story told in the New Testament.
Paul (who is traditionally regarded as the author of this text) elsewhere
explicitly compares his own congregation with the sacrificial sheep in the
Hebrew Bible, reminding his people that they must be willing to die for their
faith, for "as it is written, For thy sake we are killed all the day long; we are
accounted as sheep for the slaughter."[55] Metamyths thus perform an important
function in the self-justification of any religious tradition, the essence of which
is the perpetuation of the myth that things have not changed when, in fact, they
have.[56] These stories allow a tradition to make innovations without cutting
down its roots.

In playing with and against the Jewish tradition of sacrifice, the early
Christians were in fact going one step further in a direction that the Jews
themselves had begun long before. Let us go back for a minute to trace in
broad outline the history of sacrifice in ancient Judaism. There is, to begin
with, the widespread evidence of the killing of the scapegoat, performed long
before the Temple was established and continuing long after it had been
destroyed. Within the Hebrew Bible, there is solid evidence of the sacrifice of
animals and some evidence of the sacrifice of the firstborn human child.[57] Most
famous of all, of course, is the story of Abraham and Isaac in *Genesis* 22. The
usual situation, which Isaac refers to in all innocence, is the sacrifice of a lamb
("Behold the fire and the wood," he says to his father, "but where is the lamb
for a burnt offering?"), and, as we saw earlier, such an animal usually stands as
a surrogate for the human sacrificer himself. Isaac is to be stubstituted for this
substitute—until another lamb appears in the thicket as a substitute for this
human substitute for the basic surrogate lamb. This is the already labyrinthine
house of mirrors into which the New Testament introduces its own mirror to
end all mirrors; for surely John and Paul (like so many Christians after them,
including Kierkegaard) had Isaac in mind as the human lamb who was to be
saved by the sacrifice of Jesus.

The references to human sacrifice in the Hebrew Bible are all pejorative,
as are, indeed, almost all the references to the sacrifice of animals, a strong
indication that the practice was historically attested but no longer endorsed
by the time of the recension of the text that we have. There is also far more
explicit moralizing on this subject in the Hebrew Bible, a definite tendency
to suggest that there are preferable substitutes for the animal victim,[58] such
as words and prayers ("So will we render the calves of our lips")[59] and
obedience: "Hath the Lord as great delight in burnt offerings and sacrifices, as
in obeying the voice of the Lord? Behold, to obey is better than sacrifice, and
to hearken than the fat of rams."[60]

These texts present a view of sacrificial substitutions as arising not out
of necessity (as in the Vedic paradigm: use rice or barley when you can't get

a goat) but out of morality (as in the Hindu paradigm: use rice and barley to avoid killing a goat). Nowadays, they argue, we do things *better* than they did in those times. The argument from necessity is often recast in historical terms: we used to be able to get animals (or Soma plants) to sacrifice but we can't get them now. So, too, the argument from morality may be historicized: we used not to know it was wrong but we know it now. Both of these arguments inevitably involve us in the mythology of origins: it used to be one way and then came to be another way. And both sets of arguments appear both in scholarship about sacrifice and within the sacrificial texts themselves: both the traditions themselves and our own interpretation of the traditions often say, "We/they stopped sacrificing because we/they were forced to stop" or "We/they stopped sacrificing because we/they decided it was wrong." And sometimes they/we say both at once.

In the case of the Jews, this ambivalence leads to interesting historical problems. Within the Hebrew Bible there is, as we have just seen, ample evidence of the argument from morality. But another argument, the argument from necessity, runs right alongside it: the sacrifice ceased when the second Temple was destroyed. This argument is problematic. To begin with, it does not account for the lapse into desuetude of the ritual slaughter of the scapegoat, which took place outside the temporal or spatial confines of the Temple. Moreover, the argument from necessity implies that if the necessity is obviated, the sacrifice will be reinstated; a time will come when a new Jerusalem will be established and new Temple will be built, and then the sacrifice will be reestablished. Thus many Orthodox Jews pray to God to bring the sacrifice back to the Temple. But the argument from morality is retained by many Conservative and Reform Jews, who regard sacrifice as a "once adequate but now outmoded" form of worship and do not ask for the future restoration of the rite.[61] Indeed, the Reform argument can encompass both necessity and morality: we were forced to give up the sacrifice, but we now realize that it is immoral. And, historically speaking, it is quite likely that the anti-sacrificial moralizing that had already begun in the early books of the Hebrew Bible became more pronounced after the destruction of the Second Temple in A.D. 70.

Thus the question of surrogation was already seriously broached—and, indeed, had already begun to be problematic—in the Hebrew Bible, and it is in this context that we must view the further transformations wrought in the New Testament. It might appear from the Christian texts that a human victim has been substituted for an animal; or rather, that the lamb that was a substitute (or scapegoat, or scapelamb) for an original human victim has now been replaced by another human victim. But Christ does not fill the role of the sacrificed domestic animal; he denies and cancels that role. He himself is not a lamb; he comes to replace the lamb precisely so that the lamb—symbolic of all that is vulnerable and pure—will no longer be killed. And the ritual that celebrates this event sacrifices neither a lamb nor a man, but a wafer and a cup of wine.

Let us return for a moment to Hinduism, whose myths express a similar transition from the sacrifice of a domestic animal to the sacrifice of a vegetable, a rice cake. Even in the Vedic ritual such vegetable oblations (rice and barley) were the minimally acceptable lowest form of the sacrificial victim, the *pashu*. But then a new stage of Hinduism evolved, perhaps under the influence of Buddhism, or of the broader concept of *ahimsa* (noninjury) that became a part of both Hinduism and Buddhism. During this period, all animal sacrifices were banished from mainstream Hinduism. Though this latter transition is almost always couched in terms of morality (the rise of the concept of *ahimsa*), there may also have been an element of necessity in it: the need to answer the challenge posed by the antisacrificial polemic of Buddhism, which had converted many powerful political leaders. The Buddhists, too, may have had moral reasons to abolish the sacrifice (as they said they did); but they may also have wanted to make a clean break with Hinduism by eliminating with Vedic sacrifice the one element by which most Hindus defined themselves (as Jews defined themselves by circumcision, another transformed sacrifice).

In this form of Hinduism, which remains the basic format to the present day, the deity in the center of the Hindu temple (an aspect of Shiva or Vishnu or the Goddess) is strictly vegetarian; he accepts no blood offerings, only rice, fruits, flowers, and so forth. He is a sage. But his alter ego, the hunter and butcher, still casts his shadow in the same temple; the whole coconuts that the deity fancies bear a suspicious resemblance to human heads (an oft-noted resemblance that is sometimes explicitly mentioned in the accompanying liturgy). Even the Vedic texts treat the rice cake like an animal: "When the rice cake [is offered], it is indeed a *pashu* that is offered up. Its stringy chaff, that is the hairs; its husk is the skin; the flour is the blood; the small grains are the flesh; whatever is the best part (of the grain) is the bone."[62] And when a Vedic sacrifice was recently performed in India under the auspices of Frits Staal, and public protest prevented the sacrificers from slaughtering a goat, the rice cakes that were used in place of the goat were wrapped in leaves, tied to little leashes, and carefully "suffocated" before they were offered, a clear atavism from the Vedic sacrifice in which, as we know, a living animal was suffocated.

Moreover, while the Brahmin priest makes his vegetarian offering in the central shrine, an Untouchable priest in an outer corner of the temple courtyard, or outside the very wall of the temple compound, slaughters a goat and offers its flesh and blood to the god—or, if the distancing between the two personae is even greater, to a servant of the god, or to a demon whom the god has killed. Sometimes the vegetarian deity in the inner shrine is a god, and the carnivorous deity outside is a goddess. This arrangement in the structure of the temple translates into a spatial configuration, a synchronic opposition—from outside to inside, what can also be viewed as a historical, diachronic transition—from Vedism to Hinduism, or, indeed, an ideological conflict outside of both space and time: the conflict between the need to offer oneself to the god and the need to stay alive.

It is significant that, in both the Hindu and the Christian rituals, the substitution consists of food substances that symbolize the triumph of culture over nature. The food that transforms the worshiper from a hunter to a sage is not raw, but cooked—a symbolism that Lévi-Strauss glossed for us long ago.[63] The sacrifice addresses the problematics of food, the inescapable fact that you must kill something in order to live. This problem cannot be solved, but it can be distanced and diluted first through the substitution of substances that are less like us, more Other (vegetables instead of animals), and then through the further cultural transformation of cooking those substances.

For Christianity, bread is not only a symbolic transformation of flesh but also an elaborate, actual, physical (one might almost say magical) transformation of wheat, and wine an alchemical transformation of the grape. For India, rice functions similarly. It is significant that what substitutes for the animal in the temple ritual of worship (*puja*) is a ball of rice. For rice, which is planted and then picked and replanted several times, becomes a cultural symbol of semen and rebirth;[64] the complexity of its multiple plantings and reapings is taken as analogous to the complexity of the process of multiple rebirth. Balls of rice, called *pindas*, are used in funeral ceremonies to supply a new body for the dead man and in birth ceremonies to guarantee a male child to a woman who wishes to become pregnant.[65] The food that is regarded as a symbolic transformation of living flesh is an actual cultural transformation of a crude, raw substance into a sophisticated food that is taken as symbolic of the culture itself. Rice thus functions as a ritual expression of the triumph of agriculture over hunting.

The parallels between the Christian Eucharist and both human and animal sacrifices have been noted by many sacrificers in the process of their conversion to Christianity. The apostle John tells us that many of the disciples would no longer follow Jesus when he told them to eat his flesh.[66] From the second century, the Romans accused the Christians of ritual cannibalism. The Christians, in turn, accused the Gnostics of cannibalism and expressed particular horror of the *taurobolium* celebrated by the worshipers of Mithra in Rome in the first centuries of the Christian era: a bull would be placed on a kind of screen over a pit in which an initiate would stand, and the bull's throat would be cut so that his blood would drip down and soak the initiate. This vividly literal baptism by the blood of the bull was said to satirize and to degrade the ritual of the Eucharist and the myth of the Resurrection. In fact, it brought the Christian metaphor to life in a way that was shocking, even as the literal slaughter of Daksha or Pentheus was shocking.

The problem of the enacted metaphor of cannibalism continued to plague the Christian church. Early missionaries working among tribes where cannibalism was known but loathed ("*We* don't do that any more") found themselves in the awkward position of being regarded as proselytizers for cannibalism when they spoke of eating the body and drinking the blood of Christ. And in Papua New Guinea, where pig sacrifices were the central religious ceremony before Catholic missionaries began their work in the 1950s, the Papuan converts to Catholicism used to speak of the *agnus dei* as "the pig of god," a syncretism that startled the proselytizers but that some, at least, did not find inappropriate.[67] ("Porco dio!" in Italian is a common blasphemy.) These same converts made a more subtle connection: one of them remarked, "We are brothers and sisters eating together and sharing things among us as Jesus told us to do. That is why . . . we kill pigs."[68]

Indeed, the missionaries elsewhere encountered even more literal interpretations of the symbolism of the Mass—interpretations that went right back to the source, to the crucifixion itself. When they converted the Maya in Yucatan, in the sixteenth century, they were horrified to find that, according to one scholar, "the Maya Indians of Yucatan, after their apparent conversion, had not only continued to worship their old idols, but had returned to an intensified practice of human sacrifice in which some victims had been subjected to preliminary crucifixion."[69] This may have been a crude attempt at a syncretistic assimilation, or it may have been, as the Inquisition thought, a "mock crucifixion,"[70] like the mocking Black Masses that were being hunted down by the Inquisition in Europe at that time. Yet it was in fact a *real* crucifixion, as the Mass was not. The Mass was the "mock" crucifixion, in one sense of that word; the Maya were taking the Eucharist literally.

There were even more perverse Mayan assimilations, involving both human sacrifice and animal sacrifices that were reminiscent of the syncretism of the Papuans:

> In the course of his account of the sacrifice of two little boys, Francisco Chuc, a native priest, mentioned that a pig had also been sacrificed. Its belly had been ripped open, and a burning cross thrust into the blood-filled cavity. The Spanish scribe sought to describe this performance by recording that the pig had been "crucified."[71]

In a way, this sacrifice was less shocking than the crucifixion of a human, more progressive, moving forward one stage from human sacrifice to animal sacrifice. But in the eyes of the missionaries it was more shocking, more blasphemous, assimilating the noble, symbolic Christian Mass to the base form of a literal animal sacrifice.

The evidence for crucifixions of this sort among the Maya is massive, but as it was obtained through equally massive torture it remains suspect. Nevertheless, it raises important questions: "Whether the Maya responded to the intrusion of Spanish Catholic culture by an intensification of human sacrifice, with the incorporation, in reverence, confusion or parody, of the Christian cross, we cannot know."[72]

At the other end of the spectrum of literal versus symbolic sacrifices, a highly sensitive repugnance, even toward the *symbol,* was expressed by the Vedic priests, who argued that one must not perform a certain ceremony (involving the oblation of rice cakes) for another person, because by eating the victim, the cake, one would be eating the sacrificer's flesh.[73] The confusing complexity of these transformations was beautifully, if perhaps unconsciously, expressed by Evans-Pritchard when he spoke of his intention to limit his discussion of sacrifice to blood sacrifice, but then remarked, "On the other hand, I include as coming within the sense of bloody sacrifice offerings of cucumbers, for they are consecrated and immolated as surrogates for oxen."[74]

Nietzsche restored the literal sacrifice in his satire on the Last Supper: Zarathustra served, in place of unavailable bread, the meat of two good lambs.[75]

The Eucharist thus stands at precisely the same remove from human sacrifice as the "suffocated" rice cake in the Hindu ritual stands at its own remove from the sacrifice of a goat. Indeed, in both instances we have what is more precisely not the replacing of flesh by grain but the supercession of flesh by grain. That is, in the earliest records of both the ancient Hebrew sacrifice and the ancient Vedic sacrifice, the killing of the animal was accompanied by an offering of grain (rice and barley in the Vedic sacrifice or, in the case of the Vedic stallion, balls of rice). These sacrifices were thus ambivalent from the very start; they involved not only an animal surrogate for a human victim but the substance that first complemented and replaced that surrogate.

In another sense, of course, the Eucharist *is* the flesh and blood, and the communion is indeed a human sacrifice. This is not the place, nor am I the scholar, to review the complexities of the arguments surrounding transubstantiation.[76] But it is, perhaps, the place to show that the same complexities can be applied to the Hindu ritual. The Christian tradition views the killing of the historical Jesus as a unique event, an actual realization of the previously metaphorical sacrifice of a lamb, a realization that in a sense demythologized that metaphor. Similarly, the Hindu tradition views the episodes of Daksha and Janamejaya as unique events, the one time that the sacrificer actually was the animal victim or the god actually took the form of the animal victim, events that demythologized the Vedic ritual.

The two traditions are certainly not saying the same thing; but they are arguing with the same sort of paradoxical logic, looking back on their sources in the same self-deceptive way. The myths of Daksha and Janamejaya invert the ideological underpinnings of the sacrificial ritual; they do not ignore the concept of the sacrificial victim as symbolic of the sacrificer, or of the god, or of both, but, on the contrary, they make these concepts ludicrously literal. Such schizophrenic metamyths about rituals, like the split rituals in the Hindu temples, represent moments when the tradition says, "We used to do that, but now we do this. We used to do sacrifice, but now we don't anymore; we are better than the old religion that we have evolved out of. On the other hand, what we do now is essentially the same as what we did; what we do now is really sacrifice still, but a better kind of sacrifice."

These traditions are driving with one foot on the brake and one foot on the accelerator; they are trying to find a way to have their rice cake and eat it too. They are saying, "It is a wafer and therefore a moral improvement on human sacrifice, but it is also flesh, with all the power of the sacrifice that it came to replace; we are doing the same thing, but we are doing it differently." The bread and wine are a transformation of the original body and blood of Christ, but they are also transformed back into that body and blood in the ritual; so too, the rice cakes that replaced the goat become the goat. Without the myth about the ritual, they would remain simply bread and wine and rice cakes.

Chapter 6

Other Peoples' Myths

The Place in the Woods

We have just looked at three sets of myths about rituals. In this chapter, I wish to ask what happens when myths lose their rituals and when rituals lose their myths. At the same time, I wish to move the discourse from the realm of the adventures of characters inside the texts to the realm of our own adventures as we make use of such texts. In doing this, we will pick up the thread of chapter 3. If, as I argued there, the glass of our own religious classics is half empty, then there is another glass that is half full. If we are released from our imprisoning assumption that the only way to possess a classic is to experience it as *ours,* we may begin to possess classics that are officially "other." There still are ways in which we can possess Homer or Shakespeare, and these are ways in which we, as Westerners, can also possess the *Rig Veda*—indeed, may be able to possess it in ways in which the people who hold it sacred cannot. To do this, we must simultaneously reduce the list of the "Western" classics that we regard as our own and expand our definition of what counts as "our classics" in such a way as to make it possible to include the *Rig Veda.*

This brings us back to the problem of the elusive "we," first broached in the Introduction. In chapter 1, I spoke explicitly of the academic community, which is my community, my caste, my guild; and, within it, I addressed the smaller community of scholars of religion, and the still smaller community of historians of religions. In chapter 3, my implicit "we" was a broader aspect of that same community, the people who maintain the system of education

119

that enshrines certain works as "classics." Here I wish to broaden the base still more, to speak of all the people in America (and, to some lesser extent, in Europe) who are involved in religion itself, rather than in the study of religion, either because they are actively religious or because they are actively nonreligious. I want to leave the sages and get back to the hunters.

I have several sorts of "we" in mind here. It may prove useful to distinguish several groups of Americans who find themselves in several different stages of religious commitment, borrowing Rudolf Bultmann's term, "demythologization,"[1] but applying it to a spectrum of disaffection not merely toward myths but toward religion in general: the thoroughly un-mythologized, the un-demythologized (or still mythologized), the demythologized, and the remythologized.

We might as well exclude from the start of our discussion the thoroughly un-mythologized, the people who have never had, and never will have, any inclination to take religion seriously, the people who are tone deaf to religion; they will not be interested in myths, or religion, at all.

The un-demythologized (or still mythologized), at the other extreme, are the people who are still religious in the old-fashioned way, the devout churchgoers who have never lost what Paul Ricoeur has called their "first naiveté." There have always been many people of this sort, of course, and indeed there are now many new ones, not all of them fundamentalists. Many are not at all naive about their naiveté, either. They are religiously sophisticated and literate, aware of the flaws in the traditions to which they are committed and of the available alternative traditions, but they are still happy to worship within their own traditions. They are piscophiles at least in the sense that they love their own fish.

The demythologized are the people who have lost their first naiveté. These are the secular (or radical) humanists, a group that includes many professional scholars of religion. These are the people who believed Nietzsche when he said that God is dead; these are the post-Enlightenment rationalists, the piscophobes. This group, though less numerous than the first, may still be in many ways the dominant voice in our academic culture.

The remythologized are the people who have begun to react against secular humanism, but are still unable to return to their first naiveté. They have eaten their way through Marx and Freud and are still hungry, sometimes hungering for a second naiveté. They have ceased to be confident in their piscophobia, but they are unwilling to return to a dogmatic piscophilia. This is the final "we" that I have in mind here, perhaps more than the other two.

In the midst of this new stirring, it seems to me that the historian of religions may have a genuine contribution to make, if only by raising consciousnesses to an awareness of the many, many varieties of fish that swim in the ocean of religious story, not all of them sharks. If people are once again venturing out into the waters to fish, it may be useful for them to fish for a while in deep, exotic foreign waters. For though it may ultimately be best to fish off one's own shores, some of these waters are overfished, shallow, or historically polluted. It may prove refreshing to fish elsewhere for a while, if only to return better able to catch the fish that were always swimming there in our native harbors.

In chapter 1, we looked at the case of sages and saw the particular problems that face scholars who take other people's myths not only into their heads (as sages) but into their hearts (as hunters). Now let us look more closely at the problems that face any of us, academic as well as nonacademic hunters, if we do take seriously—in a more personal manner than the intellectual assimilation that we have dealt with thus far—the myths of other people, particularly when those myths involve rituals.

When we study other peoples' myths and rituals we may do so out of pure intellectual curiosity, to see what they believe in and do that we do not believe in or do. But sometimes we may begin to wonder what would happen if we ourselves came to believe in those myths or to perform those rituals. There are many good things that happen to us, and this is the point to which I wish ultimately to return. But first let us look at some of the potential pitfalls involved.

We are not the first ones to ask these questions; the religious that we are studying have asked them, too. Their myths provide us with some rather vivid and grim descriptions of the perilous crossing of the channel between one system of myths and rituals to another. But what about us outside the text? What happens when *we* attempt to enter into a myth and ritual? What happens when the myth and ritual infringe upon our real lives? Let us approach this problem through the mediating instance of myths performed in the theater.

The Theater of Myth

Many myths are acted out in the theater; this enactment is a moment in which myths take on the ritual aspect of communal experience. Pope John XXIII is said to have remarked that Italians go to church as if they were going to the theater, while Germans go to the theater as if they were going to church.[2] There is, of course, an essential difference between religious ritual and drama, akin to the difference in the ability of archetypal and nonarchetypal art to survive kitsch: drama, as art, must move you artistically in order to be effective, while ritual moves you to a certain extent in any case. Yet ritual, too, is performed, and it can become stupefyingly boring by virtue of that element of repetition that is also its main strength. Ritual, like myth, works better when it is well done. Of all literary forms, drama best reproduces the effects of myth, most powerfully through the catharsis of the tragic drama, but also in the surreal humor of great comedy. The voices and bodies of the actors serve to bring the mythical and supernatural alive for us on an anthropomorphic level, to make them physically real. The fourth wall is notoriously permeable, and the audience feels that the group caught up in the story on the stage is a part of the world of the audience. Oedipus and Prometheus are, after all, people like us. But then there is also something else in the mythic drama that moves in the opposite direction. Before the drama begins, the world that the actors on the stage inhabit is perceived as other than the world that the audience inhabited before the drama began. This higher world may be suggested by the masks of classical Greek, Indian, and Japanese drama and by the lighting and staging of less stylized drama; above all it is suggested by the voices and movements of inspired actors and by the words of inspired playwrights. But as the drama unfolds, the audience is lifted back through the same fourth wall onto the stage, into the other world; we are, after all, inhabitants of the supernatural world of Oedipus and Prometheus.

Drama built upon archetypes functions as the realization of a myth. In our day, drama (or film) often takes the place of the communal ritual that was a frequent (though certainly not inevitable) complement to the traditional myth. The theater in the broadest sense of the term (encompassing opera, ballet, film, and the so-called legitimate theater) is nowadays the main sacrificial arena in which myths are reenacted.[3]

Hindu literature is self-conscious about the relationship between myth and life as it is manifest in myths that are enacted in the theater. The use of aesthetic experience in salvation was the subject of much discussion in classical Indian philosophy. By seeing, and therefore participating in, the enactment of the myth of Krishna, one was led unconsciously into the proper stance of the devotee. Moreover, the viewer was not merely inspired to decide what role in the cosmic drama he or she wished to play (mother, lover, brother, or friend of Krishna); one was inspired to discover what role one *was* playing, had been playing all along, without knowing it.[4] Alf Hiltebeitel has beautifully described the way that the real world gradually absorbs the stage in Indian religious performances: "The nightlong dramas, acted out on a small patch of ground beneath the petromax lanterns, are finally unravelled at dawn on a stage that grows with the morning light to include first the surrounding outlines of village trees and buildings and then, in effect, the familiar world of the day."[5] An uncannily similar effect was produced upon me and the rest of the American audience who sat through the all-night performance of Peter Brook's production of the *Mahabharata* on the night of Halloween, 31 October, 1987. At the end, the Indian characters brought out tiny lamps and floated them on the surface of the rivers on stage; and as the sun finally rose, and we found ourselves once again not in Hastinapura but in Brooklyn, the final lamp was brought out; and it was a jack-o'-lantern.

The assumption that theatrical myths enter into the lives of the audience and change them is implicit in the argument in Aristophanes' *The Frogs*, in which dramatic poets discuss at great length the truth or falsehood of the myths in their plays and the effects that these myths have upon real life. *The Frogs* is about the theater of Dionysus (which is, in the case of the *Bacchae*, about the rituals of Dionysus). To the extent that the *Bacchae* is a meta-metamyth, *The Frogs* may be regarded as a meta-meta-metamyth.

The protagonists of *The Frogs* are playwrights. In answer to Aeschylus's accusation that Euripides had put "unholy matings" on the stage—in particular by depicting the incestuous passion of Phaedra with Hippolytus, Bellerophon with Stheneboia, and anonymous women who go to bed with their brothers—and that Euripides had called Oedipus a happy man,[6] Euripides replies that his depictions were harmless. To this Aeschylus objects, saying that married women took hemlock out of shame because of Euripides' depiction of the love of Stheneboia for her stepson Bellerophon. Here Aeschylus blurs the permeable fourth wall between the theater and reality; the audience becomes part of the drama by reacting to it. Euripides is being judged not only for the actions of "his" Bellerophon and Stheneboia, but for the actions of the "real" women who took hemlock as a result of seeing the play.

Euripides counters this with a claim that mythic drama and reality do in fact intersect, but on a different plane, and one that justifies rather than condemns his depiction of the myth: "The story I told about Phaedra was true, wasn't it?" he argues, and Aeschylus does not deny this.[7] But Aeschylus' final rebuttal takes yet another tack: he says that even true stories, when immoral, should not be put on the stage, since poets speak to young men (in the world of the theater) as the schoolmaster speaks to children (in the world of reality). Thus Aeschylus accepts the assertion that real events do lead to myths about real events (the story of Phaedra was true), but then turns around and asserts that the myths, in their turn, produce real events (forming the character of young men as the schoolmaster instructs children), for better or for worse. In chapter 2 we traced this very Greek line of reasoning back to Plato, who argued that people would use evil myths (no matter whether true or false) to construct an evil life, and good myths (again, no matter whether true or false) to construct a good life.

The assumption that the myth in the theater expresses a human truth shared by the audience is implicit in Aeschylus' accusation of Euripides: the effect of the myth of Stheneboia and Bellerophon was not to establish a social law ("Don't commit incest!") nor to reinforce an already existing social law ("Aren't you glad you don't commit incest!") nor to inspire antisocial behavior ("How about committing incest?"), but to reveal an already existing and unacceptable aspect of reality. At the very least, it created on the stage a scene that violated nature, that offended the audience's conception of what it was possible even to imagine, much as we might still be shocked by a depiction of a child being tortured or sexually abused.

But on a deeper level, the play may also have revealed another aspect of reality, one that was masked and unconsciously denied. It may have made women commit suicide out of shame at the sudden realization of their own incestuous impulses, by showing them that they were already participating in the myth of Stheneboia by virtue of their erotic relationships with their sons.[8] This is reinforced by Aristophanes' equation of the audience with the sinners in hell, a motley group who include sexual miscreants.[9]

The play within the play in *Hamlet,* a mime of stark mythical power, has the same effect on Claudius that the myth of Stheneboia had on the Greek wives: it makes Claudius face not only the fact that his guilt is known but even the fact that he is guilty; the play within the play precipitates him directly into the episode of (unsuccessful) repentant prayer. The theater does not, therefore, *construct* myths for us; it provides a space wherein we may *discover* our myths. The mythic drama serves vicariously as an escape valve to release intolerable tensions that are in fact a part of our lives. But it also enables its witnesses to experience at one remove a fantasy translated into reality. The mythic drama allows us to live as sages and as hunters at the same time, without conflict. The drama is more real than fantasy, because we can see it with our own eyes, and touch the flesh and blood actors; yet it is less real (and hence less costly) than reality.

In our world, a similar space is provided by the cinema, but without the vivid intensity supplied by the physical presence of the actors in the living theater. I have already noted the mythological atavisms in science fiction movies such as *Star Trek* and *Superman;* a whole mythology (though with a greatly reduced religious content) may also be seen in the classical genre of the Western, with its stark opposition between good and evil (the man in the white hat versus the man in the black hat), the symbiotic complementarity of the noble hero and his clownish sidekick, the ineluctible chastity of the hero (who loves his horse far more than he loves any woman), and the shameless use of sentimental music.

Great films have mythic dimensions and often become quasi-myths in our culture. They influence how life is evaluated, perceived, in fact lived. Gary Cooper in *High Noon,* Marlon Brando in *On the Waterfront* became new paradigms of individualism; Clark Gable and Carole Lombard (or her successors), Katharine Hepburn and Spencer Tracy, Humphrey Bogart and Lauren Bacall changed the relationships between men and women for generations. Among Woody Allen's many meta-films, *Play it Again, Sam* testifies to precisely this influence of Bogart upon his sexual fantasies. And even films that are less than great exert some of the power of kitsch myths: Doris Day, the eternal virgin, blighted the sex lives of millions of American girls in the fifties and sixties, and Jimmy Dean inspired a generation of inarticulate rebels. There are many good (and bad) books about the mythological role of the cinema, and I have nothing to add to this literature. I merely wish to co-opt the example of films as fuel to my more general fire.

The fact that in America, and even more so in India,[10] movie actors become successful politicians indicates the degree to which films, like other myths, become assimilated into real life. Hindi films still perform the function of mythology for Indian society. Sudhir Kakar has interpreted popular Hindi film as "a collective fantasy containing unconscious material and hidden wishes of a vast number of people. . . . Hindi films may be unreal in a rational sense, but they are certainly not untrue. . . . [They] are modern versions of certain old and familiar myths."[11] This is more literally true of Indian films than it is even of our own films, for Hindi films are often rather lurid reenactments of the sacred stories, with tacky but spectacular celestial special effects, dry ice simulating the clouds of heaven, and matinee idols playing the parts of the gods. In India, even where people do still tell the old stories in the traditional way, films begin to usurp the position of myths. It is not, therefore, as one might have thought on the basis of the Western situation, that myths flee from their classical shrines when these crash down under the assault of modern, materialistic can[n]ons, and find refuge in the cool, dark halls of cinema. No, even when the temple is still standing, the myths find another, supplementary home in the medium of film. Old archetypes never die; they just lurk quietly in the background of the sets of Hindi films.[12]

Indeed, where mythological themes are culturally so omnipresent as they are in India, it is particularly easy for a sophisticated filmmaker to select such themes as elements in a film and to feel instinctively that they will magnify the image that he wishes to project, literally, to a mass audience. One film, *Santoshi Ma,* told the story of the establishing of the cult of a goddess named Santoshi Ma; the film became so popular that the cult of the goddess (who had had, until then, only a modest local following) spread throughout India; people would offer traditional objects of worship (garlands, coconuts, and so forth) to the screen at the front of the cinema hall. In R. K. Narayan's novel *Mr. Sampath,* a filmmaker decides to reenact the story of the destruction of Kama, the god of erotic love, by Shiva, the god of yogis; and the actors playing the parts are swept up helplessly into a parallel reenactment of the story in their private lives.[13] Clearly films, like the legitimate theater, present one instance of that ephemeral swinging door of ritual through which myth and reality eternally pass one another.

Orthopraxy and Heterodoxy: Ritual without Myth

Thus films provide an important ritualistic arena for an encounter between the myths and lives of people in our culture at large. To what extent do the rituals of traditional religions still provide this for us? To what extent can the rituals of other peoples' religions provide it for us?

It has been argued that people who take into their hearts (rather than merely into their heads) the myths that they pick up promiscuously in Oriental bazaars risk a crisis of faith when these myths infect the myths of their own traditions—or, in the case of academics, a crisis of atheism when the myth of objectivity is challenged. I think that this false argument is based upon a confusion between myths and rituals. Most people may convert to myths more easily than to rituals; for most people are more orthoprax than orthodox:[14] they define themselves by their rituals, by what they do as hunters, not by their myths, by what they think as sages. People who are merely hunters may find themselves helplessly absorbed into the bodies (rituals) of others, and suffer for it. It takes the conscious effort of a sage to enter other peoples' heads (myths), but once achieved, this is a far less painful process than entering other bodies. As long as the rituals remain intact, the faith remains intact, however much the myths may change. And as long as you *do* the ritual, it does not matter *how* you do it, let alone what you are thinking while you do it. Indeed, it often appears that the very rigidity of the orthoprax structure, the inflexibility of the laws of action, frees the mind all the more.

People are usually, though not always, tied for life to the rituals that they are born with, the rituals that they grow up with, the rituals of their own religion. These rituals may be the formal rituals of an organized religion (attending Mass or a Passover celebration) or ritual in a broader sense, in the sense of any ceremony that people use when they want to bring down to them a benevolent divine presence or to ward off a malevolent one. Such rituals often stem from childhood, from the first attempts to construct deep patterns of order so as to combat the chaos of nightmare fears. And deep patterns are hard to erase.[15]

Rituals cling more obsessively than myths do. The rituals of childhood may haunt even adults who deny the power of the myths of childhood. People may still go on doing their old rituals in the same way that they have always done but explain them differently if they chance to find new myths. Or they may go on doing the rituals without any myths at all to sustain them, or modify the rituals and create new myths to sustain them.

In such circumstances, it might be argued that the ritual has ceased to have any meaning.[16] The ontological status of a ritual without a myth is hardly more than that of a forgotten dream. An example of such a ritual is the case of the Spanish Jews, who, under persecution, were forced to perform their rituals in disguised forms and in secrecy. As they celebrated the Seder inside the house, they posted a guard outside to warn them of the approach of the Inquisition authorities, and in order not to attract attention, the guards would set up a table in the sun and play cards. As time passed, some of the Jews ceased to perform the actual rituals; but every year on that day they knew it was important to set up a table outside and play cards—though they did not know why it was important. Others converted from Judaism altogether but continued to practice their new Catholic rituals in the same, now meaningless, conditions of secrecy.[17] This process is quite closely parallel to the one that Max Müller postulated for myths: through a "disease of language," the word for a god remains when its true, original, naturalistic meaning has been forgotten. On a less dramatic and more banal level, we might see an example of a ritual that has survived without its myth in the experience of all those sufferers who have no interest in or understanding of religion at all but were dragged to church, Sunday after dreary Sunday, by devout parents—and who, even as adults, may feel a pang of guilt every Sunday that they miss Mass.[18]

Can people change their old rituals when those rituals have lost their mythic meaning for them? Yes, but only with difficulty. The resistance to new translations of the Bible when it is part of the church liturgy is based in part upon orthopraxy: people do not like other people monkeying around with their rituals. The conscious construction of a ritual (like the conscious construction of a myth) is a dangerous thing. I am uneasy at modern weddings where the bride and groom patch together a liturgy from their favorite folk-songs, love poetry, and scraps of survey courses in world religions. The marriage liturgy that should be made of something old and blue suffers when it is made of things borrowed and new. Rituals, like genes, are inherited rather than acquired characterictics.

People may often, therefore, find themselves in a situation where they have kept their old rituals but have no old myths to sustain them.

Myth without Ritual

Of course, even rituals, hardier than myths, may ultimately be lost. As a counterpart to the story of the Spanish Jews who continued to perform a ritual that had lost its myth, there is another Jewish story about the survival of myth when ritual is lost:

> When the Baal Shem-Tov had a difficult task before him, he would go to a certain place in the woods, light a fire and meditate in prayer—and what he had set out to perform was done. When a generation later the "Maggid" of Mezeritz was faced with the same task he would go to the same place in the woods and say: We can no longer light the fire, but we can still speak the prayers—and what he wanted done became reality. Again a generation later Rabbi Moshe Leib of Sasov had to perform the task. And he too went into the woods and said: We can no longer light a fire, nor do we know the secret meditations belonging to the prayer, but we do know the place in the woods to which it all belongs—and that must be sufficient; and sufficient it was. But when another generation had passed and Rabbi Israel of Rishin was called upon to perform the task, he sat down on his golden chair in his castle and said: We cannot light the fire, we cannot speak the prayers, we do not know the place, but we can tell the story of how it was done. And, the story-teller adds, the story which he told had the same effect as the actions of the other three.[19]

In retelling this story, Elie Wiesel adds, "God made man because he loves stories."[20] But Gershom Scholem sees a slightly different moral: "You can say if you will that this profound little anecdote symbolizes the decay of a great movement. You can also say that it reflects the transformation of all its values, a transformation so profound that in the end all that remained of the mystery was the tale. That is the position in which we find ourselves today, or in which Jewish mysticism finds itself. The story is not ended, it has not yet become history, and the secret life it holds can break out tomorrow in you or in me."[21] The story is what survives when all else is gone; the *kleos,* the telling of the life of the hero, is all that lives when the Greek hero dies.

This Hasidic story echoes the loss of another, earlier ritual, the sacrifice. In fact, as we have seen, the argument that the sacrifice was abandoned for moral reasons outweighs, historically, the also valid argument that it was abandoned through necessity, after the destruction of the second Temple. But the Jewish myth about the loss of sacrifice through necessity prevails because it is intrinsic to the broader and deeper Jewish myth and self-image of exile, persecution, and loss. This self-image is then perpetuated in the Jewish myth about the loss of the ritual, a myth that itself takes the place of the actual sacrifice. Yet even before the destruction of the Temple, the Jewish sacrifice was entirely mythologized; the recital of the portions of the Bible dealing with sacrifice came to be regarded as the proper substitute for sacrifice. And later, such recitations became "the only generally recognized substitutes for the sacrifices offered up in the Temple."[22]

M. Gaster remarked upon a particularly poignant aspect of this phenomenon:

> Of special significance in this connexion is the lesson read from the first scroll on the second day of the New Year. It is *Genesis* 22, containing the story of the sacrifice of Isaac. This is embellished by a legend of the Rabbis in which it is stated that, for the sake of Abraham's compliance with the divine command of offering up Isaac, God would accept hereafter sacrifices of animals as an atonement for the people's sin. When Abraham asked, "What will happen if they will no longer be able to bring such sacrifices?", God replied, "Let them recite it before me, and it will be for me like unto the sacrifice."[23]

It is in the very nature of rituals not merely to fragment and proliferate, but also to condense, to simplify, to economize.[24] And one form of such simplification is to eliminate the performance of the ritual altogether, keeping only the script, the myth. Such a ritual is like a symphony that exists only in the score that one reads silently but that one never hears in an orchestral realization. Just as the mere ghost of a ritual may be retained when its myth is lost, so too the inverse may be true: the mythical afterimage of a ritual may be retained when the ritual is no longer performed. The rituals of childhood may still be performed in the unconscious minds of people who have long ago ceased actually to *do* them.

This happened in ancient India. The Vedic ritual used to be performed by many priests, one of whom merely imagined the perfect ritual in his head, checking the actual performed ritual against the mental image in order to ensure against possible errors. Eventually, certain renunciant Vedantic sects came to believe that this one priest (the Brahmin, significantly, the eponymous paradigm for all other priests) could function without the others, that it was sufficient for the worshiper only to imagine the perfect ritual in his head, without doing anything at all.[25]

The survival of a ritual without its myth (like the ritual of the Spanish Jews) means the survival of everything but the *explicit* meaning, the survival of the outside of a book whose inside has been gutted. But the misunderstood ceremony may still encapsulate a most powerful set of inarticulate meanings, having to do with community, mystery, and indeed survival itself. By contrast, the survival of a myth without its ritual (like that of Rabbi Israel in the woods) may amount to the survival of nothing *but* the explicit meaning. And if it can be maintained (as I think it can, if only in the most general sort of way) that most people are more orthoprax than orthodox, there are more people like the Spanish Jews than there are those like Rabbi Israel. People find it hard to hang on to myths without rituals.

The Shock of Recognition

Still, the problem of a myth that has outlived its ritual does arise, and when it does it is hard to resolve. Can those who have lost their old rituals, and who cannot consciously construct new ones, replace their lost or broken rituals by importing someone else's "old rituals" wholesale? People can, of course, borrow new ones; this is what conversion is all about. But such conversions are dangerous and difficult. More often, the myth simply lives on, devoid of ritual. And when those myths that are associated with rituals come loose from their ritual moorings, they lose much of their power and relevance. Many canonical stories, wrenched out of their ritual context, are no longer taken seriously.

In traditional societies, rituals often function as a physical, experiential complement to myths, and these rituals do in fact subject the initiate to various shocks—physical torture (fasting, sleeplessness, mutilation), fear, and the symbolic experience of being reborn. This is what the myth is about, the experience for which the myth has prepared not only the initiate but the community that shares vicariously in the ritual. We have seen, for instance, how the Greek tragedies were said to shock their audiences.

The crucifixion and the Eucharist have lost their power as shocking mythic images for many Christians. This was not always so. We have seen that early converts saw the Mass as an instance of cannibalism. In later Christianity, those who were accused of resisting the myth and ritual of the Eucharist by their very resistance confirmed the literalness of its power. In Germany in 1600, men and women accused of witchcraft were said to have stolen the consecrated wafers of the Mass and to have "pierced them with needles until blood flowed from them." One man testified that when he had received the Holy Sacrament at Eastertime,

> he kept it, and afterwards bit it several times so that fair-sized drops of blood were seen to come out of it. And he also stamped on the same, so that it suffered wounds and bruises. He also threw it into the fire, and the flames turned blue. He threw it into the privy on two occasions. . . . [His son] had confirmed this statement. "His father once cast the Host into the privy. In Wischlburg his father bit the Host, so that it shed blood—especially the part he had in his mouth. But they just laughed at this, and scarcely thought it worth mentioning."[26]

Thus, the witches' Black Masses *proved* the sanctity of the true mass; a witch could demonstrate that the Host was in fact the body of Christ, where the priest could not. "The bleeding of the wafer was a miraculous confirmation that it was not simply a wafer of flour and water that had been desecrated but the very body of Christ."[27] So, too, by denying Shiva, Daksha enters into the myth that will affirm Shiva's greatness, and by desecrating the sacrifice of Daksha, the false sacrifice that denies the true god, Shiva affirms the power of the true sacrifice. Hating a god, perhaps even more than loving him, can be an affirmation of faith.

The shocking Black Mass is gone, and now for many the true Mass has lost its power to shock. In some cases, the myths of the Eucharist have been destroyed by religious kitsch, even as some rituals have been destroyed by kitsch. But even in their finer forms, they have become subject to the familiarity that breeds contempt. Nowadays, only children, for whom myth is real, experience the shock of the Mass. Children taking first communion worry about eating Christ: Will the wafer taste bloody? They try to swallow it without biting it. They move behind the symbolism of the suffocated rice cake to the older, more brutal ritual that it replaced: the actual sacrifice of a domestic animal, a *pashu.*

Yet in time children grow up and become dulled to the symbolic murder. In the epilogue to George Bernard Shaw's *Saint Joan,* when King Charles dreams of meeting Joan after she has been burned at the stake, he dreams that the chaplain says he was redeemed and saved by seeing Joan burn to death. When the bishop, Pierre Cauchon, asks, "Were not the sufferings of our Lord Christ enough for you?", the chaplain says, "No. Oh no; not at all. I had seen them in pictures, and read of them in books, and been greatly moved by them, as I thought. But it was no use." Then Cauchon exclaims, "Must then a Christ perish in torment in every age to save those that have no imagination?"[28] The ideal sages would have the imagination to be saved without actually having to burn Joan at the stake.

Within the myth, characters (Pentheus, Daksha) experience the mythic shock of recognition, but we, the readers, see it coming and take it in our stride. The myth shocks the characters in it because it is *about* shock. It narrates the shock, however, in totally familiar terms, and it narrates the same shock over and over again. As we saw in our first attempts to distinguish oral and written classics, oral traditions do not *expect* to be surprised, but written traditions do. Both traditions operate in the contemporary experience of Christian and Jewish rituals, where the ritual tends to resist change or surprise while the myth about the ritual tends to be more tolerant of change. Shock and recognition play at tug of war within the myth about the ritual.

For though rituals continue to have power over those who perform them, they also begin to bore them with their unrelenting roteness. Rituals may become boring precisely for the people who really do believe in them, while other peoples' rituals, that they do not believe in, may be both terrifying and moving in ways that their own rituals are not. Jews may find the Catholic communion exciting in ways that real Catholics have long ceased to do. It is, I think, the sacrificial symbolism of the Catholic Eucharist, a symbolism that long preceded Christ, that moves me when I attend a Catholic Mass, where I can draw relatively little sustenance from any sense of *communitas* with the rest of the congregation. In the formal sense, of course, and as a cultural manifestation, the Mass will always remain for me someone else's ritual, and indeed this may be part of its attraction. But in a deeper sense, and on the level of the archetype, it is also *my* ritual, and that, too, moves me. Indeed, it may be that the very fact that most of the manifestational, specifically communal level of the Catholic Mass is closed to me forces me to respond to it on a more generally humanistic level than that on which I respond to the rituals of my own community, where I am distracted by manifestational details. But the lack of a true identification with the community has serious drawbacks.

In *illo tempore*, "archaic" man (according to the Eliadean prototype) lived the myth in a group and in a shared, traditional ritual; this was the classical myth. For the first group of "us," the un-demythologized, this may still happen. There are still Jews for whom the Passover Seder is a living gate to the Jerusalem that was and that will be, and Christians for whom Christ is entirely present in the Eucharist. But there are others, the demythologized, for whom this is no longer possible. Such people may have lost many of their own rituals or never have received any formal rituals at all as children, but they may still have their myths. As lonely as Rabbi Israel in the woods, they must often live whatever myths they have against the group, surrendering to disturbing and totally personal emotions that often threaten their existence as social animals or their common sense as the creatures of realism and materialism.

One reason why young Americans often become groupies for modern "myths" is, perhaps, a reaction against the terror of religious solipsism, the danger of lapsing into what Robert Bellah called Sheilaism, after the religion that Sheila Larson invented for herself.[29] Some people avoid Sheilaism, and save themselves the trouble of reinventing the religious wheel, by taking up the myths of an already existing religion. Now, it might be argued that other peoples' myths, used out of their true context, used to attain what has been called "a certain para-religious experience," do not in fact avoid the problem of solipsism. But this need not be so. The real danger of solipsism arises when the religious experience is entirely unmediated, even by a text. But in reading the *Bhagavad Gita* or the *Tao Te Ching*, students who have at least some inkling that the book has been loved by hundreds of believers for hundreds of years feel themselves to be in the company not only of the authors of these texts, and of the ghosts of all the Hindus and Taoists who have read them, but even of all the California hippies who have read them. An odd community, but a community nonetheless.

The rejection of the religious community into which they were born, their given ritual community, has left the majority of secularized, demythologized Americans with myths that have been stripped of their power to shock. For such people, there is nothing but an emasculated mythology of atheism and solipsism, a degraded mythology that is found not in churches but in films and childrens' books. But even in this world, where myth is bereft of ritual and has become a mere story—a religion deprived of a congregation—, it has once again begun to draw to itself a kind of secular ritual community, through pockets of cult, such as the cults that sprang up around "Star Trek" (the Trekkies) and the books of J. R. R. Tolkien ("Frodo Lives"). In fact, the possibly mythical function of science-fiction literature is supported by a ritual community of sorts—the computer covens that have sprung up all over America, Users' Groups that communicate through modems to form a *com-*

munitas and to discuss such metaphysical questions as the nature of human intelligence and the possibility of life on other planets. Their terminology is often theological, too; my favorite item is Resurrection Software, a disk used to retrieve lost files (souls), which may have been lost because the operator failed to perform the crucial operation named "Save" (*sic*). Although such groups have no commitment to the myths of "Star Trek" or Tolkien, to the extent that there is no group that will hold them responsible to live in a certain way because of these myths, individual members do, in fact, live much of their lives through such paradigms. These may be echoes of the great myths, but they are sadly faint and distant echoes.

One secular community in which some of us may still experience shared rituals as well as shared myths is the community of scholars or sages, the academic community that was the subject of chapter 1. This book is both an argument for and an instance of such a community: as the footnotes reveal,[30] it is a kind of extended record of a series of conversations with my colleagues and students. Within the academic community, we can exchange the wares of the head, as we have always done, as well as the wares of the heart, as we have sometimes done. Certainly we can exchange with one another guidance in mythical terrains where one of us knows the language and the other does not, or even where one of us knows the meaning and the other does not. But even sages must eventually come to terms with the implications of the loss of the more general ritual community of hunters.

Myths about Rituals

It might appear that we could avoid some of the calamities encountered by Pentheus and Daksha by not resisting the strange myths and rituals. We might also take the precaution of choosing myths that are not inextricably bound up with rituals. The dominance of orthopraxy over orthodoxy means that myths may be more easily acquired than rituals, particularly myths that are not associated with rituals. And there are such myths, I think. Scholars once argued that all rituals had their origins in myths. The other variant of the myth-and-ritual theory came later, with Lord Raglan and Jane Ellen Harrison, who argued that all myths stem from rituals.[31] Indeed, as we have just seen, there are many myths that are closely associated with rituals. But just as there are some rituals that are not associated with myths, so too there are many myths that are not associated with any rituals at all. Such myths may in fact be immediately accessible to people from another culture.

But even myths about rituals may be found in unexpected places, and changed, and absorbed into our personal religious systems. As a Jew teaching in a predominantly Christian divinity school, I wrestled with my own manifestation of the archetypal problem of the Jew among Others, the problem that I broached in chapter 1, and one day I had a dream about it. I dreamed that I was at a meal in the Commons Room of the Divinity School at the University of Chicago, sitting at one of the long tables as I have so often done at formal and informal dinners, with friends on either side and across from me. And suddenly I looked up and realized that I was inside the Leonardo da Vinci painting of the Last Supper, that Jesus and the disciples had come forward in time to join us now at the table in Chicago. As I realized this, the person sitting beside me said to me, "But Wendy, what is *your* religion?" and I replied, "My myths are Hindu, but my rituals are Christian."

This dream puzzled me when I awoke; why did I not say, "My rituals are Jewish?" For indeed, although, as I noted in chapter 1, I have few Jewish myths, my sense of community is primarily Jewish, and I usually participate, albeit somewhat irregularly, in the Passover ritual. Instead, I had borrowed from Christianity to make the collage or *bricolage* of my dream image. Through this indirect path, my dream also incorporated the ceremony of the sharing of the leftovers (or *prasada*) of the Hindu gods, the food distributed to the worshipers after the god has tasted them in the temple. This *prasada* is also said to incorporate the substance of the god, so that the worshiper is, as in the Christian Eucharist, eating God.[32] (There is also a Hasidic tradition of gathering for the Third Meal on the Sabbath, when the Rebbe feeds his disciples from the leavings of his plate.) For the myth of the communal meal served me simultaneously as a Jewish Seder, a Christian Eucharist, a Hindu *prasada,* and a University of Chicago dinner. My dream incorporated my four rituals (three religious and a transcendent fourth): Jewish, Christian, Hindu, and academic. The fourth, the academic, provided a kind of metareligion that transcended religions, a framework that made possible the *bricolage* of the other three. Of course, this was only a *dream* of a ritual, a story that I told myself about a ritual—a myth. I had not converted to a new ritual, merely dreamed that my usual rituals had taken on a new mythic dimension. But the Christian (particularly the Catholic) and Hindu myths had come to play a very important role in my religious thinking, to answer needs that were not answered by the ritual community into which I had been born, with implications that I had not yet not come to terms with until I had that dream.

How is it possible to assimilate a myth about a ritual without assimilating the ritual itself? Our rituals are deeply ensconced in our hearts; our myths may enter though the head—and, ultimately, come to lodge in the heart. But if our myths are in our heads and our rituals are in our hearts, what is our religion? Is it possible to patch together a religion, or even a God, like a piece of *bricolage,* or a stitched-together Frankenstein's monster? No, not if what is meant is the conscious construction of a theology, let alone a liturgy. Such wholesale imports remain undigested, unassimilated, like those French chateaux that Texan billionaires import, stone by stone, and set down in the suburbs of Dallas. Yet it seems to me that people who continue to live with their given rituals in the orthopraxy of the heart can still absorb other myths in the heterodoxy of the head.

For those of us whose own symbols may have become degraded, perhaps it is time to look for our myths somewhere else. Yet, though we know that myths are sustained by rituals, we cannot look casually to other sources to replace our lost rituals. What, then, will provide the sustaining structure for the new myths that we may find?

Chapter 7

Other Peoples' Lives

The Rabbi from Cracow

Reports of the death of mythology have been greatly exaggerated, as Mark Twain said of his own death. The work of Mircea Eliade, if nothing else, long ago established that mythology still survives, bloody but unbowed, in American culture; we have seen it in films, in children's books, and in all sorts of unexpected places. And we have not even begun to talk about the many separate mythologies of individual ethnic groups within our culture at large.[1] Yes, Virginia, there *is* an American mythology. But for most of us (the demythologized and perhaps also the remythologized), the surviving mythologies of American culture, though they may share many of the themes and even the forms of traditional mythology, no longer perform the *function* of traditional mythology. They do not shape our lives with its meanings. They neither comfort us as routinized traditional myths can do nor shock us as inspired retellings of routinized traditional myths can do.

Yet we still can be shocked by the myths of other people. If we may recover our own lost classics through a kind of "defamiliarization," allowing other peoples' classics to heighten our awareness of our problematic relationship with our own classics, surely we can take advantage of the native "defamiliarity" of other peoples' myths. If the Christian image of God as a sacrificed lamb has lost its power for some of us, we may be jolted out of our complacency by an encounter with the leonine Hindu shepherd. We may find that the Eucharist conceals within it implications that Christianity has not developed in the ways that Hinduism has, and we may begin to see those im-

135

plications better when we know the Hindu myth and ritual. For a foreign myth may reveal to us what is *not* in our own culture.

Sherlock Holmes once solved a mystery, the case of Silver Blaze, a race-horse, by using a vital clue of omission. When Inspector Gregory asked Holmes whether he had noted any point to which he would draw the Inspector's attention, Holmes replies, "To the curious incident of the dog in the night-time." "The dog did nothing in the night-time," objected the puzzled Inspector, the essential straight man for the Socratic sage. "That was the curious incident," remarked Sherlock Holmes. The fact that the dog did not bark when someone entered the house at night was evidence that the criminal was someone familiar to the dog.[2] Only when we view the Christian Eucharist through Hindu eyes, and the Vedic sacrifice through Christian eyes, does it occur to us to ask why the Christian dog does not bark at the image of God as a devouring wild animal, and the Hindu dog does not bark at the image of God as a domestic animal who offers himself up for sacrifice. It is easier to understand the role of an animal in one culture if we can see where it does *not* appear in another, and we can notice the lacuna left by an animal in one culture if we see where it does appear in another. To borrow the Zen koan, we cannot hear the sound of one hand clapping. But through the comparative method we can see the cultural blinkers that each culture constructs for its archetypes. In this way, a look at *their* divine animals makes us see things that we never noticed in *our* divine animals—either because in fact those things are not there or because it troubles us to see that they are.

The visionary power of foreign myths may help us to achieve a literal re-vision of our own scriptures in other ways, as well, to revalue parts of them that have fallen by the wayside or have been too hastily jettisoned. But in light of the problems posed by the otherness of our own classics, it might be supposed that the otherness of the religious classics of other cultures would be even more other to us than our own, other squared, as it were, and thus present quite insuperable obstacles. The academic and intellectual problems involved in attempts to bridge this otherness are considerable, as are the conflicts that arise when we take on new myths that involve new rituals and the weaknesses that arise when we take on new myths that are not associated with rituals. Can it, in fact, be done? Is it worth doing? How can it be done? What happens to us when we do it?

Since rituals are events that happen, one can find oneself *doing* a ritual. But it is also possible to find oneself *doing* the events that are described in a myth without a ritual. Here let us draw back just for a moment from the frame of our own lives as we confront the texts, and plunge back into the world of texts. There are many stories about people who enter myths without entering rituals, who take up new myths that do not demand new rituals.

Here we may distinguish four different variants. First, there are stories within our own culture about people who have discovered the story of their own lives in the myths of other people within their own culture. The prime example is that of people who have taken the myth of Jesus as their myth. Second, there are, still within our own culture, stories about people who found their myths in stories told by other cultures; if we count the Greeks as "ours" (a highly problematic thing to do, as we saw in chapter 3), Herodotus's story of Scyles is such a story. Then there are stories from other cultures, that is, stories told by peoples that we regard as other, which tell (a) how people found their life stories narrated in myths about other people within that culture (not other peoples, in their terms)—the story of Matangi and the buffalo sacrifice is such a story; and (b) how people found their life stories in myths about people that they themselves regarded as other—to the extent that Shiva is "other" to Vedic religion, the myth of Daksha is such a story.

The Rabbi from Cracow

Let us take as our text for this chapter an example of the second of our four possibilities, a text from one of our own cultures (the Jewish tradition) about the translation of a myth out of the text of another culture into the context of our own lives, a text about a transcultural transformation from myth to life. The great Indologist Heinrich Zimmer retold a well-known Hasidic tale told by Martin Buber, a version of the story of the Jew among Others.

> It is a brief story, told of the Rabbi Eisik, son of Rabbi Jekel, who lived in the ghetto of Cracow, the capital of Poland. He had remained unbroken in his faith, through years of affliction, and was a pious servant of the Lord his God.
>
> One night, as this pious and faithful Rabbi Eisik slept, he had a dream; the dream enjoined him to proceed, afar, to the Bohemian capital, Prague, where he should discover a hidden treasure, buried beneath the principal bridge leading to the castle of the Bohemian kings. The Rabbi was surprised, and put off his going. But the dream recurred twice again. After the third call, he bravely girded his loins and set forth on the quest.
>
> Arriving at the city of his destiny, Rabbi Eisik discovered sentries at the bridge, and these guarded it day and night; so that he did not venture to dig. He only returned every morning and loitered around until dusk, looking at the bridge, watching the sentries, studying unostentatiously the masonry and the soil. At length, the captain of the guards, struck by the old man's persistence, approached, and gently inquired whether he had lost something or perhaps was waiting for someone to arrive. Rabbi Eisik recounted, simply and confidently, the dream that he had had, and the officer stood back and laughed.
>
> "Really, you poor fellow!" the captain said; "Have you worn your shoes out wandering all this way only because of a dream? What sensible person would trust a dream? Why look, if I had been one to go trusting dreams, I should this very minute be doing just the opposite. I should have made such a pilgrimage as this silly one of

yours, only in the opposite direction, but no doubt with the same result. Let me tell you my dream."

He was a sympathetic officer, for all of his fierce mustache, and the Rabbi felt his heart warm to him. "I dreamt of a voice," said the Bohemian, Christian officer of the guard, "and it spoke to me of Cracow, commanding me to go thither and to search there for a great treasure in the house of a Jewish Rabbi whose name would be Eisik son of Jekel. The treasure was to have been discovered buried in the dirty corner behind the stove. Eisik son of Jekel!" the captain laughed again, with brilliant eyes. "Fancy going to Cracow and pulling down the walls of every house in the ghetto, where half of the men are called Eisik and the other half Jekel! Eisik son of Jekel, indeed!" And he laughed, and he laughed again at the wonderful joke.

The unostentatious Rabbi listened eagerly, and then, having bowed deeply and thanked his stranger-friend, he hurried straightway back to his distant home, dug in the neglected corner of his house and discovered the treasure which put an end to all his misery. With a portion of the money, he erected a prayer house that bears his name to this day.[3]

Both of the people in the story resist the idea that they must go abroad to find their treasure. The Captain laughs, as the man in Laurens van der Post's story laughed when he looked into the basket of his wife's myths. The Captain does not realize that he is actually addressing "Eisik son of Jekel" when he repeats that phrase, three times, in mockery. The Rabbi experiences "surprise" when he has his dream—again, three times—but he does not experience (or, at least, reveal) any surprise at the Captain's words. Instead, he hastens to dig in the neglected dirt of his own home, to excavate his own tradition more deeply. As Zimmer comments on this myth, "Now the real treasure . . . is never far away; it lies buried in the innermost recess of our own home; that is to say, our own being . . . but there is the odd and persistent fact . . . that the one who reveals to us the meaning of our cryptic inner message must be a stranger, of another creed and a foreign race."

The Captain, like the man in van der Post's story, finds the basket of foreign myths, his own dream about a foreign land, empty; the Rabbi looks into the basket of the Captain's dream and finds it full—full of his own treasures. Sometimes, indeed, the treasure may not be the secret that the myth reveals but *the myth itself,* the basket itself. Or, even beyond that, the treasure may be the person who gives us the basket, the Other that we come to recognize first through the myth.

The moral of the story of the Rabbi from Cracow according to Rabbi Simha Bunam of Pzhysha (the original author of the story, according to Buber) is somewhat different from the moral drawn by Zimmer: "There is something you cannot find anywhere in the world, not even at the zaddik's, and there is, nevertheless, a place where you can find it." And yet another moral is pointed in the version "retold" by Woody Allen:

Rabbi Yekel of Zans . . . dreamed three nights running that if he would only journey to Vorki he would find a great treasure there. Bidding his wife and children goodbye, he set out on a trip, saying he would return in ten days. Two years later, he was found wandering the Urals and emotionally involved with a panda. Cold and starving, the Rev was taken back to his house, where he was revived with steaming soup and flanken. . . . After telling the story, the Rabbi rose and went into his bedroom to sleep, and behold, under his pillow was the treasure he originally sought. Ecstatic, he got down and thanked God. Three days later, he was back wandering in the Urals again, this time in a rabbit suit. . . . The above small masterpiece amply illustrates the absurdity of mysticism.[4]

Let us pull back again from the inside of the text to the outer frame that we inhabit as readers of the text. Is it possible for us, too, to do what the heroes and heroines of these stories do, to move the myth from the past to the present and the future, to take up myths from within our own culture or from within another culture? I believe that we can, that it is possible to construct (or to discover) a metamyth (or a meta-metamyth) by reflecting not merely upon the classical themes of our own tradition but upon the classical themes of other peoples' traditions.

The first Westerner who made a serious effort to understand other peoples' myths was Herodotus; and he was the first, too, as we have seen, to note what could happen to people who adopted other peoples' rituals. When discussing the ideas of reincarnation held by the Egyptians, he remarked, "Let whoever finds them credible [*pistoi*] use them."[5] He will not tell us whether he himself found such stories "credible" or "useful," but we may decide for ourselves how we wish to use other peoples' myths. One can experience other peoples' lives and myths in several ways, as hunters (living them in our own lives without realizing it) or as sages (taking them into our own heads) or as hunting sages (realizing that we have entered into someone's else's myth). We may regard other peoples' myths as bizarre stories about other peoples that have nothing to do with us, as stories about how other people ought to be, as stories about us, or as stories about how we ought to be. Taking other peoples' myths seriously ultimately means recognizing that they are *our* myths, which means not only that they have a general meaning for us but that they narrate the stories of our own lives. If we make this decision, we must still decide what to do about it. Belief comes relatively easy, true acceptance a bit harder, commitment is much rarer, and the decision to act upon the myth, either in ritual or in life, is the most difficult of all.

There *is* a treasure for us to find in other peoples' myths. Though the otherness of other people's myths does provide serious obstacles to our understanding of them, it also enables us to do a kind of end-run around some of the obstacles that stand in the way of our understanding of our own myths. Foreign myths tell us things that no one else knows, strange things that are truly strange, things that our own myths never dreamed of. But they also tell us that what seems strange in our *own* myths, and even in our most private dreams, may not in fact be so strange as we fear it to be. And, finally, they sneak past our guard to tell us the things that we will not listen to from our own myths. Foreign myths may provoke a shock of recognition, a moment of *déjà vu* (or, more often, *déjà lu,* or *déjà écouté*) when we recognize in the pattern of a myth the pattern of our own life. The foreignness of the foreign text simultaneously mutes and intensifies the shock of recognition by presenting our home truths from an unexpected angle.

The *Mahabharata* seldom surprises a Hindu (or, indeed, a Jaina), and that is precisely why they love it. But hear what Peter Brook had to say about the reasons why a Western audience might love his production of the *Mahabharata:* "There is a very mysterious, extraordinary, rich, and totally unknown epic, *The Mahabharata.* One of its great virtues is that almost nobody coming to it [in the West] knows what's going to happen next. Imagine you were going to see *Hamlet* not knowing what's going to happen next."[6]

The myths of others may present to us meanings that may indeed exist in our own culture but that we tend to ignore or undervalue or resist when we encounter them in their familiar form, prophets in their own country. We see ourselves, by contrast, with abrupt clarity in what appear to us to be the shockingly distorted images of "others," images of ourselves mistranslated in the fun-house mirror of a foreign idiom, just as the Christian missionaries saw themselves "distorted" in the cannibal images of their potential converts. Myths constitute a stage on which we can see ourselves, not as others see us, but *as Others.* These images shock us both because we see that they are not like us and because we see that they are like us.

This seeming distortion allows us to realize things about ourselves that we did not or would not notice about the image that we saw in the mirror of our own culture—a mirror that we could not bear to look into with our eyes wide open because, wrongly, we thought that our own culture held up to us an accurate mirror, a mirror that was not "other." In that mirror we saw ourselves as through a glass, darkly; in other peoples' mirrors we may see ourselves face to face. When we look at strange myths we miss the faces that are familiar to us from our own myths, but strange myths also make us realize that the faces in our own myths are strange, too. They show us not only that what we thought was other is in fact familiar, but also that what we thought was familiar is in fact other.

India is particularly useful in this regard. Insofar as India is part of the Indo-European world (Sanskrit, and hence Hindi, Bengali, and so forth, being related to Greek, Latin, and so forth), she is part of our culture; she is non-other. But insofar as India is not Indo-European (as most of South India speaks Dravidian languages, unrelated to Indo-European), and is geographically, racially, and politically alien to us, she is other. To the extent that Indians think Indo-European words and hence Indo-European thoughts, we can hope to empathize with as well as understand Indian religions, to share their world order as well as their word order. But to the extent that India is not Indo-European, she challenges us to come to terms with the same radical Otherness that the anthropologists have always hoped to smoke out in Samoa or the Trobriand Islands. India thus provides an interface where the things that we understand from our own world shade off into the things that we do not understand. It is the place where we are forced to confront not only the strangeness of the things that we always knew that we did not know but the strangeness of things that we always thought that we did know.

Once we have learned what is "other" about other peoples' myths, we are equipped to turn our lights back upon ourselves, to photograph the cameraman. Gazing into them as into a shop window, we see the faces of the strange figures posed inside, and superimposed on their faces we see the reflections of our own faces looking at them. The myth that we thought was just a window turns out to be a mirror, too.

For instance, if we attempt to approach a sympathetic understanding of the myth that validates the institution of *suttee* we may be forced to examine in a new light our assumptions about death (which may not be shared by those who accept the myth of *suttee*); and if we attempt similarly to understand Hindu myths about Untouchables we may have to face up to our assumptions about many Others within our supposedly democratic society (not only strangers, children, and animals, but the insane, criminals, the poor, people with cancer, people with AIDS, gay people, black people, women, old people . . .). It is certainly hard enough to try to think like a Hindu while continuing to think like ourselves; but once we even begin to attempt it, we may find ourselves occasionally thinking like (what we think) a Hindu would think about our own society. However many removes we may be from anything like a direct encounter with reality, this cannot but be a humanizing experience.

Shooting at Pluralistic Ducks

The role of the *Mahabharata* in Indian culture faces us with an apparent paradox that is in fact a profoundly disturbing fact: that illiterate people often know their classics, while we do not know ours. Their intimacy with their own myths is often a result of the oral tradition. The telling of the story is but a stone's throw from the acting out of the story, and one *becomes* a story that one knows well, as the characters in Bradbury's *Fahrenheit 451* became their stories as soon as they lost the written form and were forced to use the oral form. But the loss of our own classics, our own oral tradition, and our own ritual tradition may become a positive factor when we come to adopt *other* peoples' myths.

Now we are not only freed *from* ritual (which we have lost) but we are also freed *for* myths. Now we may find our myths among the wide panoply of the myths that exist on the planet Earth, choosing them consciously, as individuals, instead of inheriting them unconsciously as part of an entire culture. Translations have become far more important and also far more easily available. But this easy accessibility of world mythology, the fact that one can pick up myths on the street, as it were, raises several problems of definition and of value judgments.

Our working definition of a myth made use of several criteria that were matters more of status and function than of substance. That is, a myth is a narrative that a *group regards* as having certain characteristics (age, anonymity, etc.) and that is part of a *group* of stories. Indeed, myths are often hierarchically arranged: some are most sanctified and most firmly fixed; other myths may be more temporary, or may even be sanctified only by their association with other myths. How, then, can an *individual* have a myth at all? How can an adopted myth remain a myth when it is no longer the property of the group that validated its status as a myth, or no longer nourished by the other myths which sustained it, directly or indirectly? How can it survive when it has none of the things that normally allow it to function as a myth: the group status or the context of other myths or the context of its history within the history of its new culture? These are real questions, I think, but they have real answers.

To begin with, if we take up a myth as an individual myth, we may do so in several different ways, all of which mimic the ways that it was used in the culture in which it became a myth in the first place. It may remain a private myth, or it may become a part of the mythology of the group. If it remains private, it may function either as a private charter for the action of an individual or as a metaphor through which that individual views the world. Many myths are "lived" not as moral directives ("I will do this because the myth tells me to") nor even as philosophical or theological dogmas ("I now believe this because I learned it from that story") but as patterns within which meaning is discovered or created ("I recognize what sort of a person my new acquaintance is; he is like Pentheus.") In that sense, we all do have private mythologies.[7] But a myth used in this way is a myth in only the weakest sense of the word.

As an intermediary state, a foreign myth may remain in the mind of the individual who discovers it abroad but find its nourishment there in the context of other myths from the native culture (or, indeed, from still other cultures). It could, like myths in more traditional societies, become sanctified through its association with an already sanctified myth, through finding its place in the corpus of stories that we already know. Thus we may assimilate the story of Shiva and Daksha when we realize the ways in which it resembles, partially, the more familiar story of Pentheus and Dionysus. We are all structuralists; even if we have never heard of Lévi-Strauss, we *do* what he says we do.

Finally, a myth may become a myth in the most traditional sense by being disseminated from the individual who borrows it to the culture at large. People do tell stories, after all; that is how a story gets to be a myth in the first place. And when people tell a story often enough, it may begin to take root in the general culture into which it has been transplanted, and perhaps to sprout new shoots in the form of new variants in new retellings. This may at first glance seem to contradict a caveat that I expressed in chapter 2 against the conscious creation of new myths to satisfy new political agendas. But I think the two cases are in fact distinct: the sort of assimilation that I have in mind here is not a conscious, immediate proselytizing but rather a gradual, almost incidental effect over time. I am not saying that we can or should make this happen; I am saying that it sometimes does happen, and that when it does it is a good thing, an infusion of new life into our culture.

All three of these processes imply some degree of universalism. They imply that, although the myth will inevitably lose a great deal of its power when it loses its specific cultural inflections, *something* will survive the transition, something that is rooted in a more general humanity. Not all myths have this; like fine wines, not all myths "travel well." Some of the most interesting myths remain mere curiosities (very curious curiosities) outside their parent culture, while others undergo many successful reincarnations throughout the world. The "English" Cinderella story, for instance, betrays its Chinese origins only when we do a double take on certain peculiar details that we tend ordinarily to overlook: the criterion for feminine beauty (small feet) and the substance of which the slipper is made (glass, a most impractical foot-covering until we realize that it was originally fur [*en vair* in the French of Perrault, from whom the English got the story] but was misread as glass [*en verre*]—yet another vindication of Max Müller's theory of mythology as a disease of language).

The history of the migrations of folk motifs, which began to be studied systematically in the nineteenth century, has revealed certain broad patterns of survival; like sperm swimming toward the egg, some fertilize, some do not. And so, as we all learned in sex education class in high school, there have to be an awful lot of sperm to make sure that at least one will get through the uterine obstacle course. The sperm-scatter principle seems to operate with myths as well as folktales: if you get into the import-export business with myths, you need a large inventory to account for all the merchandise that is bound to be lost in transit, but eventually you do sell *something*. And the hypothesis of certain human universals means that the impregnation of our storytelling traditions by foreign stories does not take place entirely at random.

For certain myths may take root in another context besides that provided by the myths of the culture that receives them, a more basic context composed of both the realities and the arts of the receiving culture. People will adopt into their own culture stories that tell about events that have happened to them, about the things that do happen to people in several (if not all) cultures, even when their own culture may not have told them stories about those events. This is a theme to which I shall return in a moment.

But first we must consider another potential objection to the immigration of myths. I have said that some myths travel better than others. Even if we are convinced that a myth remains a myth when it is translated from its parent culture to ours, the choice of one myth rather than another involves some sort of cross-cultural value judgment: one myth is good while another is not.

One factor in this process of selection may be art. Let us return for a moment to the question of kitsch. It may well be that, though kitsch is sometimes destructive even to our own myths, we can nevertheless often tolerate our own kitsch because the religious context in which our own myths are embedded, the personal and ritual context, the rich emotional patina that the myth has developed for us over the ages, supplies the emotional power that good art supplies for the nonmythological classics. But the kitsch of other peoples' myths may spoil them for us, as we see them so naked, stripped of their ritual costumes. It is therefore likely that we' can adopt other peoples' myths better if they are not merely good myths but classical myths, myths well expressed. This may add to the otherness of the foreign culture the otherness of any classic, giving us a double set of obstacles to surmount: the strangeness of the foreign, and the difficulty of great art. Ultimately, however, these are the myths that will make a lasting imprint upon us.

But of course, myths that appeal to our own sense of what art is may not be the ones that rank highest in the artistic criteria of the cultures that have created them. This may seem to raise a new form of the specter of cheap (not to say promiscuous) cultural relativism, which has haunted us from the very beginning of this discussion. But moral relativism is a property of action, of rituals; ontological relativism is all we need to select and judge myths. And ontological relativism is heterodox, not heteroprax. It simply requires that we entertain the possibility of a number of explanations of the meaning of any one act. Ontological relativism can harm us only if we are determined to hang on to a single explanation given to us by our own culture.

Here is where I finally part company with my colleague Allan Bloom. And I would go further, and argue that it is not enough for us to relent (as Bloom would not do) to the limited extent of admitting the possibility that our own single explanation might be replaced by another single explanation from another culture. It is not necessary to choose one single variant from many myths from many different cultures; it is far better to seek many variants.

And there are, fittingly, various arguments to support the case for cultural and religious pluralism both in our society in general and in the academic curriculum in particular. Setting aside the pious, but nonetheless valid, consideration that the planet is too small for us to remain ignorant of the civilizations of Asia and Africa, and that the bearers of those cultures increasingly dwell within our own boundaries, and that it behooves us to understand them—setting aside these nonacademic arguments, there are several obvious scholarly responses to the suggestion that we should stick to Plato. Let me recapitulate those that I have already stated, or implied, up to this point.

The fear that we will lose our own way, our own voice, by being swallowed up in the maelstrom of relativism, is a paranoid one; we may still make moral judgments, value judgments, while listening with openness to alternate worldviews. The fear that we will be unable to learn, deeply and personally, the classics of other peoples is equally unfounded; such classics are no harder than Homer for us to learn. The "common core" of our curriculum is entirely arbitrary; if you dig deeply enough from any spot on the surface of the earth, you will reach the center. Finally, there is good reason to believe that the classics of Asia, which have proved their ability to survive throughout the entire culture, not merely within the domain of a limited elite, might gain equally broad currency among us.

The value of seeking several versions of "our" myths in cultures other than our own may be illustrated by a story. It seems that two Irishmen, Paddy and Mike, were sitting all day in a duck blind, drinking from a jug of poteen (a kind of potent Irish moonshine), waiting in vain for the ducks to appear. At last, when both the daylight and the poteen were gone, a single duck flew across the evening sky. Mike groggily raised his gun and fired a shot, and the duck fell like a stone at their feet. "By God, Mike," said Paddy, "it's little less than a miracle that you could hit that duck in the state you're in." "But surely, Paddy," said Mike, "I'd be able to hit one single duck when the sky is full of the hundreds of them."

To me, this story is a kind of Irish koan or Zen shaggy dog story. The Irishmen are hunters, hunting the wild goose of truth. And since they think that the sky is full of ducks, they hit one—*even though there is really only one duck*. (Contrariwise, people who think that there is only one duck in the sky may never be able to hit it.) This parable argues for the reading of the myths of many different cultures; and it suggests that even if you believe that there is only one true answer to any great human question, you are more likely to find it if you shoot at a number of ducks—that is, if you take seriously a number of different cultures' answers to that question. The story enacts a variant of the sperm-scatter principle. There are so few interesting questions, and so many interesting answers.

In fact, I don't believe that there is only one true answer to any great human question; I believe there are many answers. In this, I agree with most Hindus and with the Jainas who told the variant of the *Mahabharata*. It might be argued that the question of how many answers there are to any great human question is itself a great human question to which I believe there is only one answer, that being that there are many answers. This is indeed a paradox (albeit a rather jesuitical one), and perhaps it should be regarded as one more of the inevitable pitfalls of relativism. But I would still argue in favor of pluralism, on the grounds that the statement that there is more than one answer is, in effect, more than one answer. Moreover, I do not mean to take a purely relativistic stance, but merely a relatively relativistic stance; I would reserve the right to prefer some answers to others.

To say that we may find useful answers to the same question in several different myths is not to say that they say the same thing, of course. Even two contradictory myths, myths that present two contradictory responses to the same basic question, may prove simultaneously useful to a single person, not just useful for different people, or at different times. This is because myth is an art, not a science; where science is afflicted by the hobgoblin of consistency, art can tolerate the spirit of contradiction. The statements made by myths are emotional as well as rational, and although emotion can cloud reason, it can also sharpen perception. Thus many emotions yield many different sharp perceptions.

The story of the Irishmen and the ducks might also be taken as a parable for another kind of eclecticism, the use of many different theories in attempting to understand any single myth or all myths. For the pluralism of India may also provide a model for the pluralism of the scholar of religion. If one can ask many different good questions about any single myth, and one can answer any of these questions in a variety of good ways, it makes sense to try several different approaches—structuralism, Freudianism, Marxism—to round up the usual hermeneutical suspects. The metaphor of the microscope[8] illustrates the uses of a multidemensional approach: you must constantly change the scale in which you view any particular phenomenon, for there are always at least two levels above and two levels below what you are looking at at any given moment. A thick theoretical description of a myth (to use Clifford Geertz's phrase) immerses the myth in a solution supersaturated with potential meanings (the only "solution" that a myth can have). Then anyone who reads that description can lower into it the string of his own questions—can go fishing for answers, in the hope that his own meanings will crystalize around his question.

The value of eclecticism in method may also be stated negatively: if the only tool you have is a hammer, every problem becomes a nail. There is an old story about this, retold by Idries Shah:

> Someone saw Nasrudin searching for something on the ground. "What have you lost, Mulla?" he asked. "My key," said the Mulla. So they both went down on their knees and looked for it. After a time the other man asked: "Where exactly did you drop it?" "In my own house?" "Then why are you looking here?" "There is more light here than inside my own house."[9]

An eclectic who searches outside of his own house has many lights with which to search, and finds many keys (not only his own) to many enigmas.

The single duck may be the true answer, the answer that corresponds to the archetype, the One, the swan of *brahman,* the god without qualities (*nirguna*), the monotheistic pantheon, the single echo of "boum" in the cave. But the flock of ducks are the illusion that makes life possible (*maya*), the manifestations, the Many, the god with qualities (*saguna*), the polytheistic pantheon, the infinitely various "exquisite echoes" in the cave. A single event may be repeated over and over again in time, in various world eras or in various rebirths. A single core of the classic myth may appear over and over again in space, in many cultures all over the planet. Both the myth and the archetype value themselves for the unique situation of each one in its own single culture; but both of them also value themselves for their ability to capture a universal truth. The unique situations form, with all the other unique situations, a flock of separate geese. Despite their similarities, they cannot be made to fly in a neat wedge formation. For the universal truth is the One Wild Goose.

The Audience inside the Story

We have encountered, in our own mythologies as well as in the myths of others, stories about people who discover the stories of their own lives in the myths of other people, often against their will. In Sophocles' *Oedipus Rex,* there is grotesque irony in the way that Iocaste assures Oedipus that he need not worry about the prediction that he would sleep with his mother, since everyone knows that this is something that men always dream about—but the man to whom such things are nothing lives most easily.[10] The fact that people do not believe in such things does not prevent them from happening. Indeed, resistance is often what precipitates the mythic event.

For, as Freud pointed out, the very vehemence of our denials often affirms our unconscious acceptance. (So too, as we have seen, the hatred of religion in the study of religion, or the hatred of a god in a myth, may betray a more powerful belief than is demonstrated by love.) Among the many examples of this phenomenon of implicit acceptance through explicit denial, let me cite two of my favorites. The Quakers do not believe that baptism has power; they do not practice it themselves. The Mormons, who practice not only baptism but the baptism of the dead, have had occasion to baptize some of their ancestors who happened to have been Quakers, to which the Quakers have strenuously objected. Yet the Quakers would not have objected unless the myth did, in fact, have power for them. A similar paradox has been pointed out in the argument in a Telugu devotional text:

> Virasaivism does not believe in *punarjanma* [rebirth] nor in *svarga* or *naraka* [heaven and hell]. . . . Nevertheless, Virasaivism does apply the concept of *naraka* to those who deviate from the pre-scribed path. For example, the *Basava Purana* states that a Saivite enters twenty-eight-hundred-million *narakas* by uttering the names of deities from other religions. . . . The context of these statements suggests that anyone who deviates from the Virasaiva path falls into the hells which are provided by the other systems.[11]

In this way, it is possible to get gobbled up by dragons that *other* people believe in.

But it is also possible to find oneself in a myth that one *does* believe in. Hindus know their myths so well that they *are* the text; they are the vehicle on which the disembodied myth is projected. The Baba of Sahawali relives the *Mahabharata* battles and summons the evil spirits of that epic to cure villagers who come to him for help. "As Draupadi was insulted by Duhshasana and Duryodhana, and Sita was abducted by Ravana [in the *Mahabharata* and the *Ramayana*], Baba dreamed that some 'bad characters' carried away his wife with the intention of assaulting her. As Bhima and Hanuman redeemed Draupadi and Sita, the two heroes also descended, in Baba's dream, to protect his wife. . . . They were available in his dreams." But when he invoked the gods, all but Shiva came to help him. Later, when Shiva came to Baba's house, Baba asked him why he hadn't come before, and Shiva answered, "I am in charge of the *pralaya,* total destruction. Had I appeared on the scene, and if I were seized with anger, the whole world would have been destroyed. It is not going to happen just now."[12] This is not only the answer to the question as to why Shiva remained otiose during Baba's hour of need; it is one of the usual answers to the moral problem of the *Mahabharata* holocaust:[13] Shiva is always absent at the decisive moments, postponing the untimely doomsday until the time is ripe. Baba predicts his own personal doomsday, however: "My head will be sacrificed. . . . It will be as it was done with Babhruvahana of the *Mahabharata.*" Or, he might have said, with Daksha of the *Mahabharata.*

In this way, the retelling of the myths takes on the function of communion rather than communication. People listen to stories not merely to learn something new (communication), but to relive, together, the stories that they already know, stories about themselves (communion).[14] Where communication is effective, communion is evocative. Where communication seeks to influence the future, communion draws upon the past. Traditional oral storytelling techniques (as well as contemporary serials) satisfy the need for communion, rather than (or in addition to) communication; the audience takes pleasure in predicting what will happen, and satisfaction in seeing it happen, rather than in being surprised or shocked.[15] Children, for whom we preserve the oral tradition, are often unable to tolerate the tension of surprise and shock. They demand to be reassured about the happy ending before they will allow the story to go on. When we take in new myths from other cultures, which are no longer able to surprise them but are able to surprise us, we experience both communion and communication.

Many intellectually pretentious adults speak of "rereading" a classic, when they are unwilling to admit that they have never read it before. Yet they are often the very people who cannot understand why other people will read the same books over and over again instead of "learning something new." Indeed, one very good way to define a classic book is as a book that one can (and must) read over and over again. The term "mythologize" appears for the very first time, in Homer's *Odyssey,* in a context where it seems to mean "to tell a story over and over again"—more precisely, to tell one's *own* story over and over again.[16] And no one who has ever been asked, by a young child, to tell for the umpteenth time "the story about the time when I fell into the lake" will ever preface a tale with the disclaimer "Stop me if you've heard this one before." Nor will anyone who has been corrected by a child in the retelling of a tale ("No, no, it was the *first* little pig who built his house of straw, not the *second*") try to "improve" an old favorite with new variations.

It is the *oral* nature of the text that makes possible the theme of the story within the story. In an oral tradition, the telling of a story is an event performed by a living person, rather than a physical object that remains stagnant. This makes it possible to regard storytelling as an *act* rather than as a *thing.* When this happens, the text—that is, the action of performing the text—can reproduce itself as an event that is part of its own plot. Odysseus both acts out his own story inside the narrative frame of the *Odyssey* and then tells it, outside the frame, in the assumed persona of a bard; but more than that, he asks another bard—a real, card-carrying bard—to tell him another part of his own, Odysseus' own, story.[17] And finally, on the outside of *that* frame, Homer was telling Odysseus' story to Greeks who already knew that story.

It is not unusual for a hero to tell his own story, or for an author to get caught up in his own story. People in the audience often get caught up in stories about other people within their own culture. In Woody Allen's short story "The Kugelmass Episode," a Jewish businessmen in New York goes into *Madame Bovary* and has an affair with Emma, whom he then takes out of the novel and into the Plaza Hotel for a disastrous weekend.[18] These events are then reflected back into the novel, prompting a perplexed Stanford professor to remark, "Well, I guess the mark of a classic is that you can reread it a thousand times and always find something new."[19] We can find many examples of this phenomenon in our contemporary literature, particularly in the theater.[20]

Max Beerbohm wrote a short story about a vain poet named Enoch Soames whom no one ever heard of or read or noticed. One day in 1897, so the story goes, Soames told Beerbohm that he longed to be projected a hundred years into the future so that he could go to the reading room (of the British Museum) just for one afternoon: "I'd sell myself body and soul to the Devil, for that! Think of the pages and pages in the catalogue: 'Soames, Enoch' endlessly—endless editions, commentaries, prolegomena, biographies—." At this point the Devil, who happened to be sitting at the next table, took him up on his offer. Soames disappeared and returned that evening to tell his tale. He had indeed been transported to 1997. There he had looked in a book on late nineteenth-century literature, published in 1992, and had found only this: "A riter ov th time, naimed Max Beerbohm, . . . rote a stauri in wich e pautraid an immajnari karrakter kault 'Enoch Soames'—a thurd-rait poit hoo beleevz imself a grate jeneus an maix a bargin with th Devvl in auder ter no wot posterriti thinx ov im! It iz a sumwot labud sattire but not without vallu, . . " Beerbohm protested: " 'Immajnari'—but here Soames was, no more imaginary, alas! than I. And 'labud'—what on earth was that? . . . And I don't write stories: I'm an essayist." Soames magically vanished; his last words were "Try to make them know that I did exist." But no one but Beerbohm noticed that he had gone, or missed him.[21]

Indian epics long ago developed this line with mind-boggling complexity. The sage Vyasa who narrates the entire *Mahabharata* also acts in it, fathering several of the central characters and appearing *ex machina* in his Brahmin persona to perform important and usually disastrous religious ceremonies.[22] He is thus not only the author of the epic *Mahabharata* but the author of the heroes of the epic; he creates stories in order to "create" people, who are born both through his invention and through his intervention. But the *Mahabharata* is also introduced by a series of stories explaining simultaneously how the events in the *Mahabharata* came to happen and how the *story* of those events came to be *told*. These stories are nested like Chinese boxes or

Russian dolls—or Indian stories. The lineage, the unbroken line of descent (*param-para*), of king Parikshit is not merely the line of his male ancestors; it is also, and more importantly, the lineage of the story, told first by an eyewitness, who told it to someone else, until it reached the present and final narrator. What *survives* (in the very name *Parikshit*, which is explicitly glossed in the epic as meaning "survivor") is the story, for most of the heroes die in the final holocaust, and the Pandavas die on their pilgrimage to the Himalayas.

Indeed, it is significant that the *Mahabharata* is, like the *Ramayana*, narrated in the course of a famous sacrifice, but with a difference. Where the *Ramayana* is told during an auspicious horse-sacrifice, the *Mahabharata* is told during an inauspicious snake-sacrifice. Now, the never completed snake-sacrifice is a surreal variant of the human sacrifice that is enacted in the great battle at the core of the epic;[23] and that sacrifice is, in its turn, haunted by the story of the archetype of all incomplete sacrifices—the story of Shiva's destruction of Daksha's sacrifice. Since the Daksha myth is, as we have seen, already a meta-metamyth, the reworking of it in the *Mahabharata* becomes a myth about a ritual about a myth about a ritual—another metamyth squared, like Aristophanes' *The Frogs*.

In the other great epic, the *Ramayana*, the reflexivity is so blatant that it sometimes becomes shocking or even comical.[24] In the introductory frame of the *Ramayana*, the author, Valmiki, meditates and sees the whole story, including events that have not yet happened.[25] After conceiving the entire work, he seeks someone to recite it, just as Vyasa sought Ganesha to write down the *Mahabharata*. The two sons of Rama, Kusha and Lava (whose names are the two halves of the noun *kushilava*, designating a wandering bard), are growing up in Valmiki's hermitage, because (as will only be told much later in the epic) Rama had banished their mother, Sita, when she was pregnant with them, and she had taken refuge with Valmiki. Valmiki teaches the entire epic to them, and they travel about singing it. Eventually they come to the court of Rama, who does not recognize them. As they sing, Rama "loses himself completely in a longing to experience his own story."[26] They tell him the entire *Ramayana*—all, that is, that has happened up to that point. After many days, Rama recognizes them and decides to send for Sita. She appears but vanishes forever into the earth, an episode which Valmiki concludes with a phrase beginning "When the princess from Videha had entered the subterranean world. . ." As Rama grieves, the god Brahma appears to him and urges him to listen to the *rest* of the story. Then his two sons sing the end of the *Ramayana*, including the death of Rama. They resume their poem with the phrase, "When the princess from Videha had entered the subterranean world. . ."

David Shulman describes what happens in the text at this moment:

> The story is over. But the shocking and moving fact is that we experience these final chapters as Rāma does—not in the backward movement of the story, but rather with past become present or future (and future presented as past). There is no visible seam separating

the text's statement that Kuśa and Lava sang the end of the poem from the actual content of this ending—the description of Rāma's depression, the golden image of Sītā, and so on. The frame has melted away, our sense of time is confused, past conflates with future—as it does already at the very beginning of the epic, in Vālmīki's proleptic vision of past and future combined—and we find ourselves once again listening with Rāma to the story of his own life, but at this point to that part of it that is still to unfold. We might ask ourselves if the 'actual' narrator, Vālmīki, is continuing his narration through the mouths of his pupils, or on his own, as it were—but does it matter?[27]

In a later Sanskrit retelling of the *Ramayana*, when Rama tells Sita not to come with him into exile in the forest, she replies in exasperation, "Many *Ramayanas* have been told many times by many Brahmins. Tell me. Is there a single one of them in which Sita does not go to the forest with Rama?"[28]

The merging of the actor inside the story into the actor who hears the story is even more characteristic of another Sanskrit version of the *Ramayana*, the *Yogavasishtha-Maharamayana*.[29] One story in this massive text tells of three demons who were created in the imagination of a great demonic magician named Shambara. Once they began to think that they were real, and not merely part of his story about them, they *became* real. Being real, they eventually died and were reborn many times as many things—a king, a sage, a deer in China, and finally as a mosquito, a mynah bird, and a lizard. But one day, the *Yogavasishtha* says, each of them will hear someone read the passage from the *Yogavasishtha* telling the story of their many former lives, beginning with their birth from the mind of Shambara; and then they will become free at last from the cycle of rebirth.[30]

An interesting twist on this theme may be seen in a story about a goddess who demands to hear a story told precisely because it is *not* her own story; because she was deprived of her chance to participate in the event, she must be satisfied with the story, just as God in the Jewish story must be satisfied with the *telling* of a myth about a ritual that can no longer be performed. This is a South Indian legend that gives a reason for the goddess' absence at the original death of Ravana:

> She herself was away killing another demon (Mahiṣāsura [the buffalo demon]). She then appeals to Śiva who grants her the boon . . . [of] a vision of Rāvaṇa's death, and not just once but repeatedly: she would be reborn again, this time as goddess Bhāgavatī and he as [the poet] Kampan, whose epic of Rāma would be enacted for her every year in her temples. . . . [These legends] explain that Kampan was born, his epic composed and then transformed into the shadow puppet play to fulfill a boon given to the goddess . . . by Śiva in order that she be pleased by the sight of Rāvaṇa's death. And this is precisely how Kampan's story of Rāma is performed in Kerala today—as a form

of worship to Bhagavatı who watches the spectacle from inside her temple.[31]

This story is told by a group of shadow puppeteers in Kerala, in a Malayalam commentary on the Tamil version of the *Ramayana* composed by the poet Kampan. And every year, for a whole week, or twenty-one days or sixty days, they put on a private performance, with no human audience, just for the goddess Bhagavati.

Stories such as these are metamyths that teach us how other cultures interpret the universal experience of storytelling—and that shed light on our attitude to our own tradition of storytelling. Those who experience nonritualized myths about other people within their own culture may avoid the double violence characteristic of the myths of conversion to another culture's rituals. (This is the first of the four options that we rehearsed at the beginning of this chapter). Shakespeare's Richard II takes up as his own myth the myth of Christ's passion—which is, as we have seen, already a metamyth about another myth and ritual. As David Grene has put it, Richard acts out a play that he constantly rewrites and plays as an alternative, personal reality competing with the reality based on historical facts.[32] But Richard II is not merely acting out a play; he is playing a myth—or, rather, playing two myths. Richard is making his own life into a myth by selecting classical fragments that correspond to the actual events of his life and then constructing a dramatic reality out of them. Yet he also perceives, in a less specific way, an entire myth to which his inner tragedy corresponds. In a broader sense, all of us, all the time, view our lives in terms of the cultural paradigms that we have inherited; what is special here is the fact that Richard realizes that he is doing it, that he explicitly identifies the myth on which he is modeling his life. It is the conscious, explicit identification of the myth of our life as a reworking of an older myth that allows us to view that life as a metamyth, that allows us to live our myth as sages rather than hunters.

Richard envisions himself as acting out the passion of Christ. This vision not only transforms the way in which he perceives his life but actually changes the course of that life, as he *chooses* the myth for his own life again and again. He does not merely *find* the myth he lives, he also *makes* it. By comparing himself to Christ betrayed by Judas, "Richard is finding his supporting script. He is finding the fragments of the myth, the outline to carry his purified emotion through the scene he is about to act—and create. He is Christ again in the holiness which is violated—but he is particularly Christ in the infidelity around him."[33]

René Girard sees Shakespeare's Richard II as the participant not only in a myth but in a ritual:

> The dethronement scene in *Richard II* can be seen as a sort of coronation performed in reverse. Walter Pater described it as an inverted rite,[34] but all rites demand that moment of inversion. The king acts as his own sacrificer, transforming himself by quasi-religious

means into a double of all his enemies and their surrogate victims as well. He is himself a traitor, in no way different from those who do him violence.[35]

Richard II was certainly not the only Christian who reenacted the myth of Christ. In a general way, of course, the paradigm of Christ's life and the concept of the *imitatio Christi* kept the myth present inside not only every saint and martyr, every mystic who received the stigmata, but every priest who reenacted the Eucharist. But even in a more specific way, the narrative *detail* of the life of Christ set a stage on which other Christians could walk. In Nikos Kazantzakis's novel *The Greek Passion,* Greek villagers who stage the Passion at Easter find themselves acting it out in real life; and they find that in real life the myth is rather different.[36] In Shusako Endo's novel *Silence* (significantly, a novel by a Japanese Catholic about a Portugese Catholic who came to Japan to convert the Japanese), the priest who thinks that he is reenacting the life of Christ betrayed by Judas discovers, at the end, the shocking fact that he himself is playing the role not of Christ but of Judas; it is he, not his enemy, who betrays Christ. Moreover, in Endo's novel, the priest who sees himself as Christ (and then as Judas) must *not* perish in torment. The priest must survive, must resist the urge to die, in order to save his people, the other disciples.

The Recognition of Myth in Life

The Greek Passion and *Silence* are stories about what happens to people who tell or live stories. Yet we who read those stories may also be absorbed into them, because our own lives do have a mythical dimension. I have argued up to this point that it is the otherness, the foreignness of certain myths that make them seem more "real" to us than our own myths. But there is also another force at work in myths to convince us of their reality, and this force seems at first glance to be at direct variance with the power of the exotic. This second force is what Eliade called the banality of myth, the persuasiveness of the banal detail, the familiar logic, that is a part of many myths.

Attempts to establish the reality of myth through the nagging little facts of "common sense" are legion in world mythology.[37] Freud has showed us how we incorporate into our dreams the seemingly meaningless details of daily life, and upon them, whenever they will bear the weight, we hang our fantasies. The details of the dream are the manifest content, which corresponds to what Jung called the manifestational aspect of a myth; the fantasies are the latent content—or, in a myth, the archetypal aspect. Lévi-Strauss has showed us how we incorporate into our myths the seemingly meaningless scraps of cultural *bricolage* and hang our paradoxes upon them. And Eliade has demonstrated that the banality of myth, like the banality of evil that Hannah Arendt taught us to acknowledge, is an intrinsic part of its power. Finally, life shows us that

when we rush into the myth of the buffalo sacrifice, we are left hauling grass
for the male buffaloes we have saved.

The common sense of myth works not against the exotic but in harness
with it to persuade us. Clifford Geertz has described how religious symbols
become realistic and persuasive through their use of factual details.[38] For
even in the most fantastic scenes, everyday human considerations and detailed
human objects anchor the grandiose in the mundane. These bathetic plunges
from the sublime to the ridiculous (or from the sacred to the profane) allow us
to ground our highest cravings in the most abject shortcomings of our human
nature. They also allow us to imagine ourselves as the heroes and heroines in
other peoples' stories, to see the events of our lives in their myths.

There are many anecdotes about scholars who became drawn into the
stories that they studied. That scholars become seduced by their own myths
has been argued by René Girard in the case of James George Frazer:

> Anyone who tries to subvert the sacrificial principle by turning it to
> derision invariably becomes its unwitting accomplice. Frazer is no
> exception. His work contributes to the concealment of the violent
> impulse that lurks within the rite of sacrifice. . . . Frazer, along with
> his rationalist colleagues and disciples, was perpetually engaged in a
> ritualistic expulsion and consummation of religion itself, which he
> used as a sort of scapegoat for all human thought. Frazer, like many
> another modern thinker, washed his hands of all the sordid acts
> perpetrated by religion and pronounced himself free of all taint of
> superstition. He was evidently unaware that this act of hand-washing
> has long been recognized as a purely intellectual, non-polluting
> equivalent of some of the most ancient customs of mankind. His
> writing amounts to a fanatical and superstitious dismissal of all the
> fanaticism and superstition he had spent the better part of a lifetime
> studying.[39]

Thus Girard's Frazer, like Pentheus, is drawn into the myth that he denies; he
is a piscophobe who drowns in his own data.

Some scholars have been absorbed more literally into their myths, and
others have been more consciously aware of their participation in the myths
they have studied. Of the first type, we may cite the case of Dennis Puleston,
an archaeologist who subscribed to the theory that the Maya had sacrificed
people by placing them on top of the castillo during thunderstorms, so
that they were struck by lightning. One day when he was on top of the
castillo he was struck by lightning and killed.[40] The Indian politician C. R.
Rajagopalachari was conscious of the role of his myths in his life: he produced
a scholarly translation of the *Ramayana* and at the same time modeled his own
autobiography, and indeed his own life, on that mythic drama, inspired in part
by the performances of the Ramlila to which he had long been exposed.[41]
Murray Emeneau, a great linguist, once recorded and published the songs of
a tribe in India called the Toda. Years later, he revisited the tribe to collect

new songs from them. And one of the songs that they sang for him was a song about a white man who had come to them and recorded their songs. He had become part of his own story.[42]

Stories such as this last anecdote also reveal another important consequence of our interaction with the myths of other cultures. By studying these myths, we do not merely affect ourselves; we affect *them*. Western scholarly attention to certain Hindu and Buddhist texts gave those texts a higher status in India itself. The royal road of myths is always a two-way street. This too, is reason to make all the greater effort to approach the myths with sympathetic understanding, in order to minimize the damage that we do by dragging them out of their own bright houses to look at them in our own dim streets—often the only place where we can hope to find the keys to them at all.

We have seen how people listen to myths about themselves told within their own culture, through the function of communion; and how people often recognize themselves, by chance, in the myths told by people from other cultures. But there is another important place where we can find our mythical meanings, a place so obvious, so literally close to home, that we overlook it, so that, paradoxically, it can once again surprise us: we can find the mythical meanings of our lives in our lives.

Now that many of us no longer find our myths in our own communal religious settings (or rituals), our own lives may be the main arena in which the mythic shock of recognition takes place. When we stumble upon the familiar pattern of a myth in our own familiar life, or the familiar pattern of our life within the familiarity of a story that we know well, we are shocked by what is most familiar. This is because the familiar detail seems to be in the wrong place, the myth in a life, or the life in a myth, and matter out of place is dirt.[43] This is the dirt, in the neglected corner of his own house, that the Rabbi from Cracow was willing to dig into for treasure but the Captain in Prague regarded as laughably banal. If we lack the imagination to be shocked by our own myths, we may be forced to learn our myths the hard way, by living through them, as hunters, instead of imagining them, as sages.[44] And if we have no rituals, we may be able to sustain new myths not with new rituals (which are, as we have seen, dangerous to meddle with) but with the new recognition of structures within our own lives. Dispossessed of our own myths and rituals, we have no scraps left with which to build the *bricolage* of our myths but the events of our own lives.

It has often been asserted that our lives are models *for* myths (to borrow yet another formulation from Clifford Geertz); what is less obvious but equally true is that our lives are often models *of* myths. The myth supplies an ideal that may be fantastic, impossible to live out literally, but that is no less useful in the construction of our lives. It is a target (positive or negative) that we can never reach, like Zeno's tortoise, but that establishes the full range of the scale in which we actually live.

Myths of this sort have a complex interrelationship with reality that could be described with such high-flying terms as cybernetic, symbiotic, or synergistic, but that is better conveyed by the simple image of the chicken-

and-egg (seed-and-tree, in the Indian metaphor).[45] Myths are sometimes told to people specifically in order to make them change their lives. When the sage Vyasa is asked to impregnate the wives of a dead king at the request of the king's brother, the mother of the dead king (who also happens to be Vyasa's mother) at first resists this suggestion. But then she is told the myth of another ancient queen who had sent her maid in her place to the bed of a similarly appointed old sage, and by hearing this story the queen is persuaded to submit to the plan.[46]

Myths told to children influence the development of their imaginations and hence constrain some of their practical decisions. Thus, anthropologists and psychologists speak of shared "nuclear fantasies" transmitted in India from mother to child and later modified by individual experience. For example, it is suggested that the shared fantasy of the demonic goddess inhibits the sexual activity of young married men in India. In this view, the myth is not a reflection of behavior but a cause of it.[47]

But then children grow up with certain cultural preoccupations that lead them to tell certain kinds of myths to their children; and the myth of the decapitating goddess is said to be based on the child's overabrupt weaning. In this view, the actual experience precedes and determines the myth. Clearly, there is some truth, and some falsehood, in both views. To the extent that myth arises out of reality and has an effect on reality, there can be no particular starting point or end point; it is a cycle. Myth and reality are caught up in a complex folie à deux.

At certain crucial moments, we seem to follow two maps at once, as if two celluloid overlays were placed upon the same page. There are times when we confront an actual experience and respond to it as we would respond to the confrontation of a myth. We recognize the myth in moments of real life because we recognize certain archetypal elements common to myth and life; and, as the banality of myth demonstrates, this happens to everyone, even to the "plain man." Jung remarked that "myth is not fiction: it consists of facts that are continually repeated and can be observed over and over again. It is something that happens to man, and men have mythical fates just as much as the Greek heroes do."[48] The combination of stark mythical themes and self-conscious banality in *Our Town* is a part of Thornton Wilder's attempt to show us the mythical qualities of our own lives.

These details of myth and life are banal in the sense that they are the sorts of things that do in fact happen to everyone. The mythical events in our lives include, but are not limited to, those formalized in the rituals called rites of passage: the experience of birth (ours or our childrens'), the sudden transition from childhood to adulthood, falling in love, marriage, death—our experience of the deaths of others and our contemplation of our own deaths. We encounter these primal echoes also in classical occasions of joy—plunging into the ocean, galloping on a young horse, climbing mountains, watching geese fly south, returning home after a long journey, listening to sublime music, watching a summer thunderstorm in the middle of the night. And the same feeling overcomes us in moments of modern tragedy—the phone call in the middle of the night, news of failure or desertion, an accident, the diagnosis of cancer, a prison sentence. The private mythic moment is crowded by ghosts whom we cannot identify consciously, but whose multiplicity we are aware of. We know that what is happening to us has happened to them, because we have heard stories about them, and so they are present with us when those things happen again to us. If there is some piece of sad news that our children have to hear in real life, news of a death or a loss, we try to let them hear it from someone we know and trust—an aunt who was with us when we first learned about death ourselves, or a teacher or a wise friend. This is what great myths are—the stories that people all over the world have come to trust with their darkest and most deeply troubling insights.

These passionate encounters with life are so classical that they often border on the trite, like something out of a cheap novel or a Hollywood confection; they may embarrass us to the point where we hesitate to acknowledge their genuine power over us. Their juxtaposition with the everyday quality of the rest of our lives makes them seem overblown, and may render bathetic both those lives and the banal details of the myth that forge the essential bond with reality. Some people, the kind we often refer to as self-dramatizing, regard every moment in an apparently ordinary life as mythical. Such a person was delightfully satirized by Edmund Wilson, in one of a number of fictional (or fictionalized) seduction scenes:

> "Who are you?" I asked. "Where do you come from?" "I'm a myth," she replied, with her coquetry. "But what part of the world do you come from? Or are you a universal myth?" "I was born in Minnesota"—I could see it was a reluctant confession—"but I've lived in the East since I was fourteen." "Have you got any Irish blood?" "My father was born in Ireland—in County Galway. My mother's people came from Sweden." "Then you *are* a universal myth: you're Brunhilde and Iseult in one."[49]

But some people really do seem to have mythical lives, just as some paranoids really are surrounded by enemies. Mythic events seem to happen more often to people who believe in the mythic dimension, who seek it out and allow it to break in on them. Or perhaps people who live through many such events become converted, even against their own common sense, to a belief in the reality of myth.

Charles Long has characterized "creative mythology" (*contra* Joseph Campbell) as a genre that results when "the individual has had an experience of his own—of order, horror, beauty, or even exhilaration—which he seeks to communicate through signs."[50] The signs that one uses are derived from the myths that one already knows, and they may not necessarily belong to one's own culture. When J. Robert Oppenheimer witnessed the explosion of the first atomic bomb, he realized that he was part of the myth of doomsday, but not his own Jewish doomsday.[51] Oppenheimer, who liked to think that he knew some Sanskrit, said that as he watched the bomb go off he recalled the verse in the *Bhagavad Gita* when Krishna reveals himself as the supreme lord, blazing like a thousand suns. Later, however, when he saw the sinister clouds gathering in the distance, he recalled another verse, in which Krishna reveals that he is death, the devourer of men.[52] Perhaps Oppenheimer's inability to face directly his own shock and guilt, the full realization and acknowledgment of what he had helped to create, led him to distance the experience by viewing it in terms of someone else's myth of doomsday. The other side of the coin of this phenomenon was demonstrated by those contemporary American critics who faulted Peter Brook's recreation of the *Mahabharata* for projecting into the Indian text references to our own impending nuclear holocaust.[53] In fact, every word of the Peter Brook script was taken from the Sanskrit text, which tells of two great warring factions each of which possesses terrible weapons capable of destroying the world. It was the critics who projected our situation onto the Indian story, unconsciously demonstrating precisely the power that great myths have: to depict a great human story in which we are compelled to see ourselves, even across the barriers of cultures. Many of the dark truths of hate, as well as the sunnier truths of love, come to us from other peoples' myths.

As Girish Karnad remarked about the critics' reaction to the Peter Brook production, "The *Mahabharata* is always about the most recent war." After Partition in 1947, when Muslims and Hindus were murdering one another, a famous Indian playwright felt that he could not write about an experience so horribly real, and so he wrote a play about the *Mahabharata;* and everyone in India knew what his play was really about. As a shared cultural metaphor, the great epic was able to distance what could not be said directly, just as myth (in Lévi-Strauss's formulation) must be fragmented to transmit a series of messages that cannot be accepted whole, and just as God (in the *Bhagavad Gita*) must mute the epiphany that cannot be tolerated directly. The myth, like the god, must mask its meanings.

Our experiences of the interface between our myths and our lives momentarily lift the artificial barrier that we have imposed between myth and reality, so that we gaze back suddenly upon the myth that we had unknowingly entered. All at once, in retrospect, we realize that by comparison, all that has gone before has not been real. The film *The Wizard of Oz* goes along for about a quarter of an hour until Dorothy arrives in the land of Oz, opens the door, and looks out into a world in glorious technicolor, and only then do we realize that we have been accepting the conventions of filming in black and white, that we had not *missed* the colors. This is how mythic moments in life retroactively transfigure our frame of reference.

In another film about a myth that takes over a life, a young dancer is made famous by a ballet created for her from a fairy tale, the story of the Red Shoes: a young girl who puts on magic red shoes is bewitched by them and is forced to dance herself to death. The dancer in the movie, unable to choose between her life (epitomized by the man she loves) and her art, puts on the red shoes for a final performance and is carried away by them over a balcony to her death under a train. The shoes (a motif that also appears in the form of the magic ruby slippers in *The Wizard of Oz*) here represent not only her own art but the art of the myth itself, that encompasses her life.

Eliade tells how, when one "lives" the myth, "one is seized by the sacred, exalting power of events."[54] He is speaking of "archaic man" and of particular ritual events, but it is true for us as well, and for myths without rituals. Most deep passions and the web of circumstances in which they appear make immediate contact with what underlies the great myths. These evocative passions often sweep along in their flood the solid, banal details that are the flotsam and jetsam of human nature and human culture—particular colors, particular animals, particular geographical places. Seemingly neutral, these things are highly charged with evocative detail to which we are helplessly drawn by a kind of centripetal force.

Even when we feel that we are finding a myth with its details right in our lives, we are also making the myth by framing it with nonarchetypal details in order to see it. But because we know how the myth goes, we then ignore those details in selecting the mythic elements of the event as the ones that we regard and retell as real. In trying to make sense of our own lives, after all, we tell ourselves stories about what has happened to us, extracting significant patterns that we have been taught to recognize or that we invent for ourselves. So too, if we are familiar with myths, when we try to make sense of our lives we select elements that can be naturally structured in a pattern that is mythic, a pattern of repetitions and irony and paradox, as we focus on the events and details and patterns that are such stuff as myths are made on. Because of, or in spite of, our conscious attempts to live a myth, or to live against a myth, mythical patterns lay hold on us when our passions reach the spot at which the myth originally asserted itself. And if we are in danger of missing or resisting our own myths when we find them in our actual lives, we may recognize them and accept them better if we have already met them in other peoples' myths.

The Roundhouse of Myths

"Archaic man"—the man who lives his myths—is an endangered but not yet extinct species. Eliade writes, "At a certain moment in history—especially in Greece and India but also in Egypt—an elite begins to lose interest in this divine history and arrives (as in Greece) at the point of no longer believing in the *myths* while claiming still to believe in the *Gods*."[55] There are still people for whom this situation prevails even now, the remythologized, people searching for their second naiveté. They may have retained or returned to a sense of the gods, or, more often, they may *want* to return to a sense of the gods, but they are not willing to return to the fundamental myths of the tradition that they have rejected. These are people for whom foreign myths may supply an essential element, giving them new stories to tell about their own gods. For the radical humanists, however, the demythologized, the problem is quite the reverse: they no longer have the gods, but they may well sense some meaning of the myths. Yet, they, too, may find foreign myths (whose gods need not be taken personally, or ritually) "useful," as Herodotus put it.

The Hindus say that the gods lived in another age, the Golden Age; in the present fallen age, the Kali Yuga, the Dark Age, all we have left is the stories of the gods. It is like a certain rather eery medical phenomenon: after a hand has been cut off, the amputee still feels sensation in the fingers that are no longer there.[56] So too, when the gods are cut off, we still *feel* the amputated divine limb in our myths and in our lives—whenever we come to the place where the gods would be if we still believed in them.

Plato argued that the old myths were dead (or should be dead); if they were not already dead when he said it, his own statement killed them for the Greeks. Nietzsche argued that the old god was dead; and if God was not in fact already dead when Nietzsche said it, Nietzsche's own words killed him for many of us:[57]

> The Meaning of Our Cheerfulness. The greatest recent event—that "God is dead," that the belief in the Christian god has become unbelievable—is already beginning to cast its first shadows over Europe. For the few at least, whose eyes—the *suspicion* in whose eyes is strong and subtle enough for this spectacle, some sun seems to have set and some ancient and profound trust has been turned into doubt; to them our old world must appear daily more like evening, more mistrustful, stranger, "older." . . . Indeed, we philosophers and "free spirits" feel, when we hear the news that "the old god is dead," as if a new dawn shone on us; our heart overflows with gratitude, amazement, premonitions, expectation. At long last the horizon appears free to us again, even if it should not be bright; at long last our ships may venture out again, venture out to face any danger; all the daring of the lover of knowledge is permitted again; the sea, *our* sea, lies open again; perhaps there has never yet been such an "open sea."[58]

For the demythologized, Nietzsche was right and Plato was wrong: when the gods died, they left behind an empty myth, a play in search of characters, a *Hamlet* without Hamlet. The idea of an empty space regarded as the abandoned container of an otiose god takes various forms in various cultures, such as the empty chair and open door left for Elijah during a Passover Seder. Wittgenstein used, for different but related purposes, the metaphor of a game of tennis played without a ball.[59] In the final ballet in the film *The Red Shoes,* which is given without anyone dancing the central part once played by the now dead dancer, a spotlight moves around the stage where she would have been, and the other dancers dance with that light and, finally, with the empty shoes. This image of the shoes standing for the dead or absent person also appears in ancient Indian religions: Rama's brother, Bharata, kept Rama's sandals on the throne during his exile to symbolize the fact that Rama still reigned, and early Buddhist art, unwilling to depict the Buddha anthropomorphically, often represented him by a pair of sandals.

Nietzsche inverts the old Platonic image of the shadows in the cave and develops this inverted imagery in another passage in which he treats the Buddha as he treated the Christian God:

> New battles: After the Buddha died, his shadow was still visible in a cave for hundreds of years—an enormous, gruesome shadow. God is dead; but such is the way of mankind that for thousands of years there will probably still be caves in which his shadow is visible. And we—we will have to overcome even his shadow, too![60]

The shadow of the Buddha in the cave is a theme taken (by what route?) from a text of Chinese Buddhism, in which the Buddha reforms a dragon in a cave and then, when the dragon asks him to remain forever in that cave, replies: "When I am about to die, I will leave you my shadow." This shadow remained in the Cavern of the Shadow:

> In old days there was a shadow of Buddha to be seen here, bright as the true form, with all its characteristic marks. In later days men have not seen it so much. What does appear is only a feeble likeness. But whoever prays with fervent faith, he is mysteriously endowed, and he sees it clearly before him, though not for long.[61]

Nietzsche twists the image around to the exact opposite direction: the divine shadow appears, unwanted, to plague the man who resists the worship of the god (as Dionysus plagued the recalcitrant Pentheus).

Plato's cave contained unreal shadows, but they were at least the shadows of true ideal forms outside the cave. The image of the Buddha is less real, like the afterimage burned on the spiritual retina by a divine star that burned out lightyears ago and like the shadows of the puppets of the Indonesian puppeteer gods; for it is the twice-removed image of a now lost belief in a god who in fact never existed at all.[62] In this, Nietzsche's cave is perhaps closer to E. M. Forster's cave, in which archetypal forms so thoroughly intermingled into one that they became meaningless. Let us now return to take a final look at that cave of archetypes.

It might be argued that such a cave is essential to the enterprise of comparing myths from different cultures. We cannot get out of the archetypal cave until we have gone into it; we must pass through it, as in a ritual of rebirth, entering it through the doorway of our own myths to come out on the other side, the world of other people's myths. We cannot communicate from one manifestation to another, but we may move back through a manifestation to the archetype, and out again into another manifestation. We share the structures of myths on one level, and on another we share the content, the fragments, the mythemes, the *bricolage* of life, with which the structures are built. The fact that other peoples' myths are simultaneously strange and familiar causes a constant shifting of the tension between centrifugal and centripetal approaches.

We can best understand one myth by translating it into another myth.[63] One of the reasons why this is so is that myths themselves are, as Claude Lévi-Strauss has pointed out, translations:

> Mythic thought operates in a unique way, using several codes. Each code brings out latent properties in a given realm of experience, allowing a comparison with other realms—in short, a *translation* from realm to realm. Imagine a text, difficult to understand in one language, translated into several languages; the combined meaning of all the different versions may prove richer and more profound than the partial, mutilated meaning drawn from each individual version.[64]

As myths are by nature designed to translate between sets of perceptions within a culture, they can easily be adapted (though Claude Lévi-Strauss certainly does not argue for this) to perform a similar function between cultures. Indeed, I would go even further and argue that we can best understand both our own myths and those of other people by translating them into other myths.

Many attempts to interpret a myth beyond the context of its own culture find their confidence of success in the assumption of a universal, archetypal level of meaning beneath the particular, manifestational meaning. The Jungian assumption that "we all have the same kind of dragons in our psyche" leads to the hope that "we can communicate, that alienation isn't the final human condition, since there is a vast common ground on which we can meet, not only rationally, but aesthetically, intuitively, emotionally."[65] Claude Lévi-Strauss has said that his ambition is "to discover the conditions in which systems of truths become mutually convertible and therefore simultaneously acceptable to several different subjects."[66] My rather more modest ambition would be to discover the conditions in which systems of meaning become not mutually convertible but at least simultaneously acceptable—or, at the very least, sympathetically comprehensible—to several different subjects.

For to understand myths we must draw them back into that internal hub where our own personal reality, our own nature, intersects with the myths preserved by tradition, by culture. This provides, in passing, a way of translating myths, but it also provides a means of addressing the far more serious problem of translating reality, of establishing a vocabulary with which to understand what goes on in the heads of other people—or fish. Myth in this sense is both solitary and communal: solitary, in that the experiences that myths tell about are among the most private and highly personal; communal, in that they are experienced by all of us. Myths provide a conceptual system through which we may understand and thereby construct a universal reality.

Myths may function as the bridges between foreign cultures. A Christian might find the myth of Krishna more easily understandable than other aspects of Indian life or religion, because of its superficial resemblance to the myth of Jesus. It was from a bridge, it may be recalled, that the Chinese philosophers viewed the fishes, and from across a bridge that the Rabbi from Cracow spoke to the Christian guard. This network of bridges may be likened to a roundhouse, the place where all the tracks of a railway meet so that the trains may pass from any one track to any other track. The mythical roundhouse is the place where we can move from the track of one person's reality to another's, passing through the myth that expresses them all. This roundhouse is a kind of cave where all the myths in the world come together, the common ground; this is the infinity where (to add another corollary to Euclid's theorem) all parallel variants meet. For Jungians the roundhouse is the collective unconscious; for structuralists it is the cognitive grid of dialectic oppositions; for Marxists it is the class struggle; for most anthropologists it is culture, or kinship; for Platonists it is the world of ideal forms outside the cave; for theologians it is God.

For mythologists, the roundhouse of myths is a place that we must reach in order to get off our track and onto someone else's track, but it is not a place to settle down into. One of the dangers of committing oneself to the myths of others, having abandoned one's own myths, is that one may spin around the roundhouse but never quite manage to make it home. Like New York, the roundhouse is a place to visit, not a place to live in. It is not a real place to stand at all; it has a status somewhat akin to Esperanto, the pseudolanguage that people once hoped would undo the damage done by the Tower of Babel, or akin to that mythical proto-Indo-European language east of the asterisk. But nobody *speaks* Esperanto natively, and no one has ever heard a proto-Indo-European word.[67] The roundhouse is the home of the invisible man that we call the archetype, the disembodied ghost of the living myth. The myth is a real thing, that one can hear or read, a thing that leaves tracks on the human mind; these are the tracks that run into the roundhouse. But the roundhouse is not real. It is a thing that *we construct* in order to get to the tracks of the myths.

The people who live in the nonexistent roundhouse that they themselves construct are the exponents of a kind of absolutism or essentialism, who believe that all the myths of the world are not only somehow related (which is a belief that I share) but somehow the same myth (a belief against which I have argued in this book). The belief in the interconnection between myths is one that I find acceptable only in a rather sharply modified version: there is indeed a common thread running through the great myths of the world, and it does arise out of the common experience of humankind. But the meaning of that experience, and therefore the meaning of the myth, changes constantly across the barriers of time and space. In myth, as in life, the Buddha's dictum holds true: all is impermanence, *anicca.*

The belief that all myths are one is in itself a postulate made by many (different!) myths. Indian myths tell us of dreams that are dreamed simultaneously by two people who dream of one another and dream all the same details of things that they have never seen in waking life.[68] These myths describe an intense heightening of the basic bond that joins all humans. The Jungians have suggested that "everybody's unconscious perfectly understands everybody else's unconscious" and that telepathic dreams occur because "when persons are bound together emotionally, the tie of love opens one unconscious to another."[69] In this view, the flint of love strikes a spark that jumps from one mind to another. It has been further suggested that the power of this emotional magnet extends across time as well as space, that there is some substantial force that, though not yet manifest, is already pregnant with the future, even as a ghost lingers by the grave of the past. This force is drawn to us across time and space, flowing backward against the current of material time in a way that cannot be measured with instruments or accounted for by our present scientific knowledge. In this view, just as the ghosts of people whom we have loved in the past may haunt our dreams, so too the shadows of people whom we will love in the future may first fall across our lives in our dreams.

The medium through which such transmissions could take place is variously described as a kind of a human substratum linking universal dreams to one another, a kind of dream ether, an all-pervading substance in which we all move like fish through water. In Jungian terms, this is the shared mental matrix of the human race, the collective unconscious; in Indian terms, it is *brahman,* ultimate reality. But dreams of this sort are, to my knowledge, recorded only in myths. That is, we do not have proof that people have such shared dreams; all we have is proof that people like to think that such a thing is possible. What is transmitted across the mental ether is therefore not dreams but myths, composed of individual human experience and art. Myths reflect our desire to believe that people really can dream the same dream, a desire that is a deep hope—a dream, if you will—that we all share. The myths that describe such experiences are shared dreams about shared dreams. The Rabbi from Cracow and the Captain share a dream, that only the Rabbi can interpret.

Through the use of the mythic ether we can find the stories of our lives in the myths of other people. And this can happen in many different ways, and to many different degrees. To the extent that we *find* our myths rather than construct them, the easiest assimilation of a strange myth into our life takes place when we stumble on a myth that expresses the life that we are already living. Though the myth does not tell us what to do in such situations, it does at least enable us to recognize them. In this, myths are quite different from paradigms. The myth of Christ's passion did not tell Richard II what to do, only how to understand what he was doing anyway. This is why, as Lévi-Strauss points out, myth is never an answer to the problems it allows us to state;[70] it merely lets us recognize these problems as mythic and therefore, by definition, impossible to solve. Yet such a myth might still make us experience our life in a different way. We go on doing the same things, but we view them differently, traveling the same road, but with a different map—sometimes better, sometimes worse (for there are, as I have argued, bad myths). In this we are like the sage who discovered that he was dreaming and went on dreaming, but with a new kind of wakefulness. Thus Arjuna in the *Bhagavad Gita* is taught to go on doing what he had always done but with an entirely different meaning, now that Krishna has revealed the truth to him.[71]

A second way of adopting a myth is the assimilation of a myth that does not exactly correspond to the life lived so far. Such a myth might not lead to change any more than the first sort, the "found myth," would. Myths function to maintain the status quo, often by expressing a situation that is the very opposite of the life situation. This mirror held up to reality may reinforce reality in several different ways. It may show us that our reality is the only viable reality by exaggerating and rejecting the alternatives. Thus the mythologies that imagine a time when there was no death resign us to our mortal fate by describing a situation of overcrowding or laziness or wickedness that is, as the myth points out, even worse than our present tragic lot. Or a myth may provide a way of blowing off steam, giving a false sense of freedom in a situation that is in fact strictly confined. The myths of Tantrism in India, with their implication that behind doors in the very next block people are drinking menstrual blood and making love to their mothers, serves as a vicarious release for many non-Tantric Hindus.[72] Similarly, rituals (always harder to pick up than myths) may serve to validate an already extant situation; to maintain such a situation while transforming one's experience of it; or to sustain it by means of the sublimation provided by its temporary inversion during the controlled time and space of the ritual.

But a myth may become a part of the new life about to be lived. Indeed, it may even contribute to the construction of that new segment of life. For some myths tell us that we must do something. Myths may ride piggyback on theology (and theology on myths); whole groups may be converted through a theological argument and be forced to accept the supporting myths as part of the package deal. But an individual may also just pick up a myth, and find himself burdened with its supporting theology. When we contemplate a great myth from another culture, even when we contemplate it through the reducing lenses of scholarship, we may be faced with the challenge that Rilke saw in the statue of Apollo—a foreign mythic image: "Du muss dein Leben ändern"—"You must change your life."[73] Such a myth achieves this effect not through logic or example (positive or negative) but by activating our emotions as it punctures our assumed world. And if such a myth does in fact move us to do something, this action, solitary though it may be, provides a kind of parallel to the action of commitment that we lost when we lost touch with our own ritual community. It remains, still, a myth without a god, a myth without a ritual, a myth without a context—ultimately, therefore, a myth without a religion. By some definitions, it is no longer a myth at all. But it still retains *something* of the power of a myth, and may take new roots in the context of our lives.

We are left, then, sometimes with no myths, sometimes with myths emasculated of their rituals, sometimes with bad myths that trap us within the cybernetic cage of our own myths/rituals and lives, each giving rise to the other. But we may break out from all of these various prisons with the help of other peoples' myths, which, coming from outside our own closed system, may provide an external influence, an anti-inertial force, to move us off our own treadmill, our own track, onto an entirely new path. New myths move us into new worlds where we can begin to think thoughts that not only were impossible to think within our old familiar world of ideas but that we could not even realize we had been unable to think in that world. In this way we are sometimes able to change both our myths and our lives—or at least to give new myths to our children.

The historians have demonstrated that there is no such thing as an even theoretically impartial observer, and the anthropologists have cynically undermined our hopes of getting inside the heads of other cultures, relativistically or otherwise. The linguists and philosophers have, finally, hopelessly defamed the character of language as a possible vehicle for mutual understanding. So we are stripped down to our naked myths, the bare bones of human experience. They may be our last hope for a nonlanguage that can free us from these cognitive snares, a means of flying so low that we can scuttle underneath the devastating radar of the physical and social sciences and skim close to the ground of the human heart.

Notes

Acknowledgments

1. *Daedalus* (Spring 1980): 93-126. See also Wendy Doniger O'Flaherty, "The Case for the History of Religions," *Daedalus* (Spring 1988): 181-186.
2. "Mythe et vie réelle dans l'oeuvre de Mircea Eliade," opening speech, XIIᵉ Congrès International de l'Académie Roumano-Americaine, Université de Paris—Sorbonne, 24 June 1987.
3. "Myths about Myths about Rituals," inaugural lecture for the Mircea Eliade Professorship in the History of Religions, University of Chicago, 14 May 1987.
4. *History of Religions* 20, 1 (August 1980): 81-111.
5. *Criterion* 24, 1 (Winter 1985): 23-25.
6. "The Good and Evil Shepherd," in *Gilgul: Essays on Transformation, Revolution, and Permanence in the History of Religions, dedicated to Zwi Werblowsky,* ed. S. Shaked, D. Shulman, and G. G. Stroumsa (Leiden, 1987), pp. 169-191.
7. The latter published in the University of Chicago *Record,* 20, 1 (10 April 1986): 43-50.
8. "The Role of Myth in the Indian Life Cycle," published in *Aditi: The Living Arts of India* (Washington, D. C., 1985), pp. 185-201; and "Impermanence and Eternity in Indian Art and Literature," to be published by the Smithsonian Institution in *Contemporary Indian Tradition: Voices on Culture, Nature, and the Challenge of Change,* ed. Carla M. Borden (Washington, D.C., 1988).
9. To be published in *The Boundary of the Text: Performing the Epics in South and Southeast Asia,* ed. Joyce Burkhalter-Fluechtiger and Laurie Sears (Ann Arbor, 1988).
10. Where Jim Foard, Ingrid Schafer, Marilyn Waldman, Lee Yearly, Nancy Falk, and Brian K. Smith gave me great help.
11. Published as "The Uses and Abuses of Other Peoples' Classics," in the *Federation Review* 9, 5 (September/October 1986): 33-41.
12. Published as "The Survival of Myth in Science Fiction," in *Mindscapes: The Geographies of Imagined Worlds,* ed. George E. Slusser and Eric Rabkin (Carbondale, Ill., 1988).
13. "The Uses and Misuses of Other Peoples' Myths," published in the *Journal of the American Academy of Religion* 54, 2 (Summer 1986): 219-239.
14. Delivered at the University of Chicago in February 1986, under the auspices of Sam Portaro, and published in *Religion and Intellectual Life* (The Journal of Associates for Religion and Intellectual Life) 4, 1 (Fall, 1986): 60-70.
15. Where I was a Visiting Canterbury Fellow. Jim Wilson, Bob Stoothoff, Colin Brown, Paul Harrison, and Hally Cederman were especially argumentative and challenging.

Introduction

1. The event of the telling of a story is one that the artists who illustrated the great Indian epic texts often chose to illustrate, in preference to (or in addition to) scenes depicting what we would more usually refer to as "actions"—the killing of demons, the epiphanies of gods. See Wendy Doniger O'Flaherty, *Dreams, Illusion, and Other Realities* (Chicago, 1984), chap. 6.
2. Martin Buber, *Tales of the Hasidim. The Early Masters* (New York, 1947), pp. v-vi.
3. In this I am in disagreement with Claude Lévi-Strauss (and others of the intellectualist school of mythology, such as Émile Durkheim and Jonathan Z. Smith), though I follow him in many other regards.
4. I do not want to say any more about method here. In a sense this whole book is an indirect discussion of method, particularly eclecticism, about which I shall say more in chapter 7. I agree with the scholar who said that method is to methodology as ideas are to ideology. I also agree with Peter Berger (in *Invitation to Sociology,* Garden City, 1963, p. 13) that "in science as in love a concentration on technique is quite likely to lead to impotence." And I agree with Samuel Butler (cited by Max Black apropos of theorizing about theorizing, in *Caveats and Critiques,* Ithaca, 1975, p. 30) that "thinking about thinking is like having an itch: the more you scratch, the more you want to scratch." (Cf. Socrates' question in Plato's *Gorgias* 494: Can a man who itches and scratches, and has abundant opportunity to do so, live happily by continually scratching?).

   But I cannot resist one parting salvo. Once, when David Shulman and I sat through a conference on methodology in the history of religions, he had a dream; he dreamed that we were in a restaurant, and the waiter brought the menu, which we perused hungrily; but when we began to order (I ordered fresh oysters and Peking duck and mangoes), the waiter interrupted: "I'm sorry, Madam," he said, "but in this restaurant, you eat the *menu.*"
5. I am limiting myself primarily to strangers as foreigners, people from another culture, though the concept of "otherness" within our own culture, strangers among us ourselves, legal or illegal aliens, is certainly a part of the mythology of otherness. There are many great works about strangers in the Western literary tradition, such as Albert Camus's novel by that title. Though I do not intend to deal here either with that tradition or with the extensive secondary literature on it, it is certainly one of the important ingredients in our own cultural presuppositions about the nature of the strange.
6. It has often been argued, throughout the history of religions, that the very defining characteristic of the Object of religion is "otherness." A discussion of this issue may be found in Charles H. Long's *Significations: Signs, Symbols and Images in the Interpretation of Religion* (Philadelphia, 1986).
7. He actually said something that sounded like "Kimo Sabe," which we took to be the world for "white man" in some mysterious Hollywood Indian dialect. In fact, I have it on good authority that when the actor who played Tonto, Jay Silverheels, discovered that "Tonto" meant "fool" in Spanish, he started calling the Lone Ranger "Kimo Sabe," which means "shit" in Mohawk.

Chapter 1.   Other Scholars' Myths:
The Hunter and the Sage

1. I shall discuss other definitions of myth in chapter 2, but for now let me cite two that are relevant to this particular usage: David Shulman has said that "a myth is an intuition dramatized by a story" (in "Terror of Symbols and Symbols of Terror:

Notes on the myth of Śiva as Sthāṇu," *History of Religions* 26,2 [November 1986]: 105), and A. K. Ramanujan has noted that "a myth is a metaphor that has been made concrete and literal" (private communication, 4 August 1985).

2. O'Flaherty, *Dreams,* chap. 4.

3. Maurice Bloomfield, "On the Art of Entering Another's Body: A Hindu Fiction Motif," *Proceedings of the American Philosophical Society* 41 (1917): 1-43. Cf. also the *Bhagavadajjuka-Prahasanam* of Bodhayana (Prayaga: Devabhas-aprakasanam, 1979). I know of one remarkable occurrence of this theme in contemporary America, and that is the film *All of Me* (based on Ed Davis's novel *Me Two*), starring Steve Martin and Lily Tomlin and directed by Carl Reiner. In this film, the soul of Tomlin's character leaves her body as she dies and enters the body of Martin's character, who still has his own soul as well and thus becomes, internally, an androgyne (the woman occupies and controls the right half of his body), while externally he remains a man. The comic possibilities of this situation (as, for instance, when he attempts to make love to another woman) are brilliantly developed throughout the film; but it is interesting to note that the figure who makes the entire transformation possible in the first place, and continues to make adjustments throughout the whole film, is an Indian guru.

4. *Yogavasishtha-Maha-Ramayana* of Valmiki, ed. W. L. S. Pansikar, 2 vols. (Bombay, 1918) 6.2.136-157.

5. See O'Flaherty, *Dreams,* pp. 231-234, for a discussion of similar myths about doomsday and ontology.

6. I have greatly abbreviated this story, which occupies 21 chapters (not 21 verses) of the Sanskrit text. In some ways, this condensation makes the story more confusing than it is when one reads it at length; in some ways, it oversimplifies it. In particular, I have omitted the fascinating but here irrelevant fact that the sage falls asleep first in order to become the householder and then falls asleep *as the householder;* thus he is actually a creature in a dream within a dream. For the implications of this nesting of dreams, see chapter 5 of O'Flaherty, *Dreams.*

7. Ranjini and Gananath Obeyesekere demonstrated the way in which a similar confusion is built into a Buddhist text about revenge and reincarnation, in a paper presented at the Association of Asian Studies, 24 March 1986.

8. See the story of the hundred Rudras and the wild goose in O'Flaherty, *Dreams,* chapter 5.

9. There is another beautiful ancient Indian metaphor for this pair: "Two birds, friends joined together, clutch the same tree. One of them eats the sweet fruit; the other looks on without eating." *Rig Veda* 1.164.20, translated by Wendy Doniger O'Flaherty in *The Rig Veda* (Harmondsworth, 1981), p. 78.

10. A. K. Ramanujan has argued, in an unpublished paper ("*Samskara* and *Death in Venice*"), that the figures of sages in India are "religious" and in the West "artists"; both are capable of seeing and being other beings.

11. Robert Louis Stevenson, *The Strange Case of Dr. Jekyll and Mr. Hyde* (London, 1886). It is interesting to note the names that Stevenson gives to these two characters: Jekyll is a *Dr.,* a sage; Hyde *hides,* like a hunter, lying in wait for his prey.

12. See O'Flaherty, *Dreams,* introduction and chapter 1. It is significant that although for a long time we defined the moment of death as the moment when the heart stopped working, we now define it as the moment when the brain stops working. I use "head" and "heart" as metaphors as they have often been used in the West, indicating rational, objective, scientific, methodological mental processes on the one hand—the thoughts of sages—and irrational, subjective, artistic, and inspirational mental processes on the other—the emotions of hunters. This is, of course, not merely anatomically incorrect; it is a logically inconsistent way of dividing up reason and emotion.

13. E. M. Forster, *A Passage to India,* the Abinger edition, edited by Oliver Stallybrass (New York, 1978), p. 287.

14. Woody Allen, "Fabulous Tales and Mythical Beasts," in *Without Feathers* (New York, 1976), p. 193.

15. This division is only roughly equivalent to the distinction that is often made, in methodological debates within the history of religions, between phenomenologists and historians. Be that as it may, I do not wish to reactivate that old controversy here.

16. Or, as the late Hans van Buitenen used to say (apparently citing a Dutch proverb), "If I were two dogs, I could play with myself." Another mythical beast that can serve well as a metaphor for the same resolution of opposing tensions in the self-image of the scholar of religion is the armadillo in Rudyard Kipling's *Just So Stories* ("Beginning of the Armadillos"), who was formed when the Stickly-Prickly Hedgehog and the Slow-Solid Tortoise combined forces in order to avoid being eaten by the baby Painted Jaguar. The Jaguar, thrown into confusion by this cross-breed, came back and complained to his mother, who said, "Son, son! . . . A Hedgehog is a Hedgehog, and can't be anything but a Hedgehog; and a Tortoise is a Tortoise, and can never be anything else." "But it isn't a Hedgehog, and it isn't a Tortoise," said the baby Jaguar. "It's a little bit of both, and I don't know its proper name." "Nonsense!" said Mother Jaguar. "Everything has its proper name. I should call it 'Armadillo' till I found out the real one. And I should leave it alone."

Yet another mythical beast of ambivalence is the Pushmi-Pullyu in *Dr. Doolittle*, a creature with a head at each end, which Winston Davis has borrowed (in *Dojo: Magic and Exorcism in Modern Japan*, Stanford, Calif., 1980) to express the tension between two sets of factors that operate when a worshiper is drawn to a particular religion.

17. *Dhvanyaloka* of Anandavardhana, with the *Dhvanyalokalocana* of Abhinavagupta, ed. D. and K. Pandurang Parab (Bombay, 1891), 2.9; cited by J. L. Masson and M. V. Patwardhan, *Aesthetic Rapture: The Rasadhyaya of the Natyashastra* (Poona, 1970), p. 21.

18. An epidemic of self-conscious discussions of this problem was touched off by Claude Lévi-Strauss in *Tristes Tropiques*, trans. John and Doreen Weightman (New York, 1974).

19. Bronislaw Malinowski, *A Diary in the Strict Sense of the Term*, trans. Norbert Guterman (London, 1967), p. 167. Clifford Geertz's essay, " 'From the Native's Point of View': On the Nature of Anthropological Understanding," in *Local Knowledge* (New York, 1983) pp. 55-70, begins with a response to Malinowski's diary.

20. Wendy Doniger O'Flaherty, *The Origins of Evil in Hindu Mythology* (Berkeley, 1976), especially chap. 6, "The Birth of Death." It was Dennis O'Flaherty who pointed out to me the relevance of my work on death to my experience of death.

21. This talent (or weakness, if you will) of a particular sort of Jew must be understood in the context of Judaism as a whole. The overwhelming majority of Jews are of a very different sort. They live and die in the religion of their birth and find it entirely sufficient unto their religious needs. They are the undemythologized (whom we shall encounter in chapter 6). I am not talking about religious conversion, let alone the anti-Semitic proselytizing of such groups as the Jews for Jesus (though it is indeed interesting to note the fascination that Indian gurus seem to have for American Jews, but this is another story—one that has in fact been well discussed by Daniel Gold in *Comprehending the Guru: Toward a Grammar of Religious Perception*, Atlanta, Ga., 1988). I have in mind, rather, the ways in which Jews have been forced, for their very survival, to *learn* other peoples' religions, and in some cases to learn *from* them as well.

22. Plato, *Republic*, book 10.

23. Robert P. Goldman, "Karma, Guilt, and Buried Memories: Public Fantasy and

Private Reality in Traditional India," *Journal of the American Oriental Society* 105, 3 (1985): 413-425.

24. A similar concept of physical traces on the transmigrating soul may be seen in Plato's *Gorgias* 524, in which a man who has been whipped bears the marks of the whip upon him when he is judged after his death.

25. My belief in the karma theory was, wrongly, challenged by Robert P. Goldman in his "Karma, Guilt, and Buried Memories."

26. One striking example of a scholar who hated what he wrote about was Julius Eggeling, who devoted his life to the massive Sanskrit text of the *Shatapatha Brahmana*, his translation of which was published in five volumes in Oxford, from 1882 to 1900. In his introduction (ix) Eggeling complained that "For wearisome prolixity of exposition, characterised by a dogmatic assertion and a flimsy symbolism rather than by serious reasoning, these works are perhaps not equalled anywhere" (cited by Wendy Doniger O'Flaherty, *Tales of Sex and Violence: Folklore, Sacrifice, and Danger in the Jaiminiya Brahmana*, Chicago, 1985, p. 4).

27. "Fire and Ice," in *The Complete Poems of Robert Frost* (New York, 1949), p. 268.

28. This is only one point of view, of course; some people find real killing endlessly fascinating. And there are those who would argue that the only way to understand what a butterfly is is to pin it to the wall, dead. But against that view I would set the parable (another version of which was told by Hans Christian Andersen) of the emperor who was given a marvelous nightingale (in some versions of the story it is a live nightingale, in some it is mechanical) that sang sublimely; in order to "understand" it, he took it apart—and of course it never sang again.

29. See James T. Laney, "The Education of the Heart." *Harvard Magazine* 88, 1 (1985): pp. 23-24.

30. Relativism is often called "cheap relativism," but in its more subtle academic forms it has proved quite expensive. For a sophisticated and complex debate on the issue of moral relativity, see Bryan Wilson, *Rationality* (Oxford, 1970), and Martin Hollis and Steven Lukes, eds., *Rationality and Relativism* (Oxford, 1982).

31. Eliade has written much about the need to see beauty in all sorts of religious phenomena; see, in particular, *The Quest: History and Meaning in Religion* (Chicago, 1969). See also my criticism of this aspect of Joseph Campbell's work, in "Origins of Myth-making Man," review of Joseph Campbell's *Historical Atlas of World Mythology, New York Times Book Review,* 18 December 1983, pp. 3, 24-25.

32. Edward Said, *Orientalism* (New York, 1978).

33. Allan Bloom, *The Closing of the American Mind* (New York, 1987). My favorite epigram on relativism is the old garbled Latin malapropism: De gustibus nihil nisi bonum.

34. Clifford Geertz, "Thick Description: Toward an Interpretive Theory of Culture," in *The Interpretation of Cultures* (New York, 1973), p. 30.

35. In this I disagree with Wilfred Cantwell Smith, who has argued, on many occasions, that any statement that one makes about Hinduism, from outside, must be at least theoretically acceptable to at least one Hindu.

36. I think this is a quote from Nietzsche, writing about Socrates. David Tracy used it in a speech at the University of Chicago on 6 November 1985. And Janet Malcolm, in discussing the resistance against the Freudian approach to the unconscious, remarked that "The unexamined life may not be worth living, but the examined life is impossible to live for more than a few moments at a time." (Janet Malcolm, *In the Freud Archives,* New York, 1984), p. 26.

37. *Twelfth Night,* 2.5.159.

Chapter 2.   Other Peoples' Lies: The Cave of Echoes

1. Daredevils in this regard seem to thrive; defining myth is a growth industry within the profession of the history of religions.
2. For a discussion of the concept of lies, particularly in the context of the study of other peoples' myths, see Charles H. Long's *Significations* (Philadelphia, 1986). Before him, Mircea Eliade, Kees Bolle, and other historians of religions also had good things to say about myths and lies.
3. Indeed, it is this usage that leads most of us to call other peoples' stories "myths," while we call our own stories history. I don't think we have to regard our own history as myth (in the ways that E. H. Carr, or Hayden White or Northrop Frye, for instance, would encourage us to do), but I think we have a misplaced faith in our secular records of the past (and, in the case of fundamentalists, in our scriptural records of the past) that we enshrine in the word "history," which word we then refuse to accord to other peoples' records, secular or scriptural. The problem with this usage was brought home to me some years ago when a scholar who happened to be a Hindu reviewed my Penguin Classic *Hindu Myths*. He began the review by saying, "The title is offensive. To the Hindu, the stories of his sacred literature are as much a reality and are as sacred as are the stories of the miracles of Christ or of Adam and Eve and Noah to the Christians" (K. S. Narayana Rao, in *Books Abroad,* 1976, p. 474).
4. Richard Huntington, "Bara Endogamy and Incest Prohibition," *Dijdragen Tot de Taal-, Land-, en Volkenkunde* 134 (1978): 42.
5. This wonderful phrase was used by President Richard M. Nixon, when he was caught out in a barefaced lie during the Watergate scandal.
6. Plato, *Timaeus* 26e.
7. I do not mean to dismiss Greek myths entirely; they are, of course, myths, like all other reworkings of myths. But they pose many problems, in part because it is never entirely clear whether they were believed by any of the people who tell them, beginning with Homer, or any of the people who heard them. Literary archaeology has resurrected many older, presumably more devout, myths, but this method still leaves us with no *text* to read.
8. In *The Quest*.
9. Plato, *Laws* 10.887.c8-e1.
10. Plato, *Timaeus* 19d. For the damnation of the poets, see also *Timaeus* 22d; *Republic* 3.394b-c and 2.380c3; *Philebus* 14a.3-5. For a good discussion of this issue, see Marcel Detienne, *The Creation of Mythology* (Chicago, 1986), pp. 86-87.
11. Plato, *Republic* 378a.
12. Plato, *Timaeus* 26b.
13. Plato, *Phaedrus* 229c.
14. Plato, *Laws* 10.887.c8-e1.
15. Plato, *Timaeus* 29d, 59d, 68d, etc.
16. Marcel Detienne, *The Creation of Mythology,* p. 82.
17. At the end of the *Republic;* and a similar myth about the voyage of the dead in the *Phaedo,* 113-14.
18. In the *Symposium*.
19. In the *Statesman* and the *Timaeus*.
20. For *muthos* used interchangeably with *logos,* see *Timaeus* 29d, 59d, 68d; for *muthos* compared negatively with *logos,* see *Timaeus* 22d (on the myth of Phaeton the son of Helios), 26c (on the myth/reality of the city of the *Republic*), etc.
21. *Phaedo* 110b.
22. *Phaedo* 113-114. Translation by David Grene.
23. *Timaeus* 29d, 30b, 44d, 68d, 72d, 48c.

24. *Timaeus* 34c, 38b, 48c, 54a-b, 55d, 72d, 68d. See also *Phaedo* 114 d. So, too, the Upanishads lapse into metaphors—and negative metaphors, at that ("Not thus, not thus")—to express what cannot in fact be said in words.
25. *Phaedo* 114d. Translation by David Grene.
26. *Republic* 10 (621b-c).
27. The paradox of the anonymous author of the myth that is regarded as the life story of each member of the community was expressed, in a very different way, by a certain politician who, in introducing his entourage to Martin E. Marty, introduced one particular man by saying, "And this is my autobiographer."
28. Claude Lévi-Strauss, *The Raw and the Cooked: Introduction to a Science of Mythology* (trans. John and Doreen Weightman, New York, 1969), p. 18.
29. I have in mind particularly, but not only, feminists who attempt to create a new mythology of the Goddess, to replace the male chauvinist God of Judaism and Christianity. There have been goddesses, of course, in human history; but their mythologies pose problems for us: They are not usually the sorts of people that modern feminists would like to model their lives upon if they got to know them a bit better; they seldom, if ever, have anything to do with actual political power for women; and, most of all, they are not *our* goddesses. Of course, it is certainly possible to *borrow* someone else's myth, to take up a foreign myth as part of one's own private worldview—this is the main point that I am attempting to make throughout this book. But to *create* a myth on purpose for other people to use is an entirely different enterprise, and one that I distrust, for reasons to which I shall return.
30. See Anders Olerud, *Le macrocosmos et le microcosmos dans le Timée de Plato: Étude de religion comparée* (Uppsala, 1951).
31. Cited by Bernard Faure, "Intertextuality, Relics, and Dreams: The Avatar of a Tradition" (paper presented at the University of Chicago, 24 March 1986).
32. Mary Barnard, *The Myth-Makers* (Athens, Ohio, 1966), p. 183. I would disagree with one point: a ritual is bound by the same temporal paradox as a myth.
33. Though this song was written by two white Yale men, it has come to be widely regarded as some sort of "Negro spiritual." Paul Robeson sang it for many years as part of his repertoire of "black songs," but finally, unable to brook some of its more racist lyrics, which depicted black people as pessimistic and defeatist, he changed them to make them more upbeat. Instead of "Ah gits weary an' sick of tryin',/Ah'm tired of livin' an' skeered of dyin'," Robeson substituted, "I keeps laughin' instead of cryin',/I must keep strivin' until I'm dyin'." In this he was treating the song not as what he well knew it to be (a copyrighted show tune) but as what it had come to be perceived to be (an anonymous folk song)—and he simply created a new oral variant.
34. Indeed, it is sometimes difficult to "move" even a conscious artistic creation like a poem. W. H. Auden discovered this when he excised from his poem "In Memory of W. B. Yeats" in the *Collected Shorter Poems 1927-1957* (London, 1966; first published in *Another Time* in 1940), three stanzas, ending:

> Time that with this strange excuse
> Pardoned Kipling and his views,
> And will pardon Paul Claudel,
> Pardons him for writing well.

Many readers, as W. J. Strachan complained in a letter to the *Times,* had these stanzas "imprinted on their memory"; Strachan went on to argue that "the poet and the artist are not invariably the best judges of their own work," and concluded with his regret that "the printed word has to be reprinted to survive." Auden's poem on Yeats was reprinted, with the excised stanzas restored (and this justified on pp. xix-xx of the introduction) in *W. H. Auden, Selected Poems,*

New Edition, ed. Edward Mendelson (New York, 1979), p. 82. We shall soon consider the good-bad poetry of Kipling; and we shall return, in chapter 3, to the paradoxical tension between the secure oral preservation of a text and the insecure written preservation of a text. For the present argument, I simply want to draw from this incident the assertation that the work of an individual artist often ceases to be his own property and is conceived, by the public at least, to belong to it.

35. Personal communication, cited in O'Flaherty, *Dreams,* p. 130.

36. Claude Lévi-Strauss, *The Jealous Potter,* trans. Bénédicte Chorier (Chicago, 1988), p. 189.

37. Lévi-Strauss, *The Raw and the Cooked,* p. 3.

38. I am indebted to Dr. Martin Stein for making me aware of this aspect of secondary elaboration, about which Freud himself had a great deal to say.

39. Mircea Eliade, *Myth and Reality* (London, 1964).

40. Personal communication from Roy Rappaport, 16 September 1987.

41. Vladimir Propp emphasized the verbal event when he analyzed the Russian fairy tales (*skazki*) in terms of "moves" rather than figures, and Stith Thompson was working in the same tradition when he described his "motifs" in terms of sentences with verbs ("hero meets talking bird") rather than in terms of nouns ("talking bird"). Jung's archetypes were usually described in terms of nouns, often representing parts of the human mental world. Eliade expanded Jung's approach to include both verbs and nouns, both events and images.

42. Leonard B. Meyer, "Creation, Archetypes, and Style Change," *Daedalus* (Spring 1988): 181. I think this is a rather unfair assessment of archetypes, but it does point to a potential problem.

43. C. G. Jung, *Psychology and the East,* trans. R. F. C. Hull (Princeton, N. J., 1978), pp. 68-69. This essay is a reprint of his "Psychological Commentary on *The Tibetan Book of the Dead."*

44. The purely archetypal phallus does appear in some myths: Plutarch (Romulus, 2) tells of a disembodied phallus that appeared on the hearth of King Tarchetius. But this phallus immediately found its way into a folktale: the oracle said that a virgin must copulate with it, and when King Tarchetius's daughter was asked to perform this task, and did not wish to do it, she sent her servant in her place; the servant eventually gave birth to Romulus and Remus. So, too, the North American Trickster keeps his disembodied phallus in a box until he needs it (Paul Radin, *The Trickster,* New York, 1972, pp. 20-22), but even here one has the details of the frame (What kind of a box? What kind of need?). The Greeks sculpted disembodied phalluses (they called them *phalloi*), but they could not resist the temptation to put little wings on them, and sometimes to carve faces on them, too.

45. Mahendra Gupta, *The Gospel of Sri Ramakrishna,* trans. Swami Nikhilananda (Mylapore, 1980), vol. 1, p. 491. The archetypal *lingam* reappears in Paul Scott's *Staying On* (London, 1977), p. 243. Mr. Bhoolabhoy, an Indian Christian, deplores the near certainty that he is about to make love once more to his horrid wife:

> "Indeed I am lost," he thought. "She will make me do it. I am not a Christian at all. I am a Hindu and she is my goddess. Every orgasm is an offering to her, and every erection is a manifestation in me of *Shiva-lingam.*" He shut his eyes so that he could not see his idol. He tried to conjure a different image. It would not come.

Thus the archetypal Hindu image casts its inexorable siren spell on the would-be convert.

46. Clifford Geertz, *Negara, The Theatre State in Nineteenth Century Bali* (Princeton, N.J., 1980), p. 105.

47. Sam Gill, *Mother Earth: An American Story* (Chicago, 1987), p. 156.
48. Barbara Myerhoff, *Peyote Hunt: The Sacred Journey of the Huichol Indians* (Ithaca, N.Y., 1974), p. 42. This is not to argue, as Frits Staal argues from the same premise, that myths (or rituals) *have* no meaning; it simply means that an essential part of that meaning can only be understood by hearing the myth itself, and cannot be teased out of it by any interpretation—aside from the interpretation that is, as I have argued, an unavoidable part of any telling of the myth.
49. C. Ramnoux, "Philosophie et Mythologie, d'Hésiode à Proclus," in Yves Bon-nefoy's *Dictionnaire des Mythologies et des Religions des Sociétés Traditionnelles et du Monde Antique* (Paris, 1981), vol. 2, p. 257. Ramnoux credits Schelling with the coining of the term.
50. Larry Sullivan used this phrase, in conversation at the University of Chicago, to describe the activity of religious studies, in general.
51. I have in mind, in particular, Joseph Campbell, or, rather, the followers of Joseph Campbell. See O'Flaherty, "Origins of Myth-Making Man."
52. Forster, *A Passage to India*, chapter 14 (pp. 138–141 of the Abinger edition).
53. Plato, *Republic*, book 7, 514-516.
54. *Phaedo* 109c-d.
55. Claude Lévi-Strauss, *Structural Anthropology* (New York, 1963), p. 210.
56. Mircea Eliade, *Patterns of Comparative Religion* (New York, 1958), pp. 431-434.
57. Cited by David Carrasco, "Transformations at the Heart of Myth: Dawning, Order, Apocalypse," in *The World and I* (July, 1987): 594-610. This list might also include the reworking of myths in novels. Though serious adult novels with mythological themes are almost invariably second-rate (Gore Vidal's *Creation*, James A. Mitchener's *The Source*, John Steinbeck's *The Pearl*, and so forth), there are notable exceptions to this, novels that satisfy the classic criteria of form, such as William Faulkner's *Fable*, the stories of Jorge Luis Borges, C. S. Lewis's *Till We Have Faces*, Ernest Hemingway's *The Old Man and the Sea*, and John Updike's *The Centaur*.
58. An example of this is the Walt Disney film *The Little One*, a maudlin distortion of the story of the donkey that carried Mary into Bethlehem. Outside of the realm of mythology, a tawdry archetype may appear in a classic manifestation, as when Enrico Caruso sang "Over There."
59. *Rig Veda* 8.1.30-34; *Mahabharata* 3.122-123; see Wendy Doniger O'Flaherty, *Śiva: The Erotic Ascetic* (Oxford, 1973), pp. 57-61.
60. A somewhat different suspension of the aesthetic sensibility in favor of the religious sensibility may be seen in the unanimous Hindu preference for Ganges water (visibly dirty, and known to be the receptacle of corpses) over pure spring water, for ritual purposes.
61. See Wendy Doniger O'Flaherty, *Women, Androgynes, and Other Mythical Beasts* (Chicago, 1980), chapter 3: "The Shazam Syndrome." It is interesting to note the peculiarly masculine nature of Wonder Woman's alter ego—Diana *Prince*, who treats her handsome suitor in an appallingly brutal fashion.
62. Wendy Doniger O'Flaherty, "Inside and Outside the Mouth of God" (*Daedalus*, Spring, 1980), 119-120.
63. See O'Flaherty, *Women*, pp. 68-70.
64. Northrop Frye, *The Secular Scripture: A Study of the Structure of Romance* (Cambridge, Mass., 1976).
65. George Orwell, "Rudyard Kipling," a review of T.S. Eliot's *A Choice of Kipling's Verse*, in *A Collection of Essays* (New York, 1954), p. 135. See also Christopher Hollis, *A Study of George Orwell: The Man and his Works* (London, 1956), especially chapter 15, "Kipling, Wells, Yeats and Koestler."
66. Orwell on Kipling, p. 137.

67. George Orwell, "Good Bad Books," in *Shooting an Elephant, and Other Essays* (New York, 1950), p. 186.
68. Orwell on Kipling, p. 137.
69. See Matei Calinescu, *Faces of Modernity: Avant-Garde, Decadence, Kitsch,* Bloomington, Ind., 1977; *Five Faces of Modernity: Modernism, Avant-Garde, Decadence, Kitsch, Post-Modernism* (Durham, N.C., 1987); and "Modernity and Popular Culture: Kitsch as Aesthetic Deception," in *Sensus Communis: Contemporary Trends in Comparative Literature,* ed. Janos Riesz et al. (Tübingen, 1986), pp. 221-226.
70. In *The New York Review of Books,* 29 May 1986.
71. Mary Douglas, "The Meaning of Myth, with Special Reference to 'La Geste d'Asdiwal,'" in *The Structural Study of Myth and Totemism,* ed. Edmund Leach (London, 1967), pp. 49-70.
72. Werner Heisenberg, *Physics and Beyond: Encounters and Conversations* (New York, 1971).
73. Anantha Murthy, in a public talk at the University of Chicago, 11 October 1985.
74. See Wendy Doniger O'Flaherty, "The Survival of Myth in Science Fiction," Keynote speech for the Eaton Conference of Science Fiction Writers, Riverside, California, 11 April 1987. Published in *Mindscapes,* ed. George E. Slusser and Eric Rabkin.

Chapter 3.   Other Peoples' Classics: Retelling the *Mahabharata*

1. I must apologize for using the term "West" as if it designated a real thing. As Jim Foard has pointed out (in conversation, June 1987), we generally mean "I" when we say "the West." One of his students once remarked, after reading Lao Tzu, that the idea of the harmony of all things "was not known in the West until the Grateful Dead." And Marilyn Waldman tells a delightful story about a Chinese who was asked, by a smug American, "Well, what do you think of Western civilization?", to which the Chinese replied, "It would be a very good thing." This remark has also been attributed to Mahatma Gandhi.
2. Herodotus, *History* 2.53.
3. David Grene, "The *Odyssey:* An Approach," in *Midway* (University of Chicago), Spring, 1969: 50.
4. For further discussions of the ways in which myths in particular, rather than classics in general, undergo transformations in different situations, see, for example, Jonathan Z. Smith, "A Pearl of Great Price and a Cargo of Yams," in *Imagining Religion* (Chicago, 1982), pp. 90-101, and Kenelm Burridge's three chapters on "Myth Dreams" in *Mambu: A Study of Melanesian Cargo Movements and Their Social and Ideological Background* (New York, 1970).
5. The creators of "Dallas" even attempted a classical mythic ploy to extricate themselves from a plot that had painted itself into a corner: they announced that the entire previous season had been dreamed by one of the characters, thus rewinding the story and taking it up again at a point before those events happened. But as this was America, not India, the listening public rose up in fury *en masse* and demanded their money back.
6. The tradition of the serial has been carried on by some of the sagas of English and American novels, such as Galsworthy's *Forsythe Saga,* Trollope's Barchester books, Faulkner's Scopes novels, Howard Fast's *Lavette Saga,* and John Updike's Rabbit trilogy. And of course there are the ongoing adventures of the great detectives, beginning with Sherlock Holmes and continuing with Miss Marple, Hercule Poirot, Ellery Queen, and Travis McGee.
7. The *New York Times,* 27 October 1987.

8. Edgar Johnson, *Charles Dickens: His Tragedy and Truth* (Boston, 1952), p. 304. And when Dickens himself died, a London costermonger's girl exclaimed, "Dickens dead? Then will Father Christmas die too?"
9. Marcia Froelke Coburn, in *Chicago* magazine (April 1985): 130.
10. Bloom, *The Closing of the American Mind.*
11. A similar objection to Bloom was voiced by Martha Nussbaum in her review of his book in *The New York Review of Books,* 5 November 1987, pp. 20-26. She quotes him as saying that "only in the Western nations, i.e., those influenced by Greek philosophy, is there some willingness to doubt the identification of the good with one's own way," and she remarks, "This statement shows a startling ignorance of the critical and rationalist tradition in classical Indian thought, of the arguments of classical Chinese thinkers, and beyond this, of countless examples of philosophical and non-philosophical self-criticism from many parts of the world. . . . I have rarely seen such a cogent, though inadvertent, argument for making the study of non-Western civilizations an important part of the university curriculum" (p. 22).
12. Roy Wagner, *Lethal Speech: Daribi Myth as Symbolic Obviation* (Ithaca, N.Y., 1978), p. 38.
13. Ray Bradbury, *Fahrenheit 451* (New York, 1953), pp. 163-165.
14. Hannah Arendt told this to David Grene, and he told it to me. This is its oral line of descent to me, its *param-para;* it may be recorded somewhere in print.
15. Lévi-Strauss, *The Raw and the Cooked,* p. 5; Edmund Leach, *Lévi-Strauss* (London, 1970), p. 59.
16. Though it did make use of earlier versions, like the Coverdale version, that were already a century old.
17. Rudyard Kipling, "Proofs of Holy Writ," *The Strand Magazine,* April 1934; reprinted in *Rudyard Kipling: Stories and Poems,* ed. Roger Lancelyn Green (London, 1970), pp. 178-190. See the discussion of this story in Wendy Doniger O'Flaherty, "On Translating Sanskrit Myths," in *The Translator's Art: Essays in Honor of Betty Radice,* ed. William Radice (Harmondsworth, 1987).
18. The two plays were produced in both of these combinations by the Court Theatre of the University of Chicago in 1971.
19. Ward Keeler, "Father Puppeteer" (Ph.D. diss., University of Chicago, 1982); and *Javanese Shadow Plays, Javanese Selves* (Princeton, N. J., 1987).
20. C. S. Lewis, *The Lion, The Witch, and The Wardrobe* (Harmondsworth, 1959), p. 173.
21. Lucy Maxym, *Russian Lacquer, Legends, and Fairy Tales* (Manhasset, N.Y., 1981), p. 11.
22. *Republic* 377a.
23. See Wendy Doniger O'Flaherty, "The Role of Myth in the Indian Life Cycle," in *Aditi* (Smithsonian, 1985).
24. For an analysis of the relationship between oral and written texts, see William A. Graham's book, *Beyond the Written Word: Oral Aspects of Scripture in the History of Religion* (Cambridge, 1987).
25. For a discussion of the oral transmission of the *Rig Veda,* see Louis Renou, *The Destiny of the Veda in India* (Delhi, 1965), pp. 25-26 and 84.
26. For this and other definitions of people beyond the Aryan pale in ancient India, see Wendy Doniger O'Flaherty, "The Origins of Heresy in Hindu Mythology," *History of Religions* 10, 4 (May 1971): 271-233; and "The Image of the Heretic in the Gupta Puranas," in *Essays on Gupta Culture,* ed. Bardwell L. Smith (New Delhi, 1983), pp. 107-128.
27. *Aitareya Aranyaka* 5.5.3; cited by Frits Staal, "The Concept of Scripture in the Indian Tradition," in *Sikh Studies: Comparative Perspectives on a Changing Tradition,* ed. Mark Juergensmeyer and N. Gerald Barrier (Berkeley, 1979), pp. 122-123.

28. *Mahabharata* (Poona, 1933-1960), 13.24.70.
29. Philip Lutgendorf, "The Life of a Text: Tulsidas's *Ramacaritamanasa* in Performance," Ph.D. diss., University of Chicago, 1986, chapter 3.
30. For a fuller discussion of the relationship between *shruti* and *smriti*, see Brian K. Smith, "Exorcising the Transcendent: Strategies for Defining Hinduism and Religion," *History of Religions* 27, 1 (August, 1987): 32-55; and "The Unity of Ritual: The Place of the Domestic Sacrifice in Vedic Ritualism," *Indo-Iranian Journal* 28 (1985): 79-96.
31. E. H. Gombrich has used the image of a barely audible radio transmission, which we cannot quite hear and which we therefore complete by projecting our own expectations onto it, to describe what happens when we fill in the sketch of a piece of art with our own projections of visual images (*Art and Illusion*, 2d ed., New York, 1961, p. 204). And we have seen above how Lévi-Strauss has used the metaphor of fragmentation to describe the process by which mythology deconstructs its inexpressible truth.
32. It is of these manuscripts that Müller remarks, in his introduction to the printed text of the *Rig Veda* (London, 1890), "The MSS. of the Rig-veda have generally been written and corrected by the Brahmans with so much care that there are no various readings in the proper sense of the word" (p. ix).
33. Frits Staal, *Agni: The Vedic Ritual of the Fire Altar* (Berkeley, 1983), vol. 1, p. xxxiii.
34. Richard Schechner, "A 'Vedic Ritual' in Quotation Marks," response to Frits Staal's response to Schechner's review of *Agni, Journal of Asian Studies* 46, 1 (February 1987): 110.
35. See Brian K. Smith, "Exorcising the Transcendent." See also Thomas B. Coburn, "'Scripture' in India: Towards a Typology of the Word in Hindu Life," *Journal of the American Academy of Religion* 42, 3 (September 1984): 435-460.
36. Alf Hiltebeitel, *The Ritual of Battle* (Ithaca, N. Y., 1976), pp. 14-15.
37. Milton Singer, *When a Great Tradition Modernizes* (New York, 1972), pp. 75-76.
38. *Mahabharata* 1.1.23 and 1.56.34.
39. This claim is also, it should be noted, made for the three Vedas, which are equated with the three worlds.
40. David Shulman, "Toward a Historical Poetics of the Sanskrit Epics," unpublished manuscript, 1985, p. 5.
41. There is, of course, a lot more that could be said about this, and much of it has been said by Michel Foucault: see his "What is an Author?" in *Textual Strategies*, ed. Josue Harari (Cornell, 1977), pp. 141-160.
42. Joyce's *Ulysses* does seem to contain an episode demonstrating this concept in the West: an idea gets out of Bloom's head in Nighttown and into everyone else's. But the idea was Bloom's to begin with; and of course, the whole *book* was Joyce's, perhaps the most idiosyncratic book ever written in English.
43. See my criticism of the so-called critical edition in my review of J. A. B. van Buitenen's translation of it, in the *Times Literary Supplement*, 15 November 1974, p. 1280; and in the *Religious Studies Review* 4, 1 (January 1978): 19-28.
44. Faure, "Intertextuality, Relics, and Dreams." The reference is to Gilles Deleuze and Felix Guattari, *Anti-Oedipus: Capitalism and Schizophrenia*, trans. Robert Hurley (New York, 1977).
45. This distinction was made by A. K. Ramanujan at the conference on the Puranas, Madison, Wisconsin, 1-4 August 1985.
46. Brian K. Smith, *Reflections on Resemblance, Ritual, and Religion* (New York, 1988) and "Ritual, Knowledge and Being: Initiation and Veda Study in India," in *Numen* 33, 1 (1986): 65-89. See also the conclusion of Hiltebeitel, *The Ritual of Battle*, pp. 359-60, on the rishis of the *Mahabharata*, the fifth Veda.
47. Lutgendorf, "The Life of a Text."
48. Louis Renou (in *The Destiny of the Veda in India*, p. 24) remarks upon this

conception of the importance of mere "recitation" and quotes P. V. Kane (*History of Dharmasastra*, p. 356): "It appears that from the beginning the Veda was confined to memory and that the majority of men versed in the Vedas cared little to know its meaning." But, as Renou goes on to remark, "Allusions are not lacking from which it would appear that despite appearances, interpretation was not entirely lost sight of."

49. See Brian K. Smith, "Ritual, Knowledge, and Being."
50. Cited by Renou, in *The Destiny of the Veda*, p. 84.
51. Faure, "Intertextuality," p. 11.
52. *Mahabharata*, appendix 1, no. 1, verses interpolated [*sic*] after line 30.
53. My argument here contradicts much of what Jack Goody says about writing and orality in *The Domestication of the Savage Mind* (New York, 1976).
54. Philip Lutgendorf, "The Life of a Text".
55. Augustine records in his *Confessions* the surprise that he experienced when he saw Ambrose reading a book *without reading aloud.* (Augustine, *Confessions,* 6.3; trans. R. S. Pine-Coffin, Harmondsworth, 1961, p. 114).
56. Joyce Burkhalter-Fluechtiger, "Literacy and the Changing Concept of Text: Women's Ramayana *Mandali* in Central India," paper delivered at the Association for Asian Studies, 22 March 1986. To be published in *The Boundary of the Text: Performing the Epics in South and Southeast Asia,* ed. Joyce Burkhalter-Fluechtiger and Laurie Sears (Ann Arbor, 1988).
57. Forster, *A Passage to India,* p. 78 of Abinger edition.
58. Letter from E. M. Forster to G. L. Dickinson, 26 June 1924, cited in Stallybrass introduction, ibid., p. xxvi.
59. See such instances in the *Yogavasishtha,* as documented in chapter 3 of O'Flaherty, *Dreams.*
60. Letter from Forster to G. L. Dickinson, 26 June 1924, cited in Stallybrass introduction to *A Passage to India,* p. xxvi.
61. O'Flaherty, *Dreams,* pp. 10-11; *Siva,* pp. 4-11, 33-39.
62. Claude Lévi-Strauss, "The Structural Study of Myth," in *Myth: A Symposium,* ed. Thomas Sebeok (Bloomington, Indiana, 1958).
63. *Shiva Purana* (Benares, 1964), 4.27.23-24; cf. *Ramayana* (Baroda, 1960-1975), 7.4.3-4 and 7.16.44; cf. also Tulsi Das's *Ramacaritamanasa,* translated by W. D. P. Hill as *The Holy Lake of the Acts of Rama* (London, 1952), C. 24.
64. Diana Eck, paper on Shiva and Shakti presented in New York City, 26 October 1985.
65. Karl Marx, *The Eighteenth Brumaire of Louis Bonaparte* (Hamburg, 1869; New York, 1963), p. 1.
66. Padmanabh Jaini, "Jaina Puranas: A Puranic Counter Tradition" (paper presented at the Conference on the Puranas, Madison, Wisconsin, 1-4 August 1985), pp. 66-71; citing a sermon by the twelfth-century sage Hemadri, cited in Prabhacandra's *Prabhavakacarita,* ed. Jinvijaya Muni, Singhi Jain Series 13 (Sholapur, 1940), pp. 187-188. I have paraphrased and condensed some of the story, though keeping the direct quotes as Padmanabh Jaini gave them.
67. *Brahmavaivarta Purana, Krishna-janma Khanda* 47.50-161; cited in Heinrich Zimmer, *Myths and Symbols in Indian Art and Civilization* (New York, 1946), pp. 3-11.
68. Theri-apadana number 22 (Kisa-gotami), in *The Apadana of the Khuddaka Nikaya,* ed. Mary E. Lilley, part 2 (London, 1925), pp. 564-567.
69. Victoria Urubshurow, "The Battle of Kurukshetra: Topologically Transposed" (paper presented at the American Academy of Religion, Boston, 7 December 1987). She cites from an unpublished manuscript based on interviews and news reports, "The Baba Project: Material Collected during 1983-1984 by T. R. Singh, J. M. Mahar, and Victoria Urubshurow."
70. These may seem inappropriate or anachronistic figures to include in the epic, but they are not really inappropriate: Hillary, like the Pandavas at the end of their lives

(except in the Jaina version that we have just seen), climbed a great Himalayan mountain; Lincoln was involved in a great civil war like the *Mahabharata* war; and Jesus Christ is often regarded as an avatar of Vishnu, like Krishna. And they are not anachronistic, as the great *Mahabharata* war continues to take place anew in our time.

71. William S. Sax, "The Pandav Lila of Garhwal" (paper presented at the American Academy of Religion, Boston, 7 December 1987), p. 6.
72. Homer, *Iliad* 6.358.
73. See O'Flaherty, *Dreams,* pp. 286-289, on surrealism.
74. Martha Cooper and Henry Chalfont, *Subway Art* (New York, 1984).
75. *Newsweek,* 19 December 1986, p. 15.
76. As described by her husband in the *Chicago Tribune,* 11 March 1987, sec. 5, p. 3.
77. *Ibid.*
78. Walter Fairservis, *The Roots of Ancient India: The Archeology of Early Indian Civilization* (London, 1971), pp. 378-381.
79. For the metaphor of the city as the illusory body, see O'Flaherty, *Dreams,* pp. 268-279.
80. See Susan Sontag, *On Photography* (New York, 1977).
81. Plato, *Phaedrus* 274d and 275d.
82. Plato, *The Seventh Letter* 341c. Although there is still some dispute as to whether Plato is in fact the author of this text, there seems to be general agreement that at the very least it expresses the views of his school.
83. Lucien Lévy-Bruhl, *The Soul of the Primitive* (London, 1928), p. 156.
84. Yves Véquaud, "The colors of devotion," *Portfolio,* February-March 1980, pp. 62-63.
85. David Dean Shulman, *The King and the Clown in South Indian Myth and Poetry* (Princeton, N.J., 1985), pp. 3-4.
86. E. Valentine Daniel, paper presented at the South Asian Conference at the University of Wisconsin in Madison, 8 November 1986.
87. Lynn Hart, paper presented at the South Asian Conference at the University of Wisconsin in Madison, 8 November 1986.
88. Frits Staal, *Agni,* vol. 2, p. 689. For the non-Vedic aspects of this extraordinary event, see Brian K. Smith, "Vedic Fieldwork," *Religious Studies Review* 11, 2 (April 1985): 136-45.
89. Letter to me from Stephen Inglis, 8 January 1987.
90. Excerpted from pp. 301-314 of Inglis's Ph.D. dissertation, "The Craft of the Ve-lar." See also his paper, "The Craft of the Velar," *National Council for Education in the Ceramic Arts Journal* 7, 7, pp. 14-19.
91. Paul B. Courtright, *Ganesha: Lord of Obstacles, Lord of Beginnings* (New York, 1985), p. 197.
92. Personal communication from Ed Dimock, February 1986.
93. Cf. Brian K. Smith, "Sacrifice and Being: Prajapati's Cosmic Emission," in *Numen* 32, 1 (1985): 79-96.
94. Shelley Errington, paper presented at the Association for Asian Studies, Chicago, 1985.
95. *Apastamba Dharmasutra* (Bombay, 1892), 2.9.24.1.

Chapter 4.   Other People as Animals:
Rudra, Lord of Sacrificial Beasts

1. For the idea of incommensurability in paradigm shifts, see Thomas Kuhn, *The Structure of Scientific Revolutions,* 2d ed. (Chicago, 1970).
2. See O'Flaherty, *Women,* chapter 6, for the myth of the bird/mare/goddess.

3. Laurens van der Post, *The Heart of the Hunter* (New York, 1961), pp. 140-146.
4. *Apology* 27 b5. Socrates here is of course primarily concerned with proving that he believes in the gods (the equation of *theoi* and *daimones* having been made as a separate point), but he uses horses as a telling example. Apparently the "concrete realities" of the divine (*daimonia pragmata*) would be such phenomena as inspiration, while the concrete realities of horses (*hippika pragmata*) would be chariot races, bits, and so forth. I take *nomizo* first in the sense of customary acquaintance and then in the sense of belief.
5. E. E. Evans-Pritchard, *Theories of Primitive Religion* (Oxford, 1965), pp. 24, 43.
6. Cited by R. Angus Downie, *Frazer and the Golden Bough* (London, 1970), p. 42.
7. Ludwig Wittgenstein, *Philosophical Investigations,* 3d ed., trans. G. E. M. Anscombe (New York, 1958), p. 223.
8. Xenophanes, frag. 15, *Die Fragmente,* ed. Ernst Heitsch (Munich, 1983).
9. See, for example, R. H. Smythe, *The Mind of the Horse* (London, 1965), Moyra Williams, *The Psychology of the Horse* (London, 1965), and, most recently, Vicki Hearne, *Adam's Task: Calling Animals by Name* (New York, 1986).
10. Chuang Chou, *Chuang-tzu,* book 17, paragraph 13, "Chuang-tzu and Hui-tzu dispute on their understanding of the enjoyment of fishes." Herbert A. Giles, trans., *Chuang Tzu: Mystic, Moralist, and Social Reformer* (London, 1926), pp. 218-219.
11. It was only after I told this story as part of my presidential address for the American Academy of Religion in Anaheim in 1985 that I learned, from Roger Corless, that my predecessor in the AAR presidency, Wilfred Cantwell Smith, had already used the fish metaphor in a similar context. He had compared methodologists to flies crawling on a goldfish bowl trying to guess what it might be like to be a fish. See W. C. Smith, "The Comparative Study of Religion," in *Inaugural Lectures* (Montreal, 1950).
12. Frits Staal, "The Meaninglessness of Ritual," *Numen* 26, 1 (1979): 4.
13. Ernst Nagel, *Logic Without Metaphysics* (Glencoe, Ill., 1956), p. 365. To which Hans-Peter Duerr replied, "Under no circumstances should one turn into a werewolf just to understand what being a werewolf is like. Under no circumstances must the werewolf's experience be comprehended." *Dreamtime: Concerning the Boundary between Wilderness and Civilization,* trans. Felicitas Goodman, (New York, 1985), p. 127.
14. Duerr, *Dreamtime,* p. 133.
15. Herodotus *History,* 1.133.
16. *Timaeus* 71.
17. E. E. Evans-Pritchard, "Some Reminiscences and Reflections on Fieldwork," *Journal of the Anthropological Society of Oxford* 4 (1973): 4.
18. Duerr, *Dreamtime,* p. 133. Such a fate may await both scholars and witches (Duerr, p. 370). For a further discussion of this issue, see "Do Witches Fly?", my review of Duerr's *Dreamtime* in the *New York Times Book Review,* 8 September 1985, pp. 10-12.
19. *Vishnu Purana* (Calcutta, 1972), 5.3.
20. Jataka 34, "Maccha-Jataka" ("Story of the Birth as a Fish") in *Jataka, with Commentary,* 7 vols., ed. Viggo Fausböll (London, 1877). I cite the translation by E. B. Cowell (Cambridge, 1895-1913).
21. Jataka 216, also called "Maccha Jataka."
22. Jataka 75.
23. *Bhojaprabandha* of Bhallala (Lucknow, 1977).
24. Arthur N. Applebee, *The Child's Concept of Story* (Chicago, 1978), p. 66.
25. As Hans-Peter Duerr remarks (in *Dreamtime,* p. 290), in reply to an article by Thomas Nagel ("What Is It Like to Be a Bat?", *Philosophical Review,* 1974: 440), "Somewhat overstating the matter, we might say that we will not know what it is like to be us until we have 'flown' with bat's wings. All human

beings do, of course, have rudimentary wings of that sort, or else nobody could understand anybody else, or even himself. Nagel should have learned that much from Wittgenstein."

26. See, for example, the way in which the monkeys in the *Ramayana* act out a dark satire of the lives of the heroes, as discussed by Jeffrey Moussaieff Masson, "Fratricide among the Monkeys: Psychoanalytic Observations on an Episode in the Valmikiramayana," *Journal of the American Oriental Society* 95 (1975): 672-678; and "Hanuman as an Imaginary Companion," *Journal of the American Oriental Society* 101 (1981): pp. 355-360.

27. See *Animal Myths and Metaphors,* ed. Gary Urton (Salt Lake City, 1985).

28. Claude Lévi-Strauss, *Totemism,* trans. Rodney Needham (Boston, 1963), p. 89: "We can understand, too, that natural species are chosen not because they are 'good to eat' but because they are 'good to think with.' " See also Stanley Tambiah, "Animals Are Good to Think About and Good to Prohibit," *Ethnology* 8, 4 (1969): 423-459.

29. For further discussions of the intimacy between humans and animals in mythology, see Jonathan Z. Smith, "Animals and Plants in Myth and Legend," s. v. "Myth and Mythology," *Encyclopaedia Britannica* (1974), Macropaedia, vol. 1, pp. 911-918.

30. Aristotle, *Nicomachean Ethics* 10.28.

31. See O'Flaherty, *Dreams,* chap. 5, for the narrative forms of the ouroboros.

32. Friedrich Nietzsche, *Thus Spoke Zarathustra,* Part 2, "The Dancing Song," in *The Portable Nietzsche,* ed. and trans. Walter Kaufmann (Harmondsworth, 1976), p. 220.

33. *Mark* 1:16-18; *John* 6:10-14.

34. A *shaphari,* the same paradigmatic minnow that got into the head of King Bhoja.

35. *Shatapatha Brahmana* (Benares, 1964), 1.8.1.1-6; *Matysa Purana* (Poona, 1907), 1.11-34; 2.1-19; Wendy Doniger O'Flaherty, *Hindu Myths* (Harmondsworth, 1975), pp. 179-184.

36. *Rig Veda* 1.114; cf. O'Flaherty, *The Rig Veda,* pp. 223-225.

37. Jacques Scheuer, "Rudra-Śiva et la destruction du sacrifice," s. v. "Sacrifice," Yves Bonnefoy, *Dictionnaire des Mythologies,* vol. 2, pp. 417-420.

38. *Atharva Veda* (Bombay, 1895), 11.2.24. See O'Flaherty, *Origins of Evil,* pp. 169-173.

39. I think it is most likely that it was the male animal, the bull, that was used, as the males of all the other species are explicitly specified, and indeed their "virility" is the point of many myths and ritual texts. Yet it should be noted that the word *go* is sexually ambiguous, and many Indo-Europeans did sacrifice cows.

40. *Atharva Veda* 11.2.9, with Sayana's commentary.

41. See Wendy Doniger O'Flaherty, "The Case of the Stallion's Wife: Indra and Vrsanaśva in the Rg Veda and the Brāhmanas." *Journal of the American Oriental Society* 105, 3 (1985): 485-498.

42. *Mahabharata* 6.5.12-14.

43. Govindaraja on Manu 1.39. In *Manu-Smrti, with Nine Commentaries,* ed. Jayantakrishna Harikrishna Dave (Bombay, 1975).

44. *Mahabharata* 2.20.8-11. Cf. 2.14.18: "What pleasure is there for the kings who are anointed and washed like sacrificial beasts in the house of Pashupati?"

45. See *Shatapatha Brahmana* 13.6.1-2; *Vajasaneyi Samhita* (Berlin, 1952), 30.1-22; *Taittiriya Brahmana* (Calcutta, 1859), 3.4.1.1 ff.

46. See the discussion of human sacrifice in Asko Parpola, "The Pre-Vedic Indian Background of the Śrauta Rituals," in Frits Staal's *Agni,* vol. 2, pp. 41-75, esp. 49-53. See, too, the article by Staal himself in volume 1. See also Albrecht Weber, "Purusamedhakandha," *Zeitschrift der Deutschen Morgenländischen Gesellschaft* 18 (1864): 277-284; "Ueber Menschenopfer bei den Indern der vedischen Zeit," *Indische Streifen* 1 (1868): 54; 75-80; H. H. Wilson, "On the Sacrifice of Human

Beings as an Element of the Ancient Religion of India," *Journal of the Royal Asiatic Society* 1852; Rajendralala Mitra, "On Human Sacrifices in Ancient India," *Journal of the Asiatic Society of Bengal* 1876. Bruce Lincoln, in *Myth, Cosmos, and Society: Indo-European Themes of Creation and Destruction* (Cambridge, Mass., 1986), p. 183 n., argues that "in practice humans were probably never offered in India, the *puruṣamedha* ('sacrifice of a man') remaining only a priest's fantasy of the sacrifice to end all sacrifices."

47. G. R. Sharma, *The Excavations at Kausambi (1957-1959)* (Allahabad, 1960), pp. 87ff.; Dieter Schlinghoff, "Menschenopfer in Kausambi," *Indo-Iranian Journal* 11 (1969): 176-198.

48. James L. Sauvé, "The Divine Victim: Aspects of Human Sacrifice in Viking Scandinavia and Vedic India," in *Myth and Law among the Indo-Europeans,* ed. Jaan Puhvel (Los Angeles, 1970), pp. 193-191; Willibald Kirfel, "Der Aśvamedha und der Purusamedha," in *Festschrift für Walther Schubring* (Hamburg, 1951), pp. 39-50.

49. *Shatapatha Brahmana* 11.7.1.3. See also *Taittiriya Brahmana* 3.9.17.4-5, where the sacrificer is consecrated as the horse.

50. *Shatapatha Brahmana* 1.2.3.6-7. See also the translations and discussions by Julius Eggeling (5 vols., Oxford, 1882); Sylvain Lévi, *La doctrine du sacrifice dans les Brahmanas* (Paris, 1966) pp. 136-137. Cf. also *Aitareya Brahmana* (Calcutta, 1896), 2.8.

51. Eggeling, p. 49 of volume 1. He goes on to editorialize: "In accordance with these notions, it would seem that man originally sacrificed his equal, as the best substitute for his self; and that, as advancing civilization rendered human sacrifices distasteful, the human victim was supplied by domestic animals, ennobled by constant contact with man; and finally by various materials of human diet" (p. 50).

52. For Dadhyanch, see *Rig Veda* 1.117.22; *Shatapatha Brahmana* 14.1.1.18-24; O'Flaherty, *Hindu Myths,* pp. 56-60. For Shunahshepa see *Aitareya Brahmana* 7.13-18 and Wendy Doniger O'Flaherty, *Textual Sources for the Study of Hinduism* (Manchester, 1988), pp. 19-24.

53. For the concept of men as the sacrificial beasts of the gods, see O'Flaherty, *Origins of Evil,* pp. 169-173.

54. For a discussion of Shiva as the Lord of Beasts, see O'Flaherty, *Origins of Evil,* pp. 171-73.

55. *Brihadaranyaka Upanishad* 1.4.10; see minor differences in the reading of the same text in the *Shatapatha Brahmana* 14.4.2.21-22. See also O'Flaherty, *Origins of Evil,* p. 91.

56. Brian K. Smith, "Ritual, Knowledge and Being," p. 70. The skin of a black antelope is worn by the Brahmin (*Ashvalayana Grihya Sutra* 1.19.10, etc.), while the Kshatriya, or warrior king, wears the skin of a tiger (*Kathaka Grihya Sutra* 11.13), for the tiger is said to be the embodiment of courage (*Shatapatha Brahmana* 12.7.2.8), the king of the wild animals (*Shatapatha Brahmana* 12.7.1.8), and the representative of the power of the warrior king within the animal kingdom (*Aitareya Brahmana* 8.6). The Vaishya, or agriculturalist, wears the skin of a goat or a cow, said to be symbolic of food (*Shatapatha Brahmana* 7.5.2.6; 7.5.2.43; 6.3.2.4).

57. *Shatapatha Brahmana* 12.7.3.20.

58. For a discussion of the relationship between village and forest, see Charles Malamoud, "Village et forêt dans l'idéologie de l'Inde brahmanique," in *Archives Européennes de Sociologie* 17 (1976): 3-20.

59. The *Taittiriya Brahmana* version of the text omits this paragraph and speaks only of the danger of using forest animals for sacrifice.

60. Here the *Taittiriya* adds, "father and son would part."

61. Cf. *Taittirya Brahmana* 3.9.1.2, where the sacrifice is completed with forest animals and the same thing happens!
62. *Shatapatha Brahmana* 13.2.4.1-4; cf. *Taittiriya Brahmana* 3.9.1-2.
63. See the discussion of *jami* and *prithak*, excessive resemblance and excessive differentiation, in Brian K. Smith's *Reflections*.
64. *Panchavimsha Brahmana* (Calcutta, 1869-74), 21.4.13; cf. *Taittiriya Brahmana* 3.8.19.1-2.
65. *Aitareya Brahmana* 3.33-34; in O'Flaherty, *Hindu Myths*, pp. 29-31. See also other versions of this myth, some cited in O'Flaherty, *Siva*, some by Jacques Scheuer in the Bonnefoy *Dictionnaire des Mythologies*.
66. Cf. the statement that animals (*pashus*, here almost certainly designating all animals, in opposition to humans, rather than sacrificial animals in opposition to wild animals) commit incest, in the story of Shunahshepa, *Aitareya Brahmana* 7.13-18.
67. *Aitareya Brahmana* 3.34. Cf. also *Panchavimsha Brahmana* 8.2.10 and *Jaiminiya Brahmana* (Nagpur, 1954), 3.261-262.
68. *Brihadaranyaka Upanishad* 1.4.1-6; translated by O'Flaherty, *Hindu Myths*, pp. 34-35. For an analysis of the implications of this passage, see O'Flaherty, "The case of the stallion's wife."
69. *Panchavimsha Brahmana* 7.9.16. Cf. also *Maitrayani Samhita* (Wiesbaden, 1970), 4.2.12.
70. *Shatapatha Brahmana* 1.7.3.1; cf. also *Gopatha Brahmana* (Leiden, 1919), 2.1.2; *Panchavimsha Brahmana* 7.9.16.
71. *Varaha Purana* (Calcutta, 1893), 33.3-24.
72. *Linga Purana* (Calcutta, 1812), 1.72.34-45.
73. *Mahabharata* 12.274.2-58. See also O'Flaherty, *Siva*, pp. 114-140; *Origins of Evil*, pp. 272-277.
74. For an analysis of this transition, see Walter Burkert's *Homo Necans* (Berlin and New York, 1972).
75. See Brian K. Smith, *Reflections*.
76. For myths about rituals as the embodiment of nightmares about the sacrifice, see O'Flaherty, *Tales of Sex and Violence*, pp. 18-23.
77. See Brian K. Smith, "Gods and Men in Vedic Ritualism: Toward a Hierarchy of Resemblance," in *History of Religions* 24:4 (May, 1985): 291-307; and *Reflections*. For substitutions for the Vedic Soma plant, see Wendy Doniger O'Flaherty, "The Post-Vedic History of the Soma Plant," in *Soma: Divine Mushroom of Immortality*, by R. Gordon Wasson and Wendy Doniger O'Flaherty (New York, 1968), pp. 95-147.
78. *Atharva Veda* 8.10.22-29; translated and analyzed in O'Flaherty, *Origins of Evil*, p. 322.
79. *Bhagavata Purana* (Bombay, 1832), 4.13-19; translated and analyzed in O'Flaherty, *Origins of Evil*, p. 324.
80. See the stories of kings, hunters, and Untouchables in chapter 4 of O'Flaherty, *Dreams*.
81. Shulman, *The King and the Clown*, pp. 83 and 85.
82. Prithu's father is also killed, though not by Prithu (who is a posthumous son). Sigmund Freud, in *Totem and Taboo*, argues that the original sacrifice was a sacrifice of the father.
83. This is one of the main arguments of Walter Burkert's *Homo Necans*. Similarly, it is often argued that hunting itself is regarded as a sacrifice in hunting societies. Thus, for example, Georges Charachidze remarks in his article on the mythology of the Northern Caucasus (in Yves Bonnefoy's *Dictionnaire des Mythologies*, vol. 1), "It must be emphasized that for all the peoples of the Caucasus hunting is the equivalent of a sacrifice, and each animal that is killed is regarded as a victim offered to the Master of Game" (p. 132).

84. Jonathan Z. Smith, "The Domestication of Sacrifice," in *Violent Origins: Ritual Killing and Cultural Formation,* by Walter Burkert, René Girard, and Jonathan Z. Smith, ed. Robert G. Hamerton-Kelly (Stanford, Calif., 1987), pp. 191-205.
85. *Jaiminiya Brahmana* 1.42-44. See O'Flaherty, *Tales of Sex and Violence,* pp. 32-49.
86. See the story of "How Men Changed Skins with Animals," *Jaiminiya Brahmana* 2.182-183, also in *Tales of Sex and Violence,* pp. 40-42. For a discussion of this genre of prevarication in other religions, see Jonathan Z. Smith, "The Bare Facts of Ritual," in *Imagining Religion* (Chicago, 1982), pp. 53-65.
87. *Rig Veda* 1.162.21; O'Flaherty, *Rig Veda,* p. 91. See also my discussion of the willingness of the sacrificed animal in "The Good and Evil Shepherd," in *Gilgul: Essays on Transformation, Revolution, and Permanence in the History of Religions, Dedicated to Zwi Werblowsky,* ed. S. Shaked, D. Shulman, and G. G. Stroumsa (Leiden, 1987), pp. 169-191.
88. Of course Hinduism has its cow-herder, Krishna, but Krishna (whom Brian K. Smith has called "Jesus in blue-face") is not a cow.
89. *Shiva Purana* 1.1.18.75-76.
90. *Shiva Purana* 2.2.33.7.
91. *Rig Veda* 1.154.2; O'Flaherty, *Rig Veda,* pp. 226-7.
92. *Ramayana,* book 3, appendix 1, no. 10, line 95.
93. *Ramayana* 5.11.50.
94. Cf. *King Lear* 4.1.36: "As flies to wanton boys are we to the gods; they kill us for their sport."
95. Edmund Leach has pointed out some fascinating linguistic aspects of this spectrum of otherness in the animal kingdom. See Edmund Leach, "Anthropological Aspects of Language: Animal Categories and Verbal Abuse," in *New Directions in the Study of Language,* ed. Eric H. Lenneberg (Cambridge, Mass., 1964), pp. 23-63.
96. T. H. White, *The Once and Future King* (London, 1962); part 1, *The Sword in the Stone.* The culmination of the animal education comes in chapter 23.
97. *Bacchae* 699-702.
98. Nietzsche, *Thus Spoke Zarathustra,* First Part, Prologue, paragraph 2; p. 123 of the Kaufmann translation.
99. Jonathan Swift, *Gulliver's Travels* (London, 1726), part 4, chapters 1 and 2. This same reversal, with the horse in charge of the human, is the theme of C. S. Lewis's *The Horse and his Boy.* Here, significantly, God (Christ) is a lion (Aslan, the Persian word for lion)—and, as Lewis points out, not a tame lion.
100. *Isaiah* 11:6-8.
101. *Vayu Purana* (Bombay, 1897), 1.8.77-88; *Digha Nikaya* (London, 1890-91), *Agganna Suttanta* 27.10 ff. See O'Flaherty, *Origins of Evil,* pp. 17-26.
102. Nietzsche, *Zarathustra,* Part IV, chapter 20, pp. 436-39.

Chapter 5.   Other Peoples' Rituals:
Daksha, Pentheus, and Jesus

1. René Girard, *Violence and the Sacred* (Baltimore and London, 1977), p. 127.
2. *Shiva Purana,* 2.2.1-43; 4.12. See also the discussion in O'Flaherty, *Siva,* pp. 111-140; *Origins of Evil,* pp. 272-320; and *Hindu Myths,* pp. 25-34. 116-125, 137-149.
3. So, too, Daksha curses the worshipers of Shiva to be heretics because they *are* heretics. See O'Flaherty, *Origins of Evil,* p. 278.
4. This is the name given to him, rather nervously and optimistically, much as the goddess of the fever of smallpox, Shitala, is called "Cool."

5. *Vamana Purana* (Varanasi 1968), 2.17-18. See pp. 278 ff. of O'Flaherty, *Origins of Evil* for other examples of texts of the Daksha myth that tell the story of Shiva's beheading of Brahma.
6. The action of Sati, Shiva's wife, becomes paradigmatic for all devoted wives, especially for those who (in many myths) burn themselves to death on their husbands' pyres (the act of *suttee*, an act whose name is derived from the name of Sati and which is legitimated by this myth).
7. Cf. *Shatapatha Brahmana* 2.2.4.1-8, 1.6.3.35-37, etc.
8. *Shatapatha Brahmana* 10.4.3.1-10. See O'Flaherty, *Textual Sources*, pp. 10-13.
9. See my discussion of the inversion of social charters in "Inside and Outside the Mouth of God," pp. 102-104.
10. See O'Flaherty, *Origins of Evil*, on Indra as performer of horse sacrifices and obstructor of horse sacrifices. For the identification of the horse with the sacrificer and with Prajapati, see *Shatapatha Brahmana* 13.1.1.1 and 13.2.1.1. For the many variants of the story of Indra's theft of the sacrificial horse of King Sagara, see *Mahabharata* 3.104-108; *Ramayana* 1.38-44; *Vishnu Purana* 4.4.1-33, etc. For a discussion of these stories, see O'Flaherty, *Women*, pp. 220-222.
11. *Harivamsha* 118.11-39.
12. See the discussion of this story in Wendy Doniger O'Flaherty, "Horses and Snakes in the Ādi Parvan of the *Mahābhārata*," in *Aspects of India: Essays in Honor of Edward Cameron Dimock*, ed. Margaret Case and N. Gerald Barrier (New Delhi, 1986), pp. 16-44.
13. See O'Flaherty, *Origins of Evil*, chapter 9, "Crowds in Heaven."
14. See O'Flaherty, *Śiva*, for the relationship between Shiva and Indra.
15. For a more detailed comparison of the two myths, see Wendy Doniger O'Flaherty, "Dionysus and Śiva: Parallel Patterns in Two Pairs of Myths." *History of Religions* 20, 1 (1980): 81-111.
16. Euripides, *Bacchae*, ed. E. R. Dodds (Oxford, 1960).
17. There remains much debate on this issue. Marcel Detienne, in his article, "Dionysos" (pp. 300-307 of vol. 1 of the Yves Bonnefoy *Dictionnaire*) argues that Dionysus is wrongly called a foreign god, since he is attested in the earliest Greek texts, even in Linear B. But I remain persuaded by W. K. C. Guthrie, in *The Greeks and Their Gods* (Boston, 1955), that there are two Dionysuses: the early one, whom Detienne has in mind, is indeed Greek and old, and is connected with Demeter; the later one, that Euripides has in mind, is a new god who came from Thrace. The two then become conflated, through the always available paradigm of the *coincidentia oppositorum*, to give us a god who is explicitly said to be both old and new, both native and foreign. Jonathan Z. Smith compares Dionysus with James Jones, leader of the Jonestown community, with regard to their spatial orientation: "The entrance of Dionysus and his band into a city is perceived, from the point of view of the city, as an invasion, as a contagious plague. It produces civil disorder and madness. Hence its official, civil interpretation will be that it is 'alien,' that it is founded by a 'charlatan and a fraud'. . . . There is *no room* for this sort of religion within *civil space*" ("The Devil in Mr. Jones," in *Imagining Religion*, Chicago, 1982, p. 113).
18. For one example among many, see *Shatapatha Brahmana* 12.7.3.20.
19. Euripides, *Bacchae*, line 1017.
20. Plutarch *Q. Gr.* 36, 299 B; cited by E. R. Dodds, introduction to his edition of the *Bacchae*, p. xviii.
21. René Girard, *Violence and the Sacred*, p. 128.
22. *Bacchae*, lines 242, 286-297; cf. 94-99. This is one of the earliest instances that I know of the theory of myth as a "disease of language," which was fully articulated twenty-four hundred years later by Max Müller.
23. See, for instance, Marcel Detienne, *Dionysos Slain* (Baltimore, 1979), pp. 68-94;

and Walter Burkert, "Orphism and Bacchic Mysteries: New Evidence and Old Problems of Interpretation," *Protocol of the 28th Colloquy of the Center for Hermeneutical Studies* (Berkeley, 1977), pp. 1-8.

24. See, for instance, Hugo Rahner's *Greek Myths and Christian Mystery* (New York, 1962).
25. Cf. Onomacritus quoted by Pausanias 8.37.3; Diodorus Siculus 3.62 and 3.68-69; Orphic Hymn 14.6; Apollodorus 3.4.3; Hyginus Fabula 182; Apollonius of Rhodes 4.1131; etc. For a discussion of the Orphic myths, see Martin L. West, *The Orphic Poems* (Oxford, 1971).
26. Ovid, *Metamorphoses* 11.1-85; Aristophanes, *Frogs,* 1032.
27. Diodorus Siculus 5.75.4; Nonnus, *Dionysiaca* 6.269.
28. E. R. Dodds, *The Greeks and the Irrational* (Berkeley, 1964), p. 155.
29. Sigmund Freud, *Totem and Taboo,* standard edition, trans. James Strachey (New York, 1950), p. 156.
30. Dodds, *The Greeks and the Irrational,* pp. 276-278; reprinted from his article, "Maenadism in the *Bacchae,*" *Harvard Theological Review* 33 (1940): 155ff. And see also W. K. C. Guthrie, *The Greeks and their Gods* (Boston, 1955), pp. 45, 149, and 157.
31. Dodds, *The Greeks and the Irrational,* p. 277, citing the scholiast on Clement of Alexandria 92 P.
32. In the introduction to the *Bacchae,* p. xvii, Dodds gives Frazer credit for this phrase and sets it in quotation marks.
33. Citing James George Frazer, *The Golden Bough: A Study in Magic and Religion,* vol. 2 (London, 1963) chap. 12.
34. Dodds, *The Greeks and the Irrational,* p. 277.
35. Dodds, introduction to the *Bacchae,* xviii.
36. Ibid., xviii-xix. Dodds cites his opinion less tentatively in his subsequent study in *The Greeks and the Irrational,* p. 278: "there once existed a more potent, because more dreadful, form of this sacrament, viz., the rending, and perhaps the eating, of God in the shape of man; and . . . the story of Pentheus is in part a reflection of that act."
37. Girard, *Violence and the Sacred,* p. 132. See also pp. 162-163.
38. Ibid., p. 251.
39. In the final scenes of the play, the lion and bull are used in symbolic contexts that further blur the line between god and mortal in an ominous way. Dionysus is called a lion only once, while Pentheus is mistaken for a lion many times; by contrast, Dionysus appears as a bull many times, Pentheus only once (at the very end of the play, when Agaue speaks of him as her "calf"). The gruesome pleasure that Pentheus's mother finds in disemboweling and beheading her son is made possible by her persistent delusion that he is a lion, or, more pointedly, the offspring of a lioness. Pentheus is not a lion; this is what makes the dismemberment so appalling. Dionysus, however, is a lion, though Pentheus never comes to realize this.
40. It is worth noting that there are two choruses in the *Bacchae,* a physical embodiment of the ambivalence of the worshipers toward the god: the chorus of original women worshipers, who love the god and are happy in his worship, and the chorus of the women of Thebes, who are seduced to his worship and come to regret it bitterly.
41. Even Herodotus, who loves myth for its own sake, dresses up the myth of the birth of Cyrus in considerable human detail. See Herodotus, *History* 1.107-112 and my discussion of this text in "Inside and Outside the Mouth of God," p. 112
42. But here too we may recognize the theme of lightning that plays such ar important role in the *Bacchae.*
43. Theodore W. Elmore, *Dravidian Gods in Modern Hinduism* (Lincoln, Neb 1915), pp. 119-120.

44. A. K. Ramanujan, "Two Realms of Kannada Folklore," in *Another Harmony: New Essays on the Folklore of India,* ed. A. K. Ramanujan and Stuart Blackburn (Berkeley, 1986), p. 73; citing Elmore.

45. I am indebted for this story to William Sax, who recorded the story and who has allowed me to use it here, changing the names of the principal actors. It is interesting to compare this report with that of Frits Staal (*Agni,* vol. 2, pp. 468-9), about which controversy still rages. Indeed, Staal's sacrifice took place in Kerala, where, according to A. K. Ramanujan, another variant of the story told by William Sax took place.

46. William S. Sax, "Chaya Maya." (Ph.D. diss., University of Chicago, 1988.)

47. Herodotus, *History* 4.78-80. Translated by David Grene, in *The History: Herodotus* (Chicago, 1987), pp. 209-210.

48. See O'Flaherty, *Women,* p. 102.

49. Philip Slater, *The Glory of Hera* (Boston, 1968).

50. Friedrich Nietzsche, *Ecce Homo* (1908), final line; p. 335 of the Walter Kaufmann translation (*On the Genealogy of Morals and Ecce Homo,* New York, 1969). Nietzsche himself provides a gloss for this line in the final paragraph (1052; March-June 1888) of *The Will to Power* (p. 542 of the Walter Kaufmann-R.J. Hollingdale translation, New York, 1968): "Dionysus versus the 'crucified': there you have the antithesis. It is *not* a difference in regard to their martyrdom—it is a difference in the meaning of it. . . . The god on the cross is a curse on life, a signpost to seek redemption from life; Dionysus cut to pieces is a *promise* of life: it will be eternally reborn and return again from destruction."

51. Cf. *Matthew* 26:2, where Jesus says to his disciples: "Ye know that after two days is the feast of the passover, and the Son of man is betrayed to be crucified." In *John* 18.39, Pilate says to the Jews: "Ye have a custom, that I should release unto you one at the passover. Will you therefore that I release unto you the King of the Jews?" In *Matthew* and *Mark,* the chief priests explicitly refrain from killing Jesus during the Passover feast, "lest there be an uproar among the people" (*Matthew* 26:4; *Mark* 14:2). In *Luke,* when the Passover approaches, the chief priests plot to kill him, "for they feared the people" (*Luke* 22:2). In *John,* Jesus is crucified over Passover weekend; as he goes to Golgotha, "it was the preparation of the passover, and about the sixth hour" (*John* 19:14); his final conversation with Judas and the disciples is explicitly said to take place "before the feast of passover, when Jesus knew that his hour was come that he should depart out of this world" (*John* 13:1).

52. Benevolence toward men is not a characteristic of Vedic or Hindu gods, until the medieval period of devotionalism (*bhakti*). (See O'Flaherty, *Origins of Evil,* chap. 4). Even then, despite the dominant image of God as a cow who loves her calf (an image already inherent in the myth of Prithu), one's relationship with God is often characterized by a mutual feeling of hate-love (*dvesha-bhakti*), fire and ice. This double-pronged power of affect is also characteristic of much scholarship in the field of religion, as we saw in chapter 1.

53. As David Tracy has remarked in a paper on "Myth, Sacrifice, and the Social Sciences," read at the Annual Meeting of the American Academy of Religion, Boston, 6 December 1987, the author of the *Epistle to the Hebrews* (whoever he was), and no one else in the New Testament, seems to have read René Girard.

54. *Hebrews* 9:12-14.

55. *Romans* 8:36, citing *Psalms* 44:22.

56. Brian K. Smith, *Reflections.* David Carrasco and Roy Rappaport have well argued that religious traditions "can actually enhance the flexibility in social structure and symbolic expression because sanctification permits previous modes of social and symbolic organization to persist in the face of innovation and change. In other words, the threatening aspects of changed conditions can be somewhat neutralized by being incorporated into sacred tradition" (David Carrasco,

Quetzalcoatl and the Irony of Empire: Myths and Prophecies in the Aztec Tradition, Chicago, 1982, pp. 106-107; citing also Roy Rappaport, *Ecology, Meaning, Religion,* Richmond, Calif., 1979, p. 148).

57. *Ezekial* 20:31, *Micah* 6:6-7; *Exodus* 22:28-30. And there is a *midrash* on the story of Abraham and Isaac that argues (in part from the Hebrew grammar: the verb going up the mountain is plural, whereas the verb going down it is singular) that Abraham really did kill Isaac, who was subsequently resurrected.

58. Or, indeed, for the human victim. It is sometimes argued that the circumcision of male children, which takes place on the same day that the sacrifice of the firstborn was to take place, is a surrogation for that rite.

59. *Hosea* 14:2.

60. 1 *Samuel* 15:22.

61. Robert L. Faherty, "Rites and Ceremonies," *Encyclopaedia Britannica,* 15th ed. (Chicago, 1985), vol. 26, p. 843.

62. *Aitareya Brahmana* 2.8-9.

63. Claude Lévi-Strauss, *The Raw and the Cooked.*

64. See pp. xvi-xvii of the introduction to Wendy Doniger O'Flaherty, *Karma and Rebirth in Classical Indian Traditions* (Berkeley, 1980); see also Marcel Detienne, *The Gardens of Adonis,* trans. Janet Lloyd (Atlantic Highlands, N.J., 1977).

65. David Knipe, "Sapindīkarana: The Hindu Rite of Entry into Heaven," in *Religious Encounters with Death, Insights from the History and Anthropology of Religions,* ed. Frank Reynolds and Earle H. Waugh (University Park, Pa., 1977), pp. 111-124.

66. *John* 6:52-66.

67. Personal communication from Mary MacDonald.

68. Mary MacDonald (Ph.D. diss., University of Chicago), 1988.

69. Inga Clendinnen, "Reading the Inquisitorial Record in Yucatan: Fact or Fantasy?" *The Americas* 38, 3 (January 1982): 327-345. p. 327.

70. Ibid., p. 341.

71. Ibid., p. 343.

72. Ibid., p. 345. Well into the nineteenth century, the Mexican sect of Penitentes, in the Western parts of the United States, performed actual crucifixions.

73. *Taittiriya Samhita* (Calcutta, 1960), 7.2.10.4; *Kathaka* 34.11. Cited by Eggeling (in reference to *Shatapatha Brahmana* 1.2.3.5, vol. 1, p. 49) in favor of the argument that the rice cake replaced an original human sacrificial victim.

74. Evans-Pritchard, *Nuer Religion,* p. 197.

75. Nietzsche, *Zarathustra,* Part IV, chapter 12, pp. 396-98: "Man does not live by bread alone, but also by the meat of good lambs, of which I have two."

76. For a classic study of the Christian Eucharist as a sacrifice, see W. Robertson Smith, *The Religion of the Semites: The Fundamental Institutions* (Aberdeen, 1888-89).

Chapter 6.   Other Peoples' Myths:
The Place in the Woods

1. Rudolf Bultmann, "New Testament and Mythology," in *The Gospel of John: A Commentary* (New York, 1941).

2. Personal communication from David Tracy, 25 February 1987.

3. Opera and ballet present myths in a form so stark and naive that they are a source of hilarity and ridicule to noninitiates, and sometimes even for people who are, at other moments, deeply moved by them. See, for example, Robert Benchley's "Opera Synopses," pp. 51-56 of *The Benchley Roundup* (New York,

1954; Chicago, 1983) and Woody Allen's "A Guide to Some of the Lesser Ballets" (pp. 18-23 of *Without Feathers,* New York, 1976). Yet myths are a serious matter for composers and opera audiences; the music fleshes out the stark themes and says what cannot be said in words. An opera without the music (that is, a plain libretto) sounds flat and obvious just as a myth told without any details (or an archetype divested of most of its manifestation) seems flat and obvious. Or, as someone (Dr. Johnson?) once remarked, things that are too silly to be said may be sung. Lévi-Strauss long ago pointed out the close analogy between the structures of myth and music. Not only do operas and myths speak the same language; they are about the same things.

But more than that: for us the otherness of opera fits well with the otherness of myth. Our operas are in Italian or German; we resist efforts to translate them into English. They sound silly in English, in part because the bare outline, the naked archetype, of a myth *does* sound silly, and in part because Englishing destroys our apprehension of the opera as exotic. It is no accident that early operas indulged in their own brand of Orientalism (*Aida, The Pearl Fishers, Lakmé,* and *Madame Butterfly*).

Of course, it is also true that Italians enjoy their operas in Italian, and Germans enjoy theirs in German. For them, the distance of the past (the setting of virtually all operatic plots) is sufficient to distance the myths. Moreover, their theater does not depend upon true realism as much as ours now does and hence is less distorted by the extravagance of the myths. But for us, in the contemporary Anglo-Saxon world, the foreign language is an extra bulwark against too intimate a confrontation with the myth. When composers do write operas in English (like Benjamin Britten's *Billy Budd* or *Peter Grimes,* or Robert Weber's *The Crucible*), they choose entirely unmythological, realistic themes. (Personal communication from Erich Leinsdorf, 29 May 1985).

4. Rupagoswamin's *Bhaktirasamritasindhu* 2.27, cited by David Haberman in "Imitating the Masters: Problems in Incongruency," *Journal of the American Academy of Religion* 53, 1 (March, 1985): 41-50.

5. Alf Hiltebeitel, "Puranas and the Mahabharata: Their Relationship in Classical and Folk Genres," paper presented at the Conference on the Puranas, Madison, Wisconsin, 1-4 August 1985, p. 11.

6. Aristophanes, *The Frogs,* 1194. Aeschylus seems to pity Oedipus as much for taking to bed an *old* woman as for the fact that she happened to be his mother.

7. Euripides may be implying a contrast between the story of Stheneboia, which was not true but drove women to commit a real act of self-destruction, and the story of Phaedra, which was true and therefore either did not lead to such an act or would have been justified even if it did.

8. For evidence that Greek mothers and sons did in fact wrestle with this problem, see Philip Slater, *The Glory of Hera.*

9. Aristophanes, *The Frogs* 141, 149, 274.

10. Arshia Sattar tells me that N. T. Rama Rao, the chief minister of Andhra Pradesh, who founded the Telugu Desam party, used to play the leading role in mythological movies, the role of Krishna or Rama; since he has assumed office, he has taken to wearing orange robes. M. G. Ramachandran, the chief minister of Tamil Nadu, has been in films for over thirty years, playing many roles including gods; he is known to use dialogues from his films in his political speeches.

11. Sudhir Kakar, "The Ties that Bind: Family Relationships in the Mythology of the Hindi Cinema," *India International Quarterly* 8, 1 (March, 1980): 11-20.

12. Wendy Doniger O'Flaherty, "The Mythological in Disguise: An Analysis of Karz," *India International Quarterly* 8, 1 (March, 1980): 23-30.

13. R. K. Narayan, *Mr. Sampath* (London, 1949). In a similar way, the characters playing out the myths in *Ariadne auf Naxos* (by Richard Strauss and Hugo von Hofmannsthal) and *Kiss Me Kate* (by Cole Porter) took on those roles in the

outer frame of "real life" depicted in these works as the lives of the singers and actors.

14. I use these terms as Frits Staal defined them, in his "Über die Idee der Toleranz im Hinduismus," *Kairos: Zeitschrift für Religionswissenschaft und Theologie* (1959): 215-218, and "The Meaninglessness of Ritual," *Numen* 26, 1 (1979): 2-22.

15. Yet the myths of childhood are also hard to erase. Recall Plato's complaint, to this effect, in the *Timaeus* 26b.

16. I disagree with Frits Staal's argument in *Numen* that *no* ritual has meaning. There have been many telling and sophisticated rebuttals of this now infamous assertion, but on the most obvious level it seems to me that the actions of which most rituals are constructed—burning something, washing something, killing something, or having sexual intercourse with something—are intrinsically highly meaningful for all human beings.

17. This is a story that I have known for years, through an oral folk tradition. I have tried in vain to find textual support for it. The closest I have come is a series of similar, though less dramatic, instances reported in Cecil Roth's *A History of the Marranos* (Philadelphia, 1932): Jews persecuted in Portugal under the Inquisition celebrated the Day of Atonement two days later than they were supposed to, as they were watched so vigilantly on the proper day, and "this curious perversion was ultimately regarded as mandatory, its origin being forgotten" (p. 183). Similarly, there are in Spain many people of Jewish origin who do not know it: "The present writer has been informed of a Spanish country gentleman who kindles a lamp in his cellar every Friday night, without knowing the reason" (p. 398).

18. It might well be argued that some religions are more orthoprax than others. Thus it has been claimed that Jews and Hindus and Catholics are more orthoprax than Buddhists or Protestants. This is a sticky question that I would prefer to sidestep here; for one thing, there are many different sorts of Jews and Protestants and so forth, some more orthoprax than others; for another thing, these arguments too often degenerate into thinly veiled bigotries. My argument here is simply that most people, in all religions, are more orthoprax than orthodox. So too, it might be said that some cultures are better than others at retaining rituals without myths. Japan certainly does this well; the ritual in itself becomes an aesthetic. The Japanese woman who hit pilgrims with a book that she did not read was performing in this way a ritual whose myth (the text of the book) was actually physically present but lost to her. In America, by contrast, ritual does not generally survive so well without myth.

19. Gershom G. Scholem, *Major Trends in Jewish Mysticism* (New York, 1941), pp. 349-50, citing the story as he heard it from S. J. Agnon.

20. Elie Wiesel, *The Gates of the Forest*, trans. Frances Frenaye (New York, 1966).

21. Scholem, *Major Trends*, p. 350.

22. M. Gaster, "Sacrifice (Jewish)," in *Encyclopedia of Religion and Ethics*, ed. James Hastings, vol. 11 (Edinburgh, 1920), pp. 24-29.

23. Ibid., p. 26, citing *Ta'an* 12a, 27; *Meg.* 31a.

24. Brian K. Smith, *Reflections.*

25. See the analysis of the imaginary sacrifice in O'Flaherty, *Dreams*, chap. 4.

26. Michael Kunze, *Highroad to the Stake: A Tale of Witchcraft*, trans. William E. Yuill (Chicago, 1987), pp. 158 and 302.

27. Ibid., p. 302.

28. George Bernard Shaw, *Saint Joan* (Harmondsworth, 1966), p. 154.

29. Robert Bellah et al., *Habits of the Heart: Individualism and Commitment in American Life* (Berkeley, 1985), pp. 221 and 234. Sheila describes her religion as "just my own little voice."

30. And footnotes reveal many of the rituals and bonds of the academic community.

See Bruce Lincoln's article on the ritual aspect of footnotes: "Two Notes on Modern Rituals," *Journal of the American Academy of Religion* 45, 2 (1977): 147-60.

31. See Joseph Fontenrose, *The Ritual Theory of Myth* (Berkeley, 1960).

32. William Sax nicely translates *prasada* as "edible grace."

Chapter 7. Other Peoples' Lives:
The Rabbi from Cracow

1. These mythologies are the province of the unexamined "we" of the earlier chapters of this book. An excellent introduction to this pluralism is provided by Catherine Albanese's *America, Religions and Religion* (Belmont, Calif., 1981).

2. Sir Arthur Conan Doyle, "Silver Blaze," in *The Annotated Sherlock Holmes,* ed. William S. Baring-Gould 2 vols. (New York, 1967), vol. 1, p. 276. As Baring-Gould remarks, "This is perhaps the most famous example of what the late Monsignor Ronald Knox felicitously termed the *Sherlockismus.*"

3. Zimmer, *Myths and Symbols,* pp. 219-221, citing Martin Buber, *Die Chassidischen Bücher* (Hellerau, 1928), pp. 532-533. I must apologize for using Heinrich Zimmer's version of this story here, when I have cited it before. It is, like the Rabbi's treasure, a native treasure that I found abroad: I had to read a book about India, by Zimmer (a Lutheran), to find that parable from my own Jewish tradition. And it played the same role for Zimmer himself, as he notes on p. 219: "When I first read this tale, some ten years ago, I realized that I had been living and acting along its lines for over a decade—ever since that moment when the millenary, spiritual treasure of Hindu myth and symbol had begun to reveal itself to me through my academic studies of Indian sacred diagrams and Mandalas."

4. Woody Allen, "Hassidic Tales, with A Guide to Their Interpretation by the Noted Scholar," in *Getting Even* (New York, 1972), pp. 52-56. That this is an enduring myth in real life, as well as in satirical literature, was demonstrated to me by an article in the *New York Times* (Sunday, 8 September 1985), stating that the Jews of Cracow, reduced by the Nazi Holocaust to a tiny community of old people, had sent to America to have a young boy come to Cracow to mark his bar mitzvah, the first bar mitzvah there in twenty years. The return of this young Jewish boy, whose great-great-grandparents had been killed near Cracow, in Auschwitz, is yet another variant of the myth, built out of the pieces of real life: the native treasure of Cracow had to be imported back from America.

5. Herodotus, *History* 2.123.

6. Peter Brook, in an interview in the *Village Voice,* 1 December 1987, p. 130. As Mimi Kramer remarked (in the *New Yorker,* 27 July 1988, p. 82), "Owing partly to Tom Stoppard, . . . we have reached a point where nothing one could possibly think of doing to or with 'Hamlet' could reasonably hope to surprise us."

7. See Dorothy Eggan, "The Personal Use of Myth in Dreams," in *Myth: A Symposium,* ed. Thomas Sebeok (Bloomington, Ind., 1958), pp. 67-75.

8. See Cyril Stanley Smith, "Metallurgical Footnotes to the History of Art," in *A Search for Structure: Selected Essays on Science, Art, and History* (Cambridge, Mass., 1981), pp. 242-305, esp. pp. 280-292.

9. Idries Shah, *The Exploits of the Incomparable Mulla Nasrudin* (New York, 1972), p. 26.

10. Sophocles, *Oedipus Rex,* 980-982.

11. Velcheru Narayana Rao, "*Bhakti* in opposition to *karma,* in the Telugu *Basava-Purana,*" paper presented at the Conference on Karma under the auspices of the

Social Sciences Research Council-American Council of Learned Societies Joint Council on South Asia, Philadelphia, 1981. See O'Flaherty, *Dreams,* p. 121.

12. Urubshurow, "The Battle of Kurukshetra," p. 8.
13. As has been suggested by Madeleine Biardeau and developed by Alf Hiltebeitel at some length, in *The Ritual of Battle.*
14. V. Narayan Rao made this distinction, in private communication.
15. V. Narayana Rao, in a public presentation at the Conference on the Puranas, Madison, Wisconsin, 3 August 1985.
16. Homer, *Odyssey* 12.450 and 12.453. In the context, it may also mean to tell a story in a stylized manner, in contrast with telling it more naturally. But of course repetition is one of the stylistic tools of the mythmaker's art.
17. Homer, *Odyssey* 8.487.
18. First published in the *New Yorker,* and reprinted in *Side Effects* (New York, 1975), pp. 61-78.
19. Ibid., p. 72.
20. Woody Allen used the Kugelmass idea again in his film, *The Purple Rose of Cairo,* in which the hero of a stereotypical (if not classic) movie moves off the screen into the life of one of his fans, and takes her back into the frame of the movie with him. (See *Three Films of Woody Allen: Zelig, Broadway Danny Rose, The Purple Rose of Cairo,* New York, 1987). In Hugo von Hofmannsthal's libretto for Richard Strauss's opera, *Ariadne auf Naxos,* the Greek tragedy of Ariadne is played simultaneously with a Viennese comic opera; the heroine of the comedy moves from the frame of her genre into the tragic opera, where she teases the mythical heroine and finally incites her to change the plot of the classic myth. Here, as in many epics (as well as many modern surrealistic novels and plays), the outer frame folds in upon the inner frame, and the author or commentator is drawn into the plot.
21. "Enoch Soames," pp. 1-48 of Max Beerbohm's *Seven Men* (London, 1919). Beerbohm, in concluding his story, surmises that it could only have happened if the author of the book on late nineteenth century literature "will not have read the later passages of this memoir," and he hopes that "some time between 1992 and 1997" somebody will have read it.
22. See Bruce L. Sullivan, "The Rishi of the Fifth Veda: Vyasa in the Mahabharata" (Ph.D. Diss., University of Chicago, 1984).
23. See O'Flaherty, "Horses and snakes." See also Hiltebeitel, *The Ritual of Battle.*
24. Indeed, reflexivity is characteristic of the two epics in relation to one another as well as to the culture as a whole. As A. K. Ramanujan has pointed out,

> Stories about stories, frame stories and nested ones, as well as various self-referential devices like plays within plays abound in Indian classical and folk-literature. . . . Whole epics tend to be repeated, remembered, reworked, renewed, not just translated but transmuted utterly, in the many languages of India. . . . The Hindu tradition is well aware of the complementarity of these two texts [the two great Sanskrit epics] . . . A clever and somewhat silly long poem was once composed in which the same words could be read two ways, to yield either the *Ramayana* or the *Mahabharata.*

See Ramanujan, "Where Mirrors are Windows: Towards an Anthology of Reflections" (paper presented at the Conference on the Direction and Limits of Reflexivity in the Axial Age Civilizations, Bad Homburg, July 1985), to be published in a forthcoming issue of *History of Religions.*
25. *Ramayana* 1.3.39.
26. *Ramayana* 1.4.36.

27. David Shulman, "Toward a Historical Poetics of the Sanskrit Epics" (unpublished MS., 1985), pp. 10-13.
28. *Adhyatma-Ramayana* (Calcutta, 1884), 2.4.77-78.
29. See O'Flaherty, *Dreams*.
30. *Yogavasishtha* 4.25-34; cited in O'Flaherty, *Dreams*, pp. 290-291.
31. Stuart Blackburn, "Epic Transmission and Adaptation: A Folk Ramayana in South India," in *The Heroic Process: Form, Function, and Fantasy in Folk Epic*, ed. Bo Almqvist (Dublin, 1987), p. 579.
32. David Grene, *The Actor in History: Studies in Shakespearean Stage Poetry* (University Park, Pa., 1988).
33. Ibid.
34. Walter Pater, *Appreciations* (London, 1957), p. 205.
35. Girard, *Violence and the Sacred*, p. 304.
36. Nikos Kazantzakis, *The Greek Passion*, trans. Jonathan Griffin (New York, 1954).
37. See the story of Noemon in the *Odyssey*, analyzed in O'Flaherty, "Inside and Outside the Mouth of God."
38. Geertz, *The Interpretation of Culture*, p. 90.
39. Girard, *Violence and the Sacred*, pp. 317-318.
40. The story of Dennis Puleston's life, including this incident, is told in his Festschrift, *Maya Subsistence: Studies in Memory of Dennis Puleston*, ed. Kent V. Flannery (New York, 1982).
41. Joanne Punzo Waghorne, *Images of Dharma: The Epic World of C. Rajagopalachari* (New Delhi, 1985).
42. A. K. Ramanujan cited this story in his presentation at the Smithsonian Institution panel "The Canvas of Culture" (Washington, D. C., 22 June 1985).
43. Mary Douglas, *Purity and Danger: An Analysis of Concepts of Pollution and Taboo* (London, 1966).
44. In Robertson Davies' *Rebel Angels* (Harmondsworth, 1983), a professor of religion who also happens to be a minister falls in love with a woman whom he recognizes as Sophia; and he says, "I suppose that if a man makes legend and forgotten belief his special and devout study he should not be surprised when legend invades his life and possesses his mind. . . . The Persians believed that when a man dies he meets his soul in the form of a beautiful woman who is also infinitely old and wise, and this was what seemed to have happened to me, living though I undoubtedly was. It is a terrible thing for an intellectual when he encounters an idea as a reality, and that was what I had done" (p. 236).
45. See O'Flaherty, *Dreams*, pp. 121-122, 252-253, 277.
46. *Mahabharata* 1.98. See Wendy Doniger O'Flaherty, "Integrated Goddesses and Split Women in Myth and Reality" (Arizona State University Lecture in Religion, April, 1986); and "Sexual Doubles and Sexual Masquerades: The Structure of Sex Symbols," *The Annual of Psychoanalysis* 17 (1988).
47. See O'Flaherty, *Women*, pp. 114-155; G. M. Carstairs, *The Twice-Born* (London, 1958), pp. 156-167.
48. C. G. Jung, *Answer to Job*, trans. R. F. C. Hull (London, 1954), p. 75.
49. Edmund Wilson, *Memoirs of Hecate County* (New York, 1942), p. 96.
50. Charles H. Long, "The Dreams of Professor Campbell: Joseph Campbell's *The Mythic Image*," *Religious Studies Review* 6,4 (October, 1980): 261-271.
51. The remarks of other scientists present on that occasion, such as General Farrell, also tended to employ mythical and theological eschatological language, but from the Western traditions.
52. Cited in Robert Jungk, *Brighter than a Thousand Suns: The Moral and Political History of the Atomic Scientists*, trans. James Cleugh (New York, 1958), p. 202.
53. Presented at the Brooklyn Academy of Music during October, November and December 1987. Mimi Kramer wrote in the *New Yorker* (2 November 1987): "Peter Brook [is] not really interested in the conflict between the Pandavas and

the Kauravas at all; he's interested in the threat of nuclear war. The warring factions in his 'Mahabharata' are *almost explicitly* likened to two rival super-powers" (p. 147). I have added the emphasis; "almost explicitly" reflects the implicit power of the myth to force us to draw personal analogies.

54. Eliade, *Myth and Reality*, p. 19.
55. Ibid., p. 111.
56. A. K. Ramanujan used this phenomenon in his poem "Prayers to Lord Murughan," in *Relations* (Oxford, 1971):

> Master of red bloodstains,
> our blood is brown;
> our collars white.
> Other lives and sixty-
> four rumoured arts
> tingle,
> pins and needles
> at amputees' fingertips
> in phantom muscle.

57. Perhaps the last word on this subject was said by Woody Allen, in a tough-guy detective story ("Mr. Big") in which the Mickey Spillane figure is hired by a beautiful blonde to find God, who is missing. He receives a call from Homicide: "Somebody with that description just showed up at the morgue. . . . He was dead when they brought Him in. . . . It's the work of an existentialist." In *Getting Even* (New York, 1974), pp. 102-111.
58. Friedrich Nietzsche, *Die fröhliche Wissenschaft, Sämtliche Werke*, vol. 3 (Berlin/New York, 1974), Aphorism 343; translated, with commentary, by Walter Kaufmann as *The Gay Science* (New York, 1974).
59. Ludwig Wittgenstein, *Last Writings on the Philosophy of Psychology*, vol. 1, ed. G. H. von Wright and Heikki Nyman, German text with English translation by C. G. Luckhardt and Maximilian A. E. Aue (Chicago, 1982), paragraph 854, p. 110.
60. Nietzsche, *Die fröhliche Wissenschaft*, p. 467, opening of book 3, paragraph 108.
61. *Si-Yu-Ki. Buddhist Records of the Western World. Translated from the Chinese of Hiuen Tsiang (A.D. 629)*, trans. Samuel Beal (London, 1884), vol. 1, pp. 93-94.
62. For some, of course, the un-demythologized, the gods still live. The gods are always dying, and some people think that they see gods that others simply fail to see. The Nietzschean argument assumes that the death of God under the attack of science and the Enlightenment was a special death from which no recovery is even theoretically possible—a death that revealed that he never existed.
63. See George Steiner, "Conversations with Lévi-Strauss," *Encounter 27*, 10 (April, 1966): 38.
64. Lévi-Strauss, *The Jealous Potter*, p. 171; italics are in the original version.
65. Ursula K. LeGuin, *The Language of the Night: Essays on Fantasy and Science Fiction* (New York, 1979), p. 79.
66. Lévi-Strauss, *The Raw and the Cooked*, p. 11.
67. Some people in the nineteenth century did, I believe, translate some of the Grimms' fairy tales into proto-Indo-European, in a pious scholarly exercise inspired, perhaps, by the belief that such stories were originally told in proto-Indo-European.
68. See O'Flaherty, *Dreams*, chapter 2.
69. Nandar Fodor, "Telepathy in Analysis," in *Psychoanalysis and the Occult*, ed. Georges Devereux (New York, 1970), p. 295, first citing J. N. Rosen. The article was first published in *The Psychiatric Quarterly* 21 (1947): 171-189.

70. Lévi-Strauss, *Structural Anthropology,* p. 229; *The Savage Mind* (London, 1966), p. 22.
71. Cf. the many stories of kings who are enlightened but return to their kingship, as cited in chapter 4 of O'Flaherty, *Dreams.* A student of mine, in an essay on her response to the *Yogavasishtha,* wrote about the theme of the person (here, Rama) who experiences a vision of otherness and enlightenment and then returns to his original life, transformed but able to go on living that same life in a new way:

> We the Western readers will most likely not be enlightened after reading this text, at least not in the sense that Rama is. . . . Our culture distances us from the text even further than its Indian audience, which finds these concepts difficult enough to handle. We must then speculate as to the degree and nature of this text's effect on the Western audience, which generally considers these ideas only in humorous contexts or at the most as mildly amusing distractions, lest they cause us too much distress.
>
>   As a Western reader exposed to such ideas for the first time, I submit that the serious *Yogavasishtha* reader's experience is parallel, without being the same, to Rama's experience. . . . When we emerge out of it, we have stretched out of our own frame of reality for a while and looked through another one. After we stop actively wrestling with the problems this frame presents, . . . we go back and live our same lives, just as Rama goes back to his princely duties. . . . Our minds have had to move over and allow for another possible reality, which exists no less certainly than our own. If this kind of perspective is gained from the *Yogavasishtha,* then we have gained what Rama gained—an outlook that gives us some degree of separation from the trivial concerns in our lives.
>
> (Margaret Vimont, "The *Yogavasishtha* and the Western Reader," essay, 13 March 1986.)

72. See O'Flaherty, *Women,* pp. 274–275.
73. Rainer Maria Rilke, "Archaïscher Torso Apollos," in *Neue Gedichte: Anderer Teil* (Leipzig, 1908). Ursula K. LeGuin applies these words of Rilke to the function of myth in *The Language of the Night,* pp. 77–78.

Bibliography

Primary Sources

INDIC LANGUAGES

Adhyatma-Ramayana. Calcutta, 1884.
Aitareya Brahmana. Calcutta, 1896.
The Apadana of the Khuddaka Nikaya. Edited by Mary E. Lilley. London, 1925.
Apastamba Dharmasutra. Bombay, 1892.
Atharva Veda. With Sayana's commentary. Bombay, 1895.
Bhagavadajjuka-Prahasanam of Bodhayana. Prayaga, 1979.
Bhagavata Purana. Bombay, 1832.
Bhojaprabandha of Bhallala. Lucknow, 1977.
Brahmavaivarta Purana. Poona, 1935.
Brihadaranyaka Upanishad. In *One Hundred and Eight Upanishads.* Bombay, 1913.
Dhvanyaloka of Anandavardhana. With the *Dhvanyalokalocana* of Abhinavagupta.
    Edited by D. and K. Pandurang Parab. Bombay, 1891.
Digha Nikaya. London, 1890-91.
Gopatha Brahmana. Leiden, 1919.
Jaiminiya Brahmana. Nagpur, 1954.
Jataka, with Commentary. 7 vols. Edited by Viggo Fausboll. London, 1877. *Jataka
    Stories.* Translated by E. B. Cowell. Cambridge, 1895-1913.
Kathaka Samhita. 3 vols. Leipzig, 1900.
Linga Purana. Calcutta, 1812.
Mahabharata. Poona, 1933-60.
Maitrayani Samhita. Wiesbaden, 1970.
Manu Smriti, with Nine Commentaries. Edited by Jayantakrishna Harikrishna Dave.
    Bombay, 1975.
Matysa Purana. Poona, 1907.
Panchavimsha Brahmana (Tandya Mahabrahmana). Calcutta, 1869-74.
Prabhavakacarita of Prabhacandra. Edited by Jinvijaya Muni. Singhi Jain Series 13.
    Sholapur, 1940.
Ramacaritamanasa of Tulsi Das. Translated from the Hindi by W. D. P. Hill, under the
    title *The Holy Lake of the Acts of Rama.* London, 1952.
Ramayana. Baroda, 1960-1975.
Rig Veda. London, 1890-1892.
Shatapatha Brahmana. Benares, 1964.
Shiva Purana. Benares, 1964.
Taittiriya Brahmana. Calcutta, 1859.
Taittiriya Samhita. Calcutta, 1960.

Vajasaneyi Samhita. Berlin, 1952.
Vamana Purana. Varanasi, 1968.
Varaha Purana. Calcutta, 1893.
Vayu Purana. Bombay, 1897.
Vishnu Purana. Calcutta, 1972.
Yogavasishtha-Maha-Ramayana of Valmiki. Edited by W. L. S. Pansikar. 2 vols. Bombay, 1918.

GREEK AND LATIN

(All texts, unless otherwise noted, are those in the Loeb Library series.)
Aristophanes. *The Frogs.*
Aristotle. *Nicomachean Ethics.*
Euripides. *Bacchae.* Edited by E. R. Dodds. Oxford, 1960.
Herodotus. *History.*
Homer. *Iliad* and *Odyssey.*
Nonnus. *Dionysiaca.*
Ovid. *Metamorphoses.*
Plato. *Apology, Gorgias, Laws, Phaedo, Phaedrus, Philebus, Republic, Statesman, Symposium, Timaeus.*
Plutarch. *The Parallel Lives.*
Sophocles. *Oedipus Rex.*
Xenophanes. *Die Fragmente.* Edited by Ernst Heitsch. Munich, 1983.
Hebrew Bible. Cited in the King James Translation.
New Testament. Cited in the King James Translation.

Secondary Sources

Albanese, Catherine. *America, Religions and Religion.* Belmont, Calif., 1981.
Allen, Woody. "Fabulous Tales and Mythical Beasts" and "A Guide to Some of the Lesser Ballets." In *Without Feathers.* New York, 1976.
———. "Hassidic Tales, with a Guide to Their Interpretation by the Noted Scholar" and "Mr. Big." In *Getting Even.* New York, 1972.
———. "The Kugelmass Episode." In *Side Effects.* New York, 1975.
———. *Three Films of Woody Allen: Zelig, Broadway Danny Rose.* New York, 1987.
Applebee, Arthur N. *The Child's Concept of Story.* Chicago, 1978.
Auden, W. H. "In Memory of W. B. Yeats." First published in *Another Time.* London, 1940. Reprinted in *Collected Shorter Poems 1927–1957.* London, 1966. Reprinted in *Selected Poems, New Edition.* Edited by Edward Mendelson. New York, 1979.
Augustine. *Confessions.* Translated by R. S. Pine-Coffin. Harmondsworth, 1961.
Barnard, Mary. *The Myth-Makers.* Athens, Ohio, 1966.
Beal, Samuel, trans. *Si-Yu-Ki. Buddhist Records of the Western World. Translated from the Chinese of Hiuen Tsiang (A.D. 629).* 2 vols. London, 1884.
Bellah, Robert, et al. *Habits of the Heart: Individualism and Commitment in American Life.* Berkeley, 1985.
Beerbohm, Max. "Enoch Soames." In *Seven Men,* pp. 1–48. London, 1919.
Benchley, Robert. "Opera Synopses." In *The Benchley Roundup,* pp. 51–56. Chicago, 1983.
Berger, Peter. *Invitation to Sociology.* Garden City, 1963.
Black, Max. *Caveats and Critiques.* Ithaca 1975.
Blackburn, Stuart. "Epic Transmission and Adaptation: A Folk Ramayana in South India." In *The Heroic Process: Form, Function, and Fantasy in Folk Epic,* edited by Bo Almqvist, pp. 569–590. Dublin, 1987.
Bloom, Allan *The Closing of the American Mind: How Higher Education Has Failed Democracy and Impoverished the Souls of Today's Students.* New York, 1987.

Bloomfield, Maurice. "On the Art of Entering Another's Body: A Hindu Fiction Motif." *Proceedings of the American Philosophical Society* 41 (1917): 1-43.

Bonnefoy, Yves. *Dictionnaire des mythologies et des religions des sociétés traditionnelles et du monde antique.* 2 vols. Paris, 1981. English edition, ed. Wendy Doniger O'Flaherty. Chicago, forthcoming.

Bradbury, Ray, *Fahrenheit 451.* New York, 1953.

Buber, Martin. *Die Chassidischen Bucher.* Hellerau, 1928.

———. *Tales of the Hasidim. The Early Masters.* New York, 1947.

Bultmann, Rudolf. "New Testament and Mythology." In *The Gospel of John, A Commentary.* New York, 1941.

Burkhalter-Fluechtiger, Joyce. "Literacy and the Changing Concept of Text: Women's Ramayana *Mandali* in Central India." Paper delivered at the Association of Asian Studies, 22 March 1986. To be published in *The Boundary of the Text: Performing the Epics in South and Southeast Asia.* Edited by Joyce Burkhalter-Fluechtiger and Laurie Sears. Ann Arbor, 1988.

Burkert, Walter. "Orphism and Bacchic Mysteries: New Evidence and Old Problems of Interpretation." *Protocol of the 28th Colloquy of the Center for Hermeneutical Studies.* Berkeley, 1977.

———. *Homo Necans.* Berlin and New York, 1972.

Burridge, Kenelm. *Mambu: A Study of Melanesian Cargo Movements and Their Social and Ideological Background.* New York, 1970.

Calinescu, Matei. *Faces of Modernity: Avant-Garde, Decadence, Kitsch.* Bloomington, Ind., 1977.

———. *Five Faces of Modernity: Modernism, Avant-Garde, Decadence, Kitsch, Post-Modernism.* Durham, N.C., 1987.

———. "Modernity and Popular Culture: Kitsch as Aesthetic Deception." In *Sensus Communis: Contemporary Trends in Comparative Literature,* edited by Janos Riesz et al., pp. 221-226. Tübingen, 1986.

Carrasco, David. *Quetzalcoatl and the Irony of Empire: Myths and Prophecies in the Aztec Tradition.* Chicago, 1982.

———. "Transformations at the Heart of Myth: Dawning, Order, Apocalypse." *The World and I* (July, 1987): 594-610.

Carstairs, G. M. *The Twice-Born.* London, 1958.

Charachidze, Georges. "Caucase du Nord: Dieux et mythes des Abkhazes, des Tcherkesses et des Ouzbykhs." In *Dictionnaire des mythologies,* edited by Yves Bonnefoy, vol. 2, pp. 129-132. Paris, 1981.

Coburn, Thomas B. " 'Scripture' in India: Towards a Typology of the Word in Hindu Life." *Journal of the American Academy of Religion* 42, 3 (September, 1984): 435-460.

Collingwood, R.G. *The Idea of History.* Oxford, 1946.

Cooper, Martha, and Chalfont, Henry. *Subway Art.* New York, 1984.

Courtright, Paul B. *Ganesha: Lord of Obstacles, Lord of Beginnings.* New York, 1985.

Davies, Robertson. *Rebel Angels.* Harmondsworth, 1983.

Davis, Winston. *Dojo: Magic and Exorcism in Modern Japan.* Stanford, Calif., 1980.

Deleuze, Gilles and Guattari, Felix. *Anti-Oedipus: Capitalism and Schizophrenia.* Translated by Robert Hurley. New York, 1977.

Detienne, Marcel. *The Creation of Mythology.* Chicago, 1986.

———. "Dionysos." In *Dictionnaire,* edited by Yves Bonnefoy, vol. 1, pp. 300-307.

———. *Dionysos Slain.* Baltimore, 1979.

———. *The Gardens of Adonis.* Translated by Janet Lloyd. Atlantic Highlands, N. J., 1977.

Dodds, E. R. *The Greeks and the Irrational.* Berkeley, 1964.

———. "Maenadism in the *Bacchae.*" *Harvard Theological Review* 33 (1940): 155 ff.

———. ed., *Bacchae.* Oxford, 1960.

Duerr, Hans-Peter. *Dreamtime: Concerning the Boundary between Wilderness and Civilization.* Translated by Felicitas Goodman. New York, 1985.

Douglas, Mary. "The Meaning of Myth, with Special Reference to 'La Geste d'Asdiwal.' " In *The Structural Study of Myth and Totemism,* edited by Edmund Leach, pp. 49-70. London, 1967.

———. *Purity and Danger: An Analysis of Concepts of Pollution and Taboo.* London, 1966.

Downie, R. Angus. *Frazer and the Golden Bough.* London, 1970.

Doyle, Sir Arthur Conan. "Silver Blaze." In *The Annotated Sherlock Holmes,* edited by William S. Baring-Gould, vol. 1, pp. 261-281. New York, 1967.

Eggan, Dorothy. "The Personal Use of Myth in Dreams." In *Myth: A Symposium,* edited by Thomas Sebeok, pp. 67-75. Bloomington, Ind., 1958.

Eggeling, Julius, trans. and ed. *Shatapatha Brahmana.* Oxford, 1882-1900.

Eliade, Mircea. *Myth and Reality.* London, 1964.

———. *Patterns of Comparative Religion.* New York, 1958.

———. *The Quest: History and Meaning in Religion.* Chicago, 1969.

Elmore, Theodore W. *Dravidian Gods in Modern Hinduism.* Lincoln, Neb., 1915.

Evans-Pritchard, E. E. *Nuer Religion.* Oxford, 1956.

———. "Some Reminiscences and Reflections on Fieldwork." *Journal of the Anthropological Society of Oxford* 4 (1973): 1-14.

———. *Theories of Primitive Religion.* Oxford, 1965.

Faherty, R. L. "Rites and Ceremonies." In *Encyclopaedia Britannica,* 15th ed., Chicago, 1985.

Fairservis, Walter. *The Roots of Ancient India: The Archeology of Early Indian Civilization.* London, 1971.

Faure, Bernard. "Intertextuality, Relics, and Dreams: The Avatar of a Tradition." Paper presented at the University of Chicago, 24 March 1986.

Flannery, Kent V., ed. *Maya Subsistence: Studies in Memory of Dennis Puleston.* New York, 1982.

Fodor, Nandar. "Telepathy in Analysis." *The Psychiatric Quarterly* 21 (1947): 171-189). Reprinted in *Psychoanalysis and the Occult,* edited by Georges Devereux, pp. 283-296. New York, 1970.

Fontenrose, Joseph. *The Ritual Theory of Myth.* Berkeley, 1960.

Forster, E. M. *A Passage to India.* Abinger edition, edited by Oliver Stallybrass. New York, 1978.

Foucault, Michel. "What is an author?" In *Textual Strategies,* edited by Josue Harari, pp. 141-160. Ithaca, N.Y., 1977.

Frazer, Sir James George. *The Golden Bough: A Study in Magic and Religion.* 8 parts; 3d ed. London, 1963.

Freud, Sigmund. *Totem and Taboo.* Standard edition, translated by James Strachey. New York, 1950.

Frost, Robert. *The Complete Poems of Robert Frost.* New York, 1949.

Frye, Northrop. *The Secular Scripture: A Study of the Structure of Romance.* Cambridge, Mass., 1976.

Gaster, M. "Sacrifice (Jewish)." In *Encyclopedia of Religion and Ethics,* edited by James Hastings, vol. 11. Edinburgh, 1920.

Geertz, Clifford. " 'From the Native's Point of View': On the Nature of Anthropological Understanding." In *Local Knowledge,* pp. 55-70. New York, 1983.

———. *Negara, The Theatre State in Nineteenth Century Bali.* Princeton, N.J., 1980.

———. "Thick Description: Toward an Interpretive Theory of Culture." In *The Interpretation of Cultures,* pp. 3-32. New York, 1973.

Giles, Herbert A., trans. *Chuang Tzu: Mystic, Moralist, and Social Reformer.* London, 1926.

Gill, Sam. *Mother Earth: An American Story.* Chicago, 1987.

Girard, René. *Violence and the Sacred.* Translated by Patrick Gregory. Baltimore and London, 1977.

Gold, Daniel. *Comprehending the Guru: Toward a Grammar of Religious Perception.* Atlanta, 1988.

Goldman, Robert P. "Karma, Guilt, and Buried Memories: Public Fantasy and Private Reality in Traditional India." *Journal of the American Oriental Society* 105, 3 (1985): 413-25.

Gombrich, E. H. *Art and Illusion.* 2d ed. New York, 1961.

Goody, Jack. *The Domestication of the Savage Mind.* New York, 1976.

Graham, William A. *Beyond the Written Word: Oral Aspects of Scripture in the History of Religion.* Cambridge, 1987.

Grene, David. *The Actor in History: Studies in Shakespearean Stage Poetry.* University Park, Pa., 1988.

———. *The History: Herodotus.* Chicago, 1987.

———. "The *Odyssey:* An Approach." *Midway* (University of Chicago, Spring 1969): 47-68.

Gupta, Mahendra. *The Gospel of Sri Ramakrishna.* Translated by Swami Nikhilananda. Mylapore, 1980.

Guthrie, W. K. C. *The Greeks and their Gods.* Boston, 1955.

Haberman, David. "Imitating the Masters: Problems in Incongruency." *Journal of the American Academy of Religion* 53, 1 (March, 1985): 41-50.

Hearne, Vicki. *Adam's Task: Calling Animals by Name.* New York, 1986.

Heisenberg, Werner. *Physics and Beyond: Encounters and Conversations.* New York, 1971.

Hiltebeitel, Alf. "Puranas and the Mahabharata: Their Relationship in Classical and Folk Genres." Paper presented at the Conference on the Puranas, Madison, Wisconsin, 1-4 August 1985.

———. *The Ritual of Battle.* Ithaca, N.Y., 1976.

Hollis, Christopher. *A Study of George Orwell: The Man and his Works.* London, 1956.

Hollis, Martin, and Steven Lukes, eds. *Rationality and Relativism.* Oxford, 1982.

Huntington, Richard. "Bara Endogamy and Incest Prohibition." *Dijdragen Tot de Taal-, Land-, en Volkenkunde* 134 (1978): 30-62.

Inglis, Stephen. "The Craft of the Velar." *National Council for Education in the Ceramic Arts Journal* 7, 7, pp. 14-19.

Jaini, Padmanabh. "Jaina Puranas: A Puranic Counter Tradition." Paper presented at the Conference on the Puranas, Madison, Wisconsin, 1-4 August 1985.

Johnson, Edgar. *Charles Dickens: His Tragedy and Truth.* Boston, 1952.

Jung, C. G. *Answer to Job.* Translated by R. F. C. Hull. London, 1954.

———. "Psychological Commentary on *The Tibetan Book of the Dead.*" In *Psychology and the East,* trans. R. F. C. Hull. Princeton, N.J., 1978.

Jungk, Robert. *Brighter than a Thousand Suns: The Moral and Political History of the Atomic Scientists.* Translated by James Cleugh. London, 1958.

Kakar, Sudhir. "The Ties that Bind: Family Relationships in the Mythology of the Hindi Cinema." *India International Quarterly* 8:1 (March, 1980): 11-20.

Kazantzakis, Nikos. *The Greek Passion.* Translated by Jonathan Griffin. New York, 1954.

Keeler, Ward. "Father Puppeteer." Ph.D. diss., University of Chicago, 1982.

———. *Javanese Shadow Plays, Javanese Selves.* Princeton, N.J., 1987.

Kipling, Rudyard. *The Jungle Books.* London, 1894 and 1895.

———. *Just So Stories for Little Children.* London, 1902.

———. "The Maltese Cat." In *The Day's Work.* London, 1898.

———. "Proofs of Holy Writ." *The Strand Magazine,* April 1934. Reprinted in *Rudyard Kipling: Stories and Poems,* edited by Roger Lancelyn Green. London, 1970.

Kirfel, Willibald. "Der Aśvamedha und der Puruṣamedha." In *Festschrift für Walther Schubring,* pp. 39-50. Hamburg, 1951.

Knipe, David. "Sapiṇḍikaraṇa: The Hindu Rite of Entry into Heaven." In *Religious Encounters with Death, Insights from the History and Anthropology of Religions,* edited by Frank Reynolds and Earle H. Waugh (University Park, Pa., 1977).

Kuhn, Thomas. *The Structure of Scientific Revolutions*. 2d ed. Chicago, 1970.
Kunze, Michael. *Highroad to the Stake: A Tale of Witchcraft*. Translated by William E. Yuill. Chicago, 1987.
Laney, James T. "The Education of the Heart." *Harvard Magazine* 88, 1 (1985).
Leach, Edmund. "Anthropological Aspects of Language: Animal Categories and Verbal Abuse." In *New Directions in the Study of Language*, edited by Eric H. Lenneberg, pp. 23-63. Cambridge, Mass., 1964.
————. *Lévi-Strauss*. London, 1970.
Le Guin, Ursula K. *The Language of the Night: Essays on Fantasy and Science Fiction*. New York, 1979.
Lévi, Sylvain. *La doctrine du sacrifice dans les Brahmanas*. Paris, 1966.
Lévi-Strauss, Claude. *The Jealous Potter*. Translated by Bénédicte Chorier. Chicago, 1988.
————. *The Raw and the Cooked*. Volume 2 of *Introduction to a Science of Mythology*. Translated by John and Doreen Weightman. New York, 1969.
————. *The Savage Mind*. London, 1966.
————. *Structural Anthropology*. New York, 1963.
————. "The Structural Study of Myth." In *Myth: A Symposium*, edited by Thomas Sebeok, pp. 50-66. Bloomington, Ind., 1958.
————. *Totemism*. Translated by Rodney Needham. Boston, 1963.
————. *Tristes Tropiques*. Translated by John and Doreen Weightman. New York, 1974.
Lévy-Bruhl, Lucien. *The Soul of the Primitive*. London, 1928.
Lewis, C. S. *The Horse and his Boy*. London, 1954.
————. *The Lion, The Witch, and The Wardrobe*. London, 1950.
Lincoln, Bruce. *Myth, Cosmos, and Society: Indo-European Themes of Creation and Destruction*. Cambridge, Mass., 1986.
————. "Two Notes on Modern Rituals." *Journal of the American Academy of Religion* 45, 2 (1977): 147-160.
Long, Charles H. "The Dreams of Professor Campbell: Joseph Campbell's *The Mythic Image*." *Religious Studies Review* 6, 4 (October, 1980): 261-271.
————. *Significations: Signs, Symbols and Images in the Interpretation of Religion*. Philadelphia, 1986.
Lutgendorf, Philip. "The Life of a Text: Tulsidas's *Ramacaritamanasa* in Performance." Ph.D. diss., University of Chicago, 1986.
MacDonald, Mary. "Exchange and Change in Mararoko: A Study in Melanesian Religion." Ph.D. Dissertation, University of Chicago, 1988.
Malamoud, Charles. "Village et forêt dans l'idéologie de l'Inde brahmanique." *Archives Européennes de Sociologie* 17 (1976): 3-20.
Malcolm, Janet. *In the Freud Archives*. New York, 1984.
Malinowski, Bronislaw. *A Diary in the Strict Sense of the Term*. Translated by Norbert Guterman. London, 1967.
Marx, Karl. *The Eighteenth Brumaire of Louis Bonaparte*. Hamburg, 1869; New York, 1963.
Masson, J. L., and M. V. Patwardhan. *Aesthetic Rapture: The Rasadhyaya of the Natyashastra*. Poona, 1970.
Masson, J. Moussaieff. "Fratricide among the Monkeys: Psychoanalytic Observations on an Episode in the Valmikiramayana." *Journal of the American Oriental Society* 95 (1975): 672-678.
————. "Hanuman as an Imaginary Companion." *Journal of the American Oriental Society* 101 (1981): 355-360.
Maxym, Lucy. *Russian Lacquer, Legends, and Fairy Tales*. Manhasset, N. Y., 1981.
Meyer, Leonard B. "Creation, Archetypes, and Style Change." *Daedalus* (Spring 1988); 177-205.
Mitra, Rajendralal. "On Human Sacrifices in Ancient India." *Journal of the Asiatic Society of Bengal* (1876).

Myerhoff, Barbara. *Peyote Hunt: The Sacred Journey of the Huichol Indians.* Ithaca, N.Y., 1974.

Nagel, Ernst. *Logic Without Metaphysics.* Glencoe, Ill., 1956.

Nagel, Thomas. "What is it like to be a bat?" *Philosophical Review* (1974).

Narayan, R. K. *Mr. Sampath.* London, 1949.

Narayana, Rao, Velcheru. "*Bhakti* in opposition to *karma,* in the Telugu *Basava-Purana.*" Paper presented at the Conference on Karma sponsored by the Social Sciences Research Council-American Council of Learned Societies Joint Council on South Asia, Philadelphia, 1981.

Nietzsche, Friedrich. *Also Sprach Zarathustra.* Vol. 4 of the *Sämtliche Werke.* Berlin/New York, 1967-77. Translated by Walter Kaufmann as *Thus Spoke Zarathustra,* in *The Portable Nietzsche.* Harmondsworth, 1976.

———. *Ecce Homo.* Translated by Walter Kaufmann in "*On the Genealogy of Morals*" and "*Ecce Homo.*" New York, 1969.

———. *Die fröhliche Wissenschaft.* Vol. 3 of the *Sämtliche Werke.* Translated by Walter Kaufmann as *The Gay Science.* New York, 1974.

———. *Götzen-Dämmerung, oder Wie man mit dem Hammer philosophiert.* Vol. 3 of the *Sämtliche Werke.*

———. *Der Wille zur Macht.* Translated by Walter Kaufmann and R. J. Hollingdale as *The Will to Power.* New York, 1968.

O'Flaherty, Wendy Doniger. "The Aims of Education." University of Chicago *Record* 20, 1 (10 April 1986): 43-50.

———. "The Case for the History of Religions." *Daedalus* (Spring, 1988): 181-186.

———. "The Case of the Stallion's Wife: Indra and Vṛṣanaśva in the Ṛg Veda and the Brāhmaṇas." *Journal of the American Oriental Society* 105, 3 (1985): 485-498.

———. "Dionysos and Śiva: Parallel Patterns in Two Pairs of Myths." *History of Religions* 20, 1 (August 1980): 81-111.

———. "Do Witches Fly?" (Review of Hans Peter Duerr's *Dreamtime.*) *New York Times Book Review,* 8 September 1985, pp. 10-12.

———. *Dreams, Illusion, and Other Realities.* Chicago, 1984.

———. "The Good and Evil Shepherd." In *Gilgul: Essays on Transformation, Revolution, and Permanence in the History of Religions, Dedicated to Zwi Werblowsky,* edited by S. Shaked, D. Shulman, and G. G. Stroumsa, pp. 169-191. Leiden, 1987.

———. "The Good Shepherd/Tiger, or, Can one have an eclectic religion?" *Criterion* 24, 1 (Winter, 1985): 23-25.

———. *Hindu Myths.* Harmondsworth, 1975.

———. "Horses and snakes in the Ādi Parvan of the *Mahābhārata.*" In *Aspects of India: Essays in Honor of Edward Cameron Dimock,* edited by Margaret Case and N. Gerald Barrier, pp. 16-44. New Delhi, 1986.

———. "The image of the Heretic in the Gupta Purāṇas." In *Essays on Gupta Culture,* edited by Bardwell L. Smith, pp. 107-128. New Delhi, 1983.

———. "Inside and Outside the Mouth of God: The Boundary between Myth and Reality." *Daedalus* (Spring, 1980): 93-126.

———. "Integrated Goddesses and Split Women in Myth and Reality." Arizona State University Lecture in Religion, April 1986.

———. "The Last Lecture: Memory, Death, and Experience." *Religion and Intellectual Life.* The Journal of Associates for Religion and Intellectual Life, 4, 1 (Fall 1986): 60-70.

———. "The Mythological in Disguise: an Analysis of 'Karz.'" *India International Quarterly* 8, 1 (March, 1980): 23-30.

———. "On Translating Sanskrit Myths." In *The Translator's Art: Essays in Honor of Betty Radice,* edited by William Radice, pp. 121-128. Harmondsworth, 1987.

———. *The Origins of Evil in Hindu Mythology.* Berkeley, 1976.

———. "The Origins of Heresy in Hindu Mythology." *History of Religions* 10, 4 (May, 1971): 271-233.

————. "Origins of Myth-making Man." (Review of Joseph Campbell's *Historical Atlas of World Mythology.*) *New York Times Book Review,* 18 December 1983.
————. "The Post-Vedic History of the Soma Plant." In *Soma: Divine Mushroom of Immortality,* by R. Gordon Wasson and Wendy Doniger O'Flaherty, pp. 95-147. New York, 1968.
————. Review of J. A. B. van Buitenen's translation of the *Mahabharata. Times Literary Supplement,* 15 November 1974, p. 1280; and *Religious Studies Review* 4, 1 (January 1978): 19-28.
————. *The Rig Veda: An Anthology.* Harmondsworth, 1981.
————. "The Role of Myth in the Indian Life Cycle." In *Aditi: The Living Arts of India,* pp. 185-201. Washington, D. C., 1985.
————. "Sexual Doubles and Sexual Masquerades: The Structure of Sex Symbols." *The Annual of Psychoanalysis* 17 (1988).
————. *Siva: The Erotic Ascetic.* Oxford, 1973.
————. "The Survival of Myth in Science Fiction." In *Mindscapes: The Geographies of Imagined Worlds,* edited by George E. Slusser and Eric Rabkin. Carbondale, Ill., 1988.
————. *Tales of Sex and Violence: Folklore, Sacrifice, and Danger in the Jaiminiya Brahmana.* Chicago, 1985.
————. *Textual Sources for the Study of Hinduism.* Manchester, 1988.
————. *Women, Androgynes, and Other Mythical Beasts.* Chicago, 1980.
————. "The Uses and Abuses of Other Peoples' Classics." *Federation Review* 9, 5 (September/October 1986): 33-41.
————. "The Uses and Misuses of Other Peoples' Myths." *Journal of the American Academy of Religion,* 54:2 (Summer 1986): 219-239.
————, ed. *Karma and Rebirth in Classical Indian Traditions.* Berkeley, 1980.
Olerud, Anders. *Le macrocosmos et le microcosmos dans le Timée de Plato; Étude de religion comparée.* Uppsala, 1951.
Orwell, George. "Good Bad Books." In *Shooting an Elephant, and Other Essays,* pp. 182-186. New York, 1950.
————. "Rudyard Kipling" (a review of T.S. Eliot's *A Choice of Kipling's Verse*). In *A Collection of Essays,* pp. 123-138. New York, 1954.
Parpola, Asko. "The Pre-Vedic Indian Background of the Śrauta Rituals." In *Agni: The Vedic Ritual of the Fire Altar,* by Frits Staal, vol. 2, pp. 41-75. Berkeley, 1983.
Pater, Walter. *Appreciations.* London, 1957.
Radin, Paul. *The Trickster.* New York, 1972.
Rahner, Hugo. *Greek Myths and Christian Mystery.* Zurich, 1957; New York, 1962.
Ramanujan, A. K. *Relations.* Oxford, 1971.
————. "Two Realms of Kannada Folklore." In *Another Harmony: New Essays on the Folklore of India,* edited by A. K. Ramanujan and Stuart Blackburn, pp. 41-73. Berkeley, 1986.
————. "Where Mirrors are Windows: Towards an Anthology of Reflections." Paper presented at the Conference on the Direction and Limits of Reflexivity in the Axial Age Civilizations, Bad Homburg, July 1985. To be published in a forthcoming issue of *History of Religions.*
Ramnoux, Charles. "Philosophie et Mythologie, d'Hésiode à Proclus." In *Dictionnaire des mythologies,* edited by Yves Bonnefoy, vol. 2, pp. 256-262.
Rappaport, Roy. *Ecology, Meaning, and Religion.* Richmond, Calif., 1979.
Renou, Louis. *The Destiny of the Veda in India.* Delhi, 1965.
Rilke, Rainer Maria. *Neue Gedichte: Anderer Teil.* Leipzig, 1908.
Roth, Cecil. *A History of the Marranos.* Philadelphia, 1932.
Said, Edward. *Orientalism.* New York, 1978.
Sauvé, James L. "The Divine Victim: Aspects of Human Sacrifice in Viking Scandinavia

and Vedic India." In *Myth and Law among the Indo-Europeans,* edited by Jaan Puhvel, pp. 173-191. Los Angeles, 1970.

Sax, William S. "The Pandav Lila of Garhwal." Paper presented at the annual meeting of the American Academy of Religion, Boston, December 1987.

———. "Chaya Maya." Ph.D. diss. University of Chicago, 1988.

Schechner, Richard. "A 'Vedic Ritual' in Quotation Marks" (response to Frits Staal's response to Schechner's review of *Agni*). *Journal of Asian Studies* 46, 1 (February 1987): 108-110.

Scheuer, Jacques. "Sacrifice. Rudra-Śiva et la Destruction du Sacrifice." In *Dictionnaire des mythologies,* edited by Yves Bonnefoy, vol. 2, pp. 417-420. Paris, 1981.

Schlinghoff, Dieter. "Menschenopfer in Kausambi." *Indo-Iranian Journal* 11 (1969): 176-198.

Scholem, Gershom G. *Major Trends in Jewish Mysticism.* New York, 1941.

Scott, Paul. *Staying On.* London, 1977.

Sewell, Anna. *Black Beauty: The Autobiography of a Horse.* Norwich, 1877.

Shah, Idries. *The Exploits of the Incomparable Mulla Nasrudin.* New York, 1972.

Sharma, G. R. *The Excavations at Kausambi (1957-1959).* Allahabad, 1960.

Shaw, George Bernard. *Saint Joan.* Harmondsworth, 1966.

Shulman, David Dean. *The King and the Clown in South Indian Myth and Poetry.* Princeton, N.J., 1985.

———. "Terror of Symbols and Symbols of Terror: Notes on the Myth of Śiva as Sthānu." *History of Religions* 26, 2 (November 1986): 101-124.

———. "Toward a Historical Poetics of the Sanskrit Epics." Unpublished manuscript.

Singer, Milton. *When a Great Tradition Modernizes.* New York, 1972.

Slater, Philip. *The Glory of Hera* (Boston, 1968).

Smith, Brian K. "Exorcising the Transcendent: Strategies for Defining Hinduism and Religion." *History of Religions* 27, 1 (August 1987): 32-55.

———. "Gods and Men in Vedic Ritualism: Toward a Hierarchy of Resemblance." *History of Religions* 24, 4 (May 1985): 291-307.

———. *Reflections on Resemblance, Ritual, and Religion.* New York, 1988.

———. "Ritual, Knowledge and Being: Initiation and Veda Study in India." *Numen* 33, 1 (1986): 65-89.

———. "Sacrifice and Being: Prajāpati's Cosmic Emission." *Numen* 32, 1 (1985): 79-96.

———. "The Unity of Ritual: The Place of the Domestic Sacrifice in Vedic Ritualism." *Indo-Iranian Journal* 28 (1985): 79-96.

———. "Vedic Fieldwork." *Religious Studies Review* 11, 2 (April 1985): 136-45.

Smith, Cyril Stanley. "Metallurgical Footnotes to the History of Art." In *A Search for Structure: Selected Essays on Science, Art, and History,* pp. 242-305. Cambridge, Mass., and London, 1981.

Smith, Jonathan Z. "Animals and Plants in Myth and Legend." In "Myth and Mythology," *Encyclopaedia Britannica,* 15th ed., vol. 24, pp. 720-724.

———. "The Bare Facts of Ritual." In *Imagining Religion,* pp. 53-65. Chicago, 1982.

———. "The Devil in Mr. Jones." In *Imagining Religion,* pp. 102-120.

———. "The Domestication of Sacrifice." In *Violent Origins: Ritual Killing and Cultural Formation,* by Walter Burkert, René Girard, and Jonathan Z. Smith; edited by Robert G. Hamerton-Kelly, pp. 191-205. Stanford, Calif., 1987.

———. "A Pearl of Great Price and a Cargo of Yams." In *Imagining Religion,* pp. 90-101.

Smith, W. Robertson. *The Religion of the Semites: The Fundamental Institutions.* Aberdeen, 1888-89.

Smith, Wilfred Cantwell. "The Comparative Study of Religion." In *Inaugural Lectures.* Montreal, 1950.

Smythe, R. H. *The Mind of the Horse.* London, 1965.

Sontag, Susan. *On Photography.* New York, 1977.

Staal, Frits. *Agni: The Vedic Ritual of the Fire Altar.* 2 vols. Berkeley, 1983.

———. "The Concept of Scripture in the Indian Tradition." In *Sikh Studies: Compara-tive Perspectives on a Changing Tradition,* edited by Mark Juergensmeyer and N. Gerald Barrier, pp. 121-124. Berkeley, 1979.

———. "The Meaninglessness of Ritual." *Numen* 26, 1 (1979): 1-18.

———. "Über die Idee der Toleranz im Hinduismus." *Kairos: Zeitschrift für Religion-swissenschaft und Theologie* (1959): 215-218.

Steiner, George. "Conversations with Lévi-Strauss." *Encounter* 27, 10 (April, 1966): 38ff.

Stevenson, Robert Louis. *The Strange Case of Dr. Jekyll and Mr. Hyde.* London, 1886.

Sullivan, Bruce L. "The Rishi of the Fifth Veda: Vyasa in the *Mahabharata.*" Ph.D. Diss., University of Chicago, 1984.

Swift, Jonathan. *Gulliver's Travels.* London, 1726.

Tambiah, Stanley. "Animals Are Good to Think About and Good to Prohibit." *Ethnology* 8, 4 (1969): 423-59.

Tracy, David. "Myth, Sacrifice, and the Social Sciences." Paper read at the Annual Meeting of the American Academy of Religion, Boston, 6 December 1987.

Urton, Gary, ed., *Animal Myths and Metaphors.* Salt Lake City, 1985.

Urubshurow, Victoria. "The Battle of Kurukshetra: Topologically Transposed." Paper presented at the annual meeting of the American Academy of Religion, Boston, 7 December 1987. Citing an unpublished manuscript, "The Baba Project: Material Collected during 1983-1984 by T. R. Singh, J. M. Mahar, and Victoria Urubshurow."

van der Post, Laurens. *The Heart of the Hunter.* New York, 1961.

Véquaud, Yves. "The colors of devotion." *Portfolio,* February-March 1980.

Waghorne, Joanne Punzo. *Images of Dharma: The Epic World of C. Rajagopalachari.* New Delhi, 1985.

Wagner, Roy. *Lethal Speech: Daribi Myth as Symbolic Obviation.* Ithaca, N. Y., 1978.

Weber, Albrecht. "Puruṣamedhakandha." *Zeitschrift der Deutschen Morgenländischen Gesellschaft* 18 (1864): 277-284.

———. "Ueber Menschenopfer bei den Indern der vedischen Zeit." *Indischen Streifen* 1 (1896): 54-80.

West, Martin L. *The Orphic Poems.* Oxford, 1971.

White, T. H. *The Once and Future King.* London, 1962.

Wiesel, Elie. *The Gates of the Forest.* Translated by Frances Frenaye. New York, 1966.

Williams, Moyra. *The Psychology of the Horse.* London, 1965.

Wilson, Bryan. *Rationality.* Oxford, 1970.

Wilson, Edmund. *Memoirs of Hecate County.* New York, 1942.

Wilson, Horace Hayman. "On the Sacrifice of Human Beings as an Element of the Ancient Religion of India." *Journal of the Royal Asiatic Society* (1876).

Wittgenstein, Ludwig. *Last Writings on the Philosophy of Psychology.* Volume 1, edited by G. H. von Wright and Heikki Nyman. German text with English translation by C. G. Luckhardt and Maximilian A. E. Aue. Chicago, 1982.

———. *Philosophical Investigations.* 3d ed. Translated by G. E. M. Anscombe. New York, 1958.

Zimmer, Heinrich. *Myths and Symbols in Indian Art and Civilization.* New York, 1946.

Index

A

Abraham and Isaac, 100, 113-14, 128, 189
Academic. *See* Scholar
Acharya, Indian sage or teacher, 65-66
Adam and Eve, 39, 172. *See also* Eden, Garden of
Aeschylus, 123, 190
Advertisements, 38-39, 49
After image. *See* Ghost; Mirror; Shadow; Trace
Agaue, mother of Pentheus, 103-4, 108, 111, 187
Agnichayana, the ceremony of building the Vedic fire-altar, 58, 72, 83. *See also* Staal, Frits
Agriculture, 89-92, 115-16
Ahimsa (noninjury), 85, 89, 92, 115. *See also* Violence
Albanese, Catherine, 192
Alice in Wonderland, 55, 81, 94
Allen, Woody, 11, 124, 138-39, 149, 190, 193, 195
Altar, 58, 71 72, 83, 90. *See also* Agnichayana
Ambivalence, 20, 104, 114, 118, 170, 187. *See also* Contradiction; Schizophrenia
America, 4-5, 13-14, 18, 29, 38-40, 48, 53, 56, 70, 120, 122, 124, 131-32, 135, 157-58, 170, 176, 189, 191-92
Amnesia. *See* Forgetfulness; Memory
Anantha Murthy, Kannada poet, 42
Animals, 1-3, 75-96, 136, 141, 159. *See also* Ants; Armadillo; Bear; Boar;
Bull; Buffalo; Cat; Cow; Deer; Dog; Dolphin; Donkey; Dragon; Elephant; Fish; Geese/goose; Horse; Lion; Monkey; Ox; Pig; Sheep; Snake; Theriomorphism; Tiger; Wolf
eating of. *See* Eating
sacrifice of. *See* Sacrifice, animal
talking, 76, 78-79, 93-96
Anonymity, 26, 28-29, 59, 123, 142, 173
Anthill, 42
Anthropologist, 2, 11-12, 21, 35, 50, 67, 76, 78, 141, 156, 163, 166. *See also* Douglas; Evans-Pritchard; Frazer; Geertz; Leach; Lévi-Strauss; Lévy-Bruhl; Malinowski; Radcliffe-Brown
Anthropomorphism, 81, 88, 92, 99, 121, 160. *See also* Theriomorphism
Ants, 66, 69, 87, 94
Apollo, 165. *See also* Dionysus
Archaism, 29, 42, 46-47, 50-53, 55, 101, 131, 159
Archetype and manifestation, 34-37, 39, 42, 46, 68, 81, 121-22, 125, 130-31, 136, 146, 150, 153, 156, 159, 161-63, 174-175, 190
Arendt, Hannah, 52, 153, 177
Argument, 2-6, 21, 26, 33, 67, 113-14, 118, 122, 125, 132, 144, 191. *See also* Logos
Aristophanes, 122-23, 150
Aristotle, 81
Arjuna, a hero of the *Mahabharata*, 164

207

F

55, 61, 67-68, 119, 135-36, 140,
155, 169, 175, 177, 189, 194, 196.
See also America
film, 124. *See also* Lone Ranger
White, Hayden, 172
White, T. H., 94
Whitman, Walt, 41
Whore, 7, 39
Wiesel, Elie, 127
Widow, burning of. See *Suttee*
Wife, 8, 32, 66, 68, 75, 79, 87, 110,
147, 156. *See also* Sati; Sita; *Suttee*
Wild animal (*mriga*), 82-93, 98, 104,
108, 110, 136
Wilde, Oscar, 70, 109
Wilder, Thornton, 156
Wilderness, 82. *See also* Forest; Jungle
Wild vs. tame, 78, 81, 82-96, 108, 136,
185. *See also* Culture, vs. nature
Wilson, Bryan, 171
Wilson, Edmund, 157
Wilson, Woodrow, 29
Wine, 18, 29, 39, 85, 104, 112-18, 143.
See also Blood; Drunkenness
Witchcraft, 129, 181
Wittgenstein, Ludwig, 76, 160, 182
Wizard of Oz, The, 55, 158-59
Wolf, 94-95, 181. *See also* Mowgli;
Romulus and Remus
Woman, 4, 194. *See also* Feminism;
Goddess; Mother; *Suttee;* Whore;
Widow; Wife
Scarlet, 18
Star, 75
Wonder, 39

Women, 4, 14-15, 21, 38, 53-57, 63,
104, 141, 194
painters. *See* Painting
Woods. *See* Forest; Jungle
World Parliament of Religions, 19
World War II, 20, 30, 41, 52. *See also*
Holocaust
Writing, 40, 46, 57-58, 61-64, 67-71,
130. *See also* Illiteracy; Orality

X

Xenios, epithet of Zeus of the
Strangers, 3
Xenophanes, 76

Y

Yoga, yogi, 7, 10, 38, 98, 125
Yogavasishtha, a Sanskrit text, 7, 9,
151, 196

Z

Zagreus, 105, 107
Zeus, 3, 103, 105
Zimmer, Heinrich, 137-38, 192
Zoo, 39, 95
Zoologist, zoology, 2, 77, 93